FUT

MAX DUBLIN

FUTUREHYPE

THE TYRANNY OF PROPHECY

A DUTTON BOOK

DUTTON

Published by the Penguin Group
Penguin Books USA Inc., 375 Hudson Street, New York, New York 10014,
U.S.A.
Penguin Books Ltd, 27 Wrights Lane, London W8 5TZ, England
Penguin Books Australia Ltd, Ringwood, Victoria, Australia
Penguin Books Canada Ltd, 2801 John Street, Markham, Ontario, Canada L3R
1B4
Penguin Books (N.Z.) Ltd, 182–190 Wairau Road, Auckland 10, New Zealand

Penguin Books Ltd, Registered Offices: Harmondsworth, Middlesex, England

Published by Dutton, an imprint of New American Library, a division of Penguin
Books USA Inc. Originally published in different form in Canada by Penguin
Books Canada Ltd.

First Dutton Printing, April, 1991
1 2 3 4 5 6 7 8 9 10

🏛 REGISTERED TRADEMARK—MARCA REGISTRADA

LIBRARY OF CONGRESS CATALOGING IN PUBLICATION DATA:
Dublin, Max, 1947–
Futurehype : the tyranny of prophecy / Max Dublin.
p. cm.
Reprint. Originally published: Harmondsworth : Viking, 1989.
1. Forecasting. I. Title.
CB158.D83 1991
303.49—dc20   90–48461
CIP
0-525-24968-0
Printed in the United States of America
Set in Times Roman

Designed by Steven N. Stathakis

The following are used by permission:

Robert Aldridge, First Strike! The Pentagon's Strategy for Nuclear War (Boston:
South End Press), 1983.

Herman Kahn and B. Bruce-Briggs, Things to Come: Thinking about the 70s
and 80s (New York: MacMillan), 1972.

Alan Turing, "Computing Machinery and Intelligence", in Alan Ross Anderson,
Minds and Machines (Englewood Cliffs, N.J.: Prentice-Hall), 1964.

FOR MY PARENTS
ROSE AND MORRIS

ACKNOWLEDGMENTS

Research for this book was begun during the year I was appointed as the first Institute Fellow at the Ontario Institute for Studies in Education in Toronto. I am indebted to Malcolm Levin, Dwight Boyd, George Geis and Ian Winchester for offering me collegial hospitality at that time and in ensuing years. For useful research leads and/or comments on the manuscript I would like to thank John Briner, Phoebe Chytiri, Mary Damianakis, Gina Feldberg, Michael Fullan, Trevor Hancock, Jane Jacobs, Robert Kuttner, David Levine, Orlando Patterson and James Rosenfield. Special thanks to Isabelle Gibb of the Institute library. I am also indebted to Nancy Anderson, Robert Bick, Deanne Bogdan, Niall Byrne, John Eisenberg, Michael Laing, Elizabeth McLuhan, Richard Rockefeller and Harold Troper who have, at different stages in the book's development, given me the yin and yang of moral support; and I am particularly grateful to my auditors in Cambridge, John Bowles, John Carey, Janet Levoff, Andrew Morvay, Nita Sembrowich and

Siki Cat, for giving me some needed encouragement and feedback at a crucial stage in the writing. Finally, I want to thank Iris Skeoch, Kevin Mulroy and Mitch Horowitz of Penguin Books, whose editorial feedback has substantially contributed to the book's improvement, and Morton Mint who saw the merits of this book while it was still at an early stage of development. Chapters seven and eight, in slightly different form, were first delivered as lectures at the Coolidge Center for Environmental Leadership and at the Center for Society Technology and Values, respectively.

Events, by definition, are occurrences that interrupt routine processes and routine procedures; only in a world in which nothing of importance ever happens could the futurologist's dream come true. Predictions of the future are never anything but projections of present automatic processes and procedures, that is, of occurrences that are likely to come to pass if men do not act and if nothing unexpected happens; every action, for better or worse, and every accident necessarily destroys the whole pattern in whose frame the prediction moves and where it finds its evidence.

—HANNAH ARENDT, *On Violence*

. . . most of the research now going on about the future tends to advocate further increases in the institutionalization of values . . .

—IVAN ILLICH, *Deschooling Society*

We [Devils] want a man hag-ridden by the Future—haunted by visions of an imminent heaven or hell upon earth—ready to break [God's] commands in the Present if by so doing we make him think he can attain the one or avert the other—dependent for his faith on the success or failure of schemes whose end he will not live to see. We want a whole race perpetually in pursuit of the rainbow's end, never honest, nor kind, nor happy *now* but always using as mere fuel wherewith to heap the altar of the Future every real gift which is offered them in the Present.

—C.S. LEWIS, *The Screwtape Letters*

CONTENTS

FUTUREHYPE

. . . the Erewhonians are a meek people, easily led by the nose, and quick to offer up common sense at the shrine of logic.

—SAMUEL BUTLER

PROLOGUE: THE POWER OF PROPHECY

The impetus to write this book originally came from the desire to shed some light on a number of troubling contradictions that were impressed on me a few years ago while I was working as a government consultant. At that time, I was hired to help a special task force to complete a unique report, the sort of long-range planning document which modern-day corporate executives and bureaucratic officials, aping their military counterparts, like to call a *strategic plan*. Because long-range planning is today closely integrated with forecasting, while working for this task force I was eventually asked to take a hard look at what our different types of prophets have to say about the future.

Predicting the future has become so integral to the fabric of modern consciousness that few people feel compelled to question it, and fewer still feel the need to defend it. And yet, in surveying the landscape of modern prophecy, it was

shocking to discover how much of what even our most respectable prophets have to say about the future is blatantly
false, that is, either deeply flawed intellectually, or morally
questionable, or both. It is true that their predictions and
visions are logical, up to a point, but when you look at them
closely, many of even the most respectable prophecies today
still fly in the face of common sense and/or common decency.
And there seem to be no real people in these visions of the
future, no real life in the rich and sometimes puzzling way
in which we experience it—only banal abstractions of life
and neat little caricatures of people.

Since it is obvious that our prophets and our prophetic
leaders in government, in the media and in industry have a
powerful impact on our lives, and since so much of what
they say turns out to be false, in the end I found myself
thinking more and more not so much about *what* they have
to say, but *how* they say it. I became concerned about the
nature of their appeal, the techniques and rhetoric that make
our prophets credible and persuasive, and also about how
prophecy shapes our world and how we think about the
future. The more I learned about modern prophecy, and the
more I thought about the role our prophets have come to
play in the development of our world, the more contradictions I discovered, and the more striking—and troubling—
did these contradictions appear.

The first of these contradictions to strike me, and perhaps the one that really got me going on this book, goes
something like this: on the one hand, a great many present-
day prophets—perhaps John Naisbitt, one of the current
lions among pop futurologists, is most prominent among
these—have proclaimed that present trends allow for almost
endless possibilities for developing the world of the future;
on the other hand, however, many of the same futurologists—and Naisbitt is noteworthy here too—also take great
pains to explain to their followers that the world of the future
will only be *thus and so.* And sometimes they even go on to
warn that those who are not willing to prepare for this specific
future, or for a short list of possible futures, will run into
any number of difficulties and dangers, and perhaps be hopelessly left behind. As Naisbitt himself has put it in this somewhat benign, but ultimately rather patronizing warning:

"Trends tell you the direction the country is moving in. The decisions are up to you. But trends, like horses, are easier to ride in the direction they are already going. When you make a decision that is compatible with the overarching trend, the trend helps you along. You may decide to buck the trend, but it is still helpful to know it is there."[1]

Endless possibilities, but very few real choices—unless, of course, you are willing to run the risks and pay the costs of "bucking trends."

Not everyone has such a respectful, if not worshipful, view of trends. George Orwell, who many people have mistakenly considered to be a prophet, was actually, in his time, a severe detractor of modern prophets, and especially of trend-chasers like Naisbitt.[2] In a long essay about James Burnham, a prominent American futurologist and trend-follower of his time, Orwell cast a very different light on trend-chasing when he made the following criticism of Burnham's political predictions: "The prediction that Russia would gang up with Japan against the U.S.A. was written early in 1944, soon after the conclusion of a new Russo-Japanese treaty. The prophecy of Russian world conquest was written in the winter of 1944, when the Russians were advancing rapidly in eastern Europe while the Western Allies were still held up in Italy and northern France. It will be seen that at each point Burnham is predicting *a continuation of the thing that is happening.*" (emphasis in original)[3]

However, Orwell's critique went much further than merely pointing out the intellectual fallacy of "predicting a continuation of the thing that is happening." Orwell argued that this way of thinking was the consequence of a moral failing. He wrote: "The tendency to do this is not simply a bad habit, like inaccuracy or exaggeration, which one can correct by taking thought. It is a major mental disease, and its roots lie partly in cowardice and partly in the worship of power, which is not fully separable from cowardice."[4] Later in this critique Orwell went on to elaborate how our experience teaches us that such predictions are false and to describe how the worship of power works in political prophecies, but his observations are generally applicable to all sorts of prophecies, not only the political ones. He wrote:

Power worship blurs political judgement because it
leads, almost unavoidably, to the belief that present
trends will continue. Whoever is winning at the
moment will always seem to be invincible. . . . This
habit of mind leads also to the belief that things
will happen more quickly, completely, and cata-
strophically than they ever do in practice. The rise
and fall of empires, the disappearance of cultures
and religions, are expected to happen with earthquake suddenness, and processes which have barely
started are talked about as though they were already at an end. . . . The slowness of historical
change, the fact that any epoch always contains a
great deal of the last epoch, is never sufficiently
allowed for. Such manner of thinking is bound to
lead to mistaken prophecies, because, even when
it gauges the direction of events rightly, it will mis-
calculate their tempo. Within the space of five years
Burnham foretold the domination of Russia by
Germany and of Germany by Russia. In each case
he was obeying the same instinct: the instinct to
bow down before the conqueror of the moment, to
accept the existing trend as irreversible.[5]

It might be nice to think that the differences between how
Orwell and Naisbitt think about trends are merely intellectual, a gentleman's disagreement to be sorted out over drinks
at the club: one thinks trends are to be exploited; the other
thinks this amounts to worshipping the conqueror of the
present moment. But the reason that this and the other contradictions of modern prophecy that I will be discussing in
this book are *not* merely intellectual is that predictions are
not merely exercises of the mind. Predictions have power:
there is no rhetorical or propaganda device more powerful
than prophecy. Predictions do not simply describe the
world—they *act* on it. How do they do this? For one thing,
predictions are seldom neutral, seldom merely descriptive.
Usually predictions—even weather forecasts—are also prescriptive; they contain a strong element of advice and warning. The advice and warning inherent in Naisbitt's forecasting

are not unique in modern prophecy—in fact, they are quite characteristic of it—but often the advice is much stronger, and the warning more dire, than those I quoted above.

But even when predictions have no advice or warning built into them, they still act powerfully on their audiences because they naturally function in the same way that promises do in the sense that they create expectations, and there is no question but that people will act on the basis of these kinds of expectations. But false predictions—and, as I will show in this book, most predictions, except for the most obvious and short-range ones do, in fact, turn out to be false—are like false promises, that is to say, they act like lies. And false predictions are destructive in the same way that lies are because, when uttered with conviction, they disarm and inspire us and put us into false positions. Furthermore, these false positions, like all false positions, encourage us to act in ways we never would if we really understood where we stood and what we were doing, in ways that are typically self-defeating.

There are all sorts of self-defeating things that false predictions may encourage us to do, but usually the false positions into which they put us will be a result of the fact that, because of the promise inherent in a prediction, we will act irresponsibly to the present. Acting irresponsibly to the present can take many forms. False predictions can lead us to abandon something of the present—something that we have known, valued, understood and lived with over the years, and something that is still worthwhile and viable if only we would continue to give it the effort and attention it deserves—in favor of something "better" that we neither know, nor value, nor yet properly understand but which, we are told, will be a great good in the future. And sometimes we abandon not just one but many things for the sake of the one that is yet to be, for this is often the nature of "building the world of the future." From the railroads in our transportation system, to the humanities in our education system, to innumerable viable industries we hasten to dissociate ourselves from worthwhile endeavors that enrich our lives in large part because their demise has been predicted and we do not want to be "left behind." Or we hasten to associate ourselves with questionable, sometimes dangerous, but in any case unproven endeavors simply because their rise has been predicted. When you think about it, it is extraordinary what we are willing to relinquish in the world of the present in order to usher in what our prophets tell us will be the world of the future—and, what is much the same thing, what we neglect for the same reasons. But the rashness and destructiveness of this kind of lemming-like behavior is seldom apparent to us because our prophets lead us to believe that to follow them is to do something brave and good. They tell us that the thing of the future is better than the thing of the past and present—or at least it is the next necessary step—and the panic, simple-mindedness and vain self-assurance which they inspire make us behave irresponsibly.

These facts were vividly brought home to me in a disturbing story I heard when I was working on an oral history project in Jamaica, a number of years before I began analyzing the thinking of our modern prophets. The story was an account of an episode in Jamaican history that occurred during the early part of this century in one of Kingston's outlying districts called August Town. In 1920 a prophet by the name of Bedward, who was based in August Town, began to preach all over Jamaica, predicting the end of white rule and his direct ascent with his followers to heaven. Bedward's message was that World War I and a major earthquake, which happened also to have occurred at that time, were signs that his prophecy was about to be fulfilled. He urged the people to give up their worldly goods and follow him. And, perhaps to his credit as a sincere, though deluded, prophet, he was very precise in his predictions. He predicted that he would make his ascent exactly at a certain time on December 31, 1920. Many people believed him. Many people—even many whose recent ancestral memory included landless slavery—sold or gave their land away, left their homes, donned white robes and gathered with him in August Town. Even the whites took this prophecy seriously. Shortly before the fateful day the Kingston *Gleaner* reported:

> Yesterday there was great excitement at the Railway. Every train brought in a large number of peo-

ple, men, women and children all bound for August Town. But they came from Colon as well, on a steamer travelling across seas to see their "Lord of August Town" ascend. In King Street all tram-cars travelling to Hope Gardens were besieged by men, women and children, some infants in arms, others hardly able to help themselves, but they were all bundling in with their clothes, baskets and fowls. All have sold out to come up and see the Lord and Master do the disappearing trick. There are still more to come.[6]

But they did not see Bedward do the "disappearing trick." Instead they saw him use the characteristic delaying tactics that the cult-prophet employs when his predictions fail to materialize. A few days before the day of his predicted ascent Bedward resorted to high drama: he swung one of his female followers from a tree to see if her faith was strong enough to make her fly, but when she failed to learn to fly he proclaimed it was too weak. When the predicted day of ascent finally arrived—but without the predicted result—he naturally pushed the date forward and kept doing so until the month of May. But these postponements could do nothing for his followers, many of whom had given up their land and livelihood, had given up everything for the promise of something better—in this case nothing less than heaven. Some were eventually arrested for vagrancy. Most of them were too ashamed to return to their homes, so they settled there in August Town, and some of their descendants live there to this day.†

This incident in Jamaica's history certainly was not earthshaking, but though it occurred as part of a fleeting religious movement and may sound somewhat droll, it is still

† When I was told this story, the narrator and I stood before a beautiful poinciana tree that insisted on growing defiantly amidst the rubble on which this wretched community was built. The poinciana tree seemed to me to be a reminder of the verdant tropical bush which is so abundant in the rural areas these people had abandoned to follow their false prophet. But not everyone has the ability to remember, for better or for worse, that which has been lost or abandoned. For example, when literacy is relinquished, one loses, even within a single generation, a great deal of the ability to remember and appreciate what was lost.

quite symbolic of our rather more secular lives. Though we
live today in a world whose self-image is decidedly secular,
we still have our civil religions, based largely on technology,
money and power. The Bedwardite vignette represents in
miniature and in stark relief the widespread, sometimes subtle, but often profound effect of prophecy on our lives. Predictions are capable of harmfully misleading not only
relatively small groups of people, like Bedward's followers,
but entire societies and even whole civilizations—and sometimes in the most monumental and decisive ways. Wars have
been started on the basis of prophecy, and so have economic
and social movements, large and small.

Because it is capable of influencing us this way, modern
prophecy, in all of its different manifestations, should be
considered a force in its own right—a force which, like all
sources of power, is liable to be abused. It does not merely
monitor the development of our civilization, as futurologists
like John Naisbitt like to claim it does, but actually shapes
it, often in decidedly harmful ways. By saying this, however,
I have a great deal more in mind than the now commonplace
observation that polling often affects the outcome of elections or, for example, that Naisbitt's futurological boosterism
has given extra impetus to the growth and economic development of Tampa, Florida, which he predicted would be one
of the "cities of the future." The effect of prophecy on a
society is much more powerful than this. Because of its
power, there is, and always has been, a great deal of manipulative, exploitative and destabilizing potential in prophecy—and often this is precisely what false prophecy is all
about. Of course it can also be about simple foolishness.
During the course of this book I will describe a number of
prophecies of our time that have been either manipulative
or foolish, and sometimes both. In each case it will be obvious how the prophecy feeds on and appeals to the worse
parts of our nature. What should also be clear is the extent
to which prophecy in our time, though often claiming on the
basis of science to be an objective business which transcends
any system of values or ethics, nevertheless still plays a highly
value-ridden part in our political and economic debates.
However, while claiming to be objective and scientific,

modern-day prophecy merely uses the mantle of science to strengthen and legitimate itself while masking its ideological content.

It is characteristic of science, in its quest for objectivity, to exclude and avoid ethical considerations. Therefore it is natural for modern prophecy, which has scientific pretensions, to do the same thing. But a prophecy with scientific pretenses, and especially one which on this basis often manages to avoid or mask ideological and ethical issues rather than facing them head-on, is a disturbing development in the history of the world. There have always been false prophets, but before scientism began to obscure ethical questions by claiming to transcend them, all forms of prophecy were deeply and explicitly grounded in ethical thinking, for the simple reason that they were a part of religious practice. Prophets were spiritual leaders and foretelling the future was only one part of the extremely complex roles they played in their nations and societies. One only has to recall the prophets of ancient Greece and Israel during what may be regarded as the golden age of prophecy to realize how integral this grounding used to be.

Consider, for example, the role that prophecy played in the life and times of King Oedipus of Thebes.[7] We are all familiar with the bare bones of this story. A young man kills a stranger, who turns out to be his father, and through a series of quirks becomes king and marries another stranger, who turns out to be his mother. For commiting these crimes he dooms himself to a miserable destiny of blindness and exile. What is interesting, however, is how all of this is revealed, for the most important work of revelation is left to a prophet by the name of Tiresias. Tiresias, the famous blind prophet of Oedipus's kingdom of Thebes, far from thrusting himself into the political fray, as our modern prophets like to do, was actually at the outset a very reluctant oracle. In fact, when first questioned by Oedipus, Tiresias was adamantly unwilling to talk. He knew the truth would eventually come out, that it would bring doom to his king and shame to the city, and so the prophet preferred not to be the one to break this terrible news. Describing his predicament, Tiresias himself says in Sophocles's version of this story, "Alas, how terrible is wisdom when/It brings no profit to the man that's wise!"[8]

But Oedipus, true to character, immediately became incensed with Tiresias for this reluctance. It was only at this point, when Oedipus had once again displayed his famous temper, that Tiresias hinted at all of the crimes that would eventually be revealed. Ultimately it was Oedipus's temper, now brandished at Tiresias himself, that reminded the prophet of the original source of this tragedy, the earlier occasion when Oedipus had lost his temper and killed another old man during an altercation on the road, a stranger who turned out to be his father. "You blame my temper," the prophet reproached King Oedipus, "but do not see / your own that lives within you."[9]

In the end, when Tiresias was forced to reveal the source of present misery and to foretell the coming doom of King Oedipus, he did so by way of a moral chastisement. Tiresias did not merely glibly predict the future for Oedipus, he did it in the context of raising explicit moral issues. He not only predicted that horrible things were in store for Oedipus but he also explained that it was the King's own reprehensible behavior that had doomed him. Tiresias indicted Oedipus in the harshest way possible by maintaining that it was nothing less fundamental than Oedipus's own character, his unruly temper, that had shaped his destiny. Character is destiny said Tiresias to King Oedipus; I predict that all of these horrible things will happen to you and they will happen as a consequence of the way you have lived your life.

Like Tiresias, most of the Old Testament prophets also chastised the Children of Israel, reminding them of their moral shortcomings. In the case of the Hebrew prophets, however, the prophecy-cum-chastisement took a somewhat different form: the call of the prophet was often an exhortation to the Israelites to better themselves so that they would be worthy of the great destiny that had been prepared for them, so that it would not be delayed by their undesirable behavior. Moses, the first and greatest of these prophets, forced them to wander through the desert for forty years to expiate their sin and prepare themselves for their destiny. Elijah, in his turn, called upon them to live a more spiritual life, and Isaiah censured them for materialism and land-grabbing.† Isaiah said, "Woe to those who add house to house/and join field to field/until everywhere belongs to them/and they are the sole inhabitants of the land." (Isaiah, 5:8).

In a sense the *foresight* which these ancient prophets possessed was fundamentally part of their more general and profound *insight* into human nature. It was a vehicle for making an honest and open moral argument about the future. There have always been charlatans in the prophecy business, but moral intelligence based on a profound understanding of the complexity of human nature has always been an integral part of true prophecy. In modern prophecy, however, this is hardly the case. Trendiness and the managerial/technological juggernaut that drives most modern forecasting generally have little if anything to do with ethics. Elijah predicted of the Children of Israel, "You will be a light unto the nations." Today our prophets are just as likely to predict, "You will sell computer chips, or armaments or banking services to the nations."

Typically, the only thing that is left of a moral argument in the prophecy of our times is lip service to progress and a great deal of the power of prediction to make us act is based on the rhetoric of progress. However, contrary to popular conceptions—conceptions which are often promoted by futurologists themselves for obvious self-serving reasons—prediction has very little, if anything, to do with progress. In fact, in our time prediction has often acted as a hindrance to real progress. This is true because, first of all, governments often use rosy predictions as a mechanism for avoiding coming to grips with the intractable problems of the present. A great deal of time, energy and money is spent making and fostering these kinds of predictions—and the often foolish interventions that are based on them—instead of taking responsibility for the present situation and tackling the

† Nowhere is the power of prophecy more evident than in the history of the Jewish people. On the positive side, the prophecy of the return to the promised land served as a binding force to preserve the Jewish culture and identity and to sustain the Jewish people for millennia. However on the negative side it also acted, and tragically acts to this day, as one of the main legitimating reasons behind the claim that is made by some sectors of Israeli society to the right of permanent occupation of the territories that were captured during the Six Day War.

problems at hand. Second, and perhaps more important, predictions often retard progress: when one speaks of progress it is important to be specific because we do not all agree on what it is, and because progress in one area often means regress in another. For example, although the arms race is now presumably over, its progress was characteristically based on predictions of future military superiority or a future state of "parity." Since the end of World War II this kind of futuristic propaganda served as an excuse for constantly postponing the talks and negotiations that were necessary to create progress in peace.†

Divorced from the progressivism of earlier periods, prophecy has also largely lost what was left, as recently as the turn of this century, of the moral and ethical basis for gazing forward. Because of this rupture we have developed an ethic about forecasting that is often self-serving but ethically indifferent. Fitting ourselves into a vulgar Darwinian definition of our humanity, in following our false prophets we are always "adaptive" and "exploitative" creatures rather than morally purposive ones. Therefore we are not so much concerned about what the future will be because, on the basis of our values, we want it to be a certain way, rather we want to know what the future will be because we think this is the only way we can protect ourselves and perhaps take advantage of it. Worse than this, many people have come to think that the future must be good merely because it is the next step, because it is there, because the next step is said to be inevitable. In our time false prophecy consistently substitutes the ethic of inevitability for the ethic of responsibility. What this amounts to—instead of futuregazing tied to truly progressive thinking—is a bland, pervasive, sterile and rather mechanical *futurity*. The future is the place to go to and we should want to go there simply because it is the next place to go.

† In spite of the fact that the cold war has largely died down, the end of the arms race is greatly exaggerated: in spite of the disarmament treaties of the last few years new weapons systems are still scheduled to come on board until the end of the century. A conference of NATO defense ministers in April 1990 issued a communique that the Alliance will continue to adhere to its first strike policy because they are unwilling to relinquish a policy that has supposedly served them so well in the past. This is a typical incidence in which "clinging to the past" is called "looking to the future."

Because it so often puts us into false positions and encourages us to make blind bargains, prophecy today has become an instrument for violating the very future it claims to predict, and which it sometimes even claims to protect. It creates an attenuation of the many possible futures that actually *can* be for the sake of the future that, in the mind of the usually self-appointed prophet, *should* be. Even those of our prophets like Naisbitt, who flutter the banner of endless possibilities use it only as a hook, as a rhetorical device and as a distraction from the limited choices, from the very narrow road, along which they are encouraging us to follow.

Therefore the real issues that are raised by the role of modern prophecy in our lives have ultimately to do with the relationship between the virtual infinity of real possibilities for development which exist compared to the few that are presented and promoted by our prophets. These are ultimately issues about freedom, growth, diversity and fulfilment. A certain course of development may be "logical" to a certain extent—even pathological developments and the transformations and transactions of decline follow a logical course—but it is never "in the nature of things," that is, it is never the only logical way to go. There is nothing inherently logical about the way we are developing now or the way the world has ever developed. Development is now and has always been an interplay between our values and the many possibilities contained in the world before us, and, contrary to a great deal of conventional wisdom, it has always been more of an improvised and creative rather than planned affair. We are continually impoverishing and betraying both our present and our future by following the narrow and ultimately restrictive paths that are pointed out by our present-day prophets. We are constantly impoverishing ourselves by abandoning what we value and have mastered in favor of what we do not yet even understand. Thereby we destroy the richness and diversity of our skills and resources: the very tools that could ensure that our futures are at least as rich as the present, and might even help us to adapt to the real world that will unfold for us.

Even true science, whose power is based on its predictive capabilities, has discovered many areas in which it is incapable of making predictions, but outside of the realm of true science there are very few neutral predictions in this world. In fact, since predictions are often heavily laden with the values of our prophets, when we buy into the world which they project before us—and thereby help make their prophecies self-fulfilling—we fulfill not ourselves but them. Fulfilling the visions of the prophets of our time has meant not only buying into banal technological utopias, but also into their vain fantasies of controlling everything from recessions to nuclear wars.

The pathological strain in modern prophecy is as broad as it is deep. It might be nice to think that it is restricted to the so-called lunatic fringe, but who can distinguish the mainstream from the lunatic fringe if a prominent politician like Henry Kissinger has envisioned that we could control nuclear wars using the psychological precepts of game-theory, while a distinguished computer scientist like Edward Feigenbaum imagines that one day we will be able to solve the problem of loneliness by using robot companions?†

In today's world we are witnessing a deadening convergence of purposes. This convergence is putting all of us in jeopardy because not only, as the saying goes, are the nations of the world all rushing to put all of their developmental eggs in one basket, they are also all trying, as much as possible, to put them into one and the same basket. There are many sources for this unhealthy convergence, but modern prophecy is undoubtedly one of the most powerful. In the long run, individual and national development which is not truly open-ended—ready both to preserve what has already been mastered and continues to be valued, as well as to pursue an infinite variety of possibilities, and not merely the ones our prophets claim to see so clearly—is bound to be dead-ended. A rich civilization—one that is masterful in a great variety of present endeavors and not merely dreaming about

† So much has futurology become woven into the fabric of our culture, now it is indeed often difficult to distinguish establishment futurology from the kind that is popularized in the media. Members of the Board of Directors of *The Futurist*, which is a pop-futurology magazine with a large following, include: former U.S. Secretary of Agriculture, Orville Freeman; former U.S. Secretary of Health, Education, and Welfare, John Gardner; former Secretary of Defense and President of the World Bank, Robert McNamara; and former Chairman of the U.S. Atomic Energy Commission, Glenn T. Seaborg.

how well it will do in the future based on one or two new ones—is one that takes an immeasurable amount of time and patience to attain; once it is relinquished, even for a relatively short period of time, it is immeasurably difficult to regain. There is a great deal of talk about decline today, especially with respect to the superpowers. Although their obituaries are rather premature, one thing the superpowers do have in common—one might call it their common enemy from within—is that they have both been particularly susceptible to the propaganda of prophets who have persistently narrowed their field of vision.

Since what is always at stake in our relationship with our prophets is nothing less than what we want to become, and since the very act of prediction has the power to influence what we will become, the questions we must pose for ourselves in this relationship are these: Will we make our own choices, or will we accept the ready-made ones with which they present us, and based on which, if they are leaders in positions of power, they often act in our behalf? Will we buy into their dreams, or will we assert the right that is the precursor to real growth, the right to dream our own dreams?

Dreaming our own dreams, that is, pursuing a diverse and rich economic and cultural development, may appear to be a luxury in our time when we are possessed by the need to predict the future in order to be purposive in conquering it. In fact it is not a luxury but one of the most compelling of necessities. It is necessary because of the diversity it promotes. It is one of the few things that can keep our civilization diverse enough so that, as time unfolds, we retain choices through the skills and knowledge that we have preserved and developed by continual cultivation.

As to our modern prophets themselves, all of the earlier ages of prophecy would have been ashamed to own up to them. The reader will not find an Isaiah, a Tiresias, or even a Cassandra or Merlin among them, but he will find, insofar as they have any moral conviction, that they are constantly inviting us to worship the ancient idol of "progress." But this is only an empty piety because the sticky and complex debate about what progress at this or any other point in time might actually mean is an issue for which they have neither the moral intelligence nor, usually, even the *patience* in which to engage. They legitimate this idol worship and make it respectable by cloaking themselves in the mantle of science, even though they are not true scientists. They also sometimes claim to be humanists, but this claim is also hollow. In fact, most of the prophets of our time have no deep tradition to draw upon or with which to ground themselves in their extremely ambitious and influential enterprise. C.S. Lewis has said of such actors that they are "merely modern . . . the severities both of abstraction and of high human tradition have passed them by."[10] Yet what is most remarkable about them, but not surprising given the nature of their training, is how impressionable they are. Though a great many of them are simply wide-eyed technophiles or mechanical extrapolators, some are obviously fools and charlatans. And, though the self-interest and the quest for power are self-evident in some modern prophets, in others these motives are disguised in self-righteous disclaimers about the public interest.

Self-interest and the quest for power: this, of course, is what false prophecy is and always has been about. But I hope it will be obvious by the end of this book that I have written it not merely to demonstrate how banal, simple-minded, and self-serving many of the most influential of our present-day prophets are. Some of that will be necessary as I go along, but my main purpose is to help make my readers more alive to the real possibilities, to the real variety of choices we can make to shape our present—and ultimately, of course, our future—according to the way we want to live, not according to the way others, in the guise of prophecy, say we ought to live. In the end, I shall be arguing that there are better vehicles than prophecy, not only for deciding where we want to go, but for affecting individual growth and social, economic and cultural development. These ways pertain to an ethic of responsibility that insists on the necessity of making the most of the present, in mastering its challenges in our personal, corporate and national lives. By elucidating the role that prophets play in our society and in our lives, by explaining their motives, their ideology and the aspects of our psychology that make us want to listen to them, it is my hope that this book will help people to become more thoughtful and critical about where we are going and why we are going there.

NOTES

1. John Naisbitt, *Megatrends* (New York: Warner Books, 1982), p. xxxii.
2. It may surprise those who have only read his fiction to learn that Orwell wrote a powerful diatribe against futurology, because he himself dabbled in prophecy for many earlier years. For example, even as late as 1945 Orwell predicted, wrongly as it turned out, that Churchill and the Conservatives would win the post-war general election. Perhaps it was because he himself so often made mistaken predictions that Orwell rethought the prophecy issue. If one reads his papers one learns that *1984* was written not so much to serve as a prediction of future society, but rather as a critique of the present society in which he lived, a speculation of what could happen if it continued its present course. The propagandized state, the state on a permanent war footing, the state which insistently intrudes on private life, was already going strong in Orwell's time and, due to the effects of World War II and its immediate aftermath, was particularly evident in 1948, when Orwell finished this novel. (The title of the book, of course, is simply a reversal of the last two digits of the year when it was completed. He had earlier toyed with the idea of calling the book *The Last Man in Europe*.) Unfortunately, using the device of future projection to gain a critical perspective on the present can now be seen, with hindsight, to have been a questionable practice on Orwell's part. Having finally passed the monumental year whose number he used for the title of this book, the sad irony is that so many people treat it as a test that has been passed—it has come and gone and was not nearly as bad as Orwell is said to have predicted it would be in his fiction—in spite of the fact that all of the major criticisms implicit in the novel have been increasingly vindicated over time.
3. George Orwell, "James Burnham and the Managerial Revolution," in *Collected Essays, Journalism and Letters* (New York: Harcourt Brace Jovanovich, 1968), vol. 4, pp. 172–173.
4. Orwell, p. 173.
5. Orwell, p. 174.
6. Quoted by Martha Beckwith in *Black Roadways* (New York: Negro Universities Press, 1969), p. 169. Beckwith actually met Bedward just before his predicted ascent. I have drawn on her classic and reliable version to refresh my memory and validate the stories I heard personally many years later.
7. It is a great pity that the story of Oedipus has been reduced in the modern popular imagination to the deeply colored and rather narrow psychological interpretation given to it by Freud. As interesting as Freud's tale of father/son rivalry and juvenile eroticism may be, the original story, as it is told in the literature of ancient Greece, is far richer, more subtle and grounded in a more complex morality.
8. Sophocles, *Oedipus the King* (trans. David Grene), in *Greek Tragedies* (Chicago: University of Chicago Press, 1973), Volume 1, p. 123.
9. Sophocles, p. 124.
10. C.S. Lewis, *That Hideous Strength* (London: Pan Books, 1983), p. 109.

If each epoch is as a matter of course better than the last, then any crime or folly that pushes the historical process forward can be justified. Between, roughly, 1750 and 1930 one could be forgiven for imagining that progress of a solid, measurable kind was taking place. Latterly this has become more and more difficult . . .

—GEORGE ORWELL

PROPHECY AS PROPAGANDA

It has always been compelling to think about the future—it is, after all, the repository of our hopes and vision. But the future is also the repository of our fears because it raises monumental questions: What will become of us and our descendants? Will we be fulfilled or depleted by the lives we are going to live? Will we succeed or fail? In our time, an unusually large and ever growing number of people will readily admit to an anxious concern about these questions and about what the future may bring. In fact, it is not too much to say that we are living at a time when a pervasive concern about the future has become no less than an obsession. This obsession has many sources, but undoubtedly it stems mainly from an almost universal unease about the present, based both on its failures and on its general lack of stability. Therefore most people, even those who by the terms of the entire history of the world are doing very well, nevertheless still feel at risk, in jeopardy; they feel that the future may hold something unpleasant in store for them in the form of a loss or undesirable change in their economic, social, or personal lives.

And yet, though anxiety about the future is particularly pronounced in our time, it is certainly not a new or extraordinary phenomenon. It has occurred many times throughout history whenever social, economic, political and technological changes have altered generally stable relationships and thus produced a climate of instability. René Dubos has observed that "There have always been timid souls who believed that adaptation to the future would be difficult, painful, and perhaps impossible. . . . In 1575, four centuries before the phrase 'future shock' was coined, there was published in Paris a small book† by an author who worried . . . about the disturbances caused by the new knowledge and technologies of his time, and even more about what was in store for the future."[1] So even though we may be inclined to convince ourselves that our times are unique and wholly unprecedented, pervasive anxiety about the future has recurred so often in history, and has been so common at *all* times, that it should be regarded as part of the human condition.

This is not to say, however, that this anxiety does not present its problems. Not only does apprehension about the future take its toll on our emotions, it also makes us vulnerable; we are as easily victimized by it as by any other of our fears. There have always been those who are ready— even eager—to play on our apprehensions about the future, and sometimes even to capitalize on them.

Forever feeding our anxiety about the future are words—words coming from the mouths of our modern-day prophets and carelessly repeated by opportunistic and impressionable journalists, academics, advertisers and politicians, some of whom like to play the role of prophet themselves. Prophecy makes good press. We are forever being told by the media that some sort of fad or recent development will be *the wave of the future,* or *megatrend.* We are told that one particular factor will make or break the economic future of a given nation, be it that vague and peculiar abstraction "competitiveness," which is currently being ban-

† *De la Vicissitude ou Variété des Choses dans l'Univers,* by Louis Le Roy.

died about in the United States; free trade with the United
States, which is presently the favorite panacea/bogeyman in
my own country, Canada; or enterprise zones, which have
recently played a similar role in China. Most countries have
their own version of the magic formula that will be decisive.
We are also constantly being told that some recent medical
discovery will lead, in the not too distant future, to the cure
for the most endemic health problems, and many of us want
to believe this, in spite of the fact that the cures for cancer,
cardiovascular disease, mental illness and other complex syndromes seem to be incessantly receding into the horizon.
And we are constantly being sent on chases after the professions of the future—communications, computer programming, investment banking—only to find the market rather
overcrowded when we finally arrive in it, or to discover that
we never really wanted to do that kind of work in the first
place. Yet, no matter how many wild-goose chases we are
sent on, we are ever eager for the hunt.

But whatever else we may believe of all these words
about the future, many people find at least this much inescapable: that the present rate of change is unprecedented in
the history of the world. From this often repeated assertion
we conclude that we should all be preparing ourselves to live
in revolutionary futures, futures which will occur within our
very own lifetimes. Yet the merits and flaws of these revolutionary futures are seldom discussed so much as is their
inevitability.

Many of those who listen to the pronouncements and
read the literature produced by our futurological gurus feel
that significant changes are indeed *inevitable* and will produce the future difficulties or traumas that everyone would
naturally want to avoid. But a great many of those who follow
our modern-day prophets have also come to feel that, if we
can predict now what the future will be like, we will be able
to *control* it, or at least prepare for it in advance by anticipatory actions consisting mainly of avoiding dangers and/or
securing our present position. (These are the types of measures which, according to the conventions of military strategy,
are commonly referred to as *defensive*.) Others—it is difficult
to know whether we should call them optimists or oppor-
tunists—follow our prophets in the hopes of enhancing their

own positions by capitalizing on insights about the inevitable transformations that are supposed to be in store for us. (These would be considered *offensive* measures according to the conventions of military strategy.)

When thinking of the future in these ways, *control* is always the objective. We play a sort of cat-and-mouse game with the future: we act as if it has a life of its own, one which is quite separate from the lives we are living in the present and somehow malevolent and threatening, somehow opposed to us. In our desire to control the world of the future, we are constantly trying to outwit, outmaneuver, or at least adapt to it—before it even exists.

The masters of this peculiar game are, of course, those who are also most likely to play on our apprehensions about the future: our prophets. They not only predict but talk a great deal about *controlling* the future. John von Neumann, one of the fathers of computer science, made a number of predictions about computers in his time. One of these was that by the present time computers would have made weather data so manageable and manipulable, and would thereby have enhanced our knowledge about the weather so greatly, that we would not only be masters at predicting it, we would also be able to control it. Though this was a false prediction, at least theoretically von Neumann was right about controlling the future with the help of predictions. Within limits and under certain conditions, scientists can indeed make predictions about natural phenomena. And sometimes, with clever interventions in the natural order, they can also bring about certain outcomes. The sustained nuclear reaction upon which atomic energy is based is the classic example of this. But to bring about predictable outcomes in the natural order, two conditions are necessary. First, that order must be profoundly understood, and second, the intervention must be doable. The reason that even today, in the future von Neumann was trying to predict, we can still forecast weather only four or five days in advance and do little if anything to change it, is that neither of these conditions has yet been met with respect to the weather system, even with the help of tremendous computing power. Though it is far more accessible to our unaided senses, the weather system is even more incomprehensible and—in spite of clever fantasies of elab-

orate cloud seeding—also far more difficult to control than
the subatomic system. And of course human civilization—
that is, the human system with its social, economic and technological components—though in some ways tied to the natural order, is even still more complicated and difficult to
control than the weather system because it is also subject to
the irrational aspects of human nature as well as to free will.

Because of its extraordinary complexity and deep-seated
irrationalities, predictions about the human order, outside
of the shortest time frame, and beyond those having to do
with the most fundamental biological imperatives, are usually wrong. They are wrong because, even today, they are
usually no more than simple linear projections, or what Orwell called "a continuation of the thing that is happening."
Typically, the "thing that is happening" eventually slows
down or stops happening entirely or changes its meaning in
our lives; really remarkable changes are seldom if ever predicted. Consider the remarkable, yet unpredictable, developments that have occurred even since the end of the last
World War: the rise of Japan as the leading economic power;
the huge hole that has developed in the ozone layer; the
appearance of the AIDS virus; President Sadat going to Je-
rusalem; the rise to power in the Soviet Union of a radical
reformist like Gorbachev and the ensuing liberation of Eastern Europe. Not one of these unpredictable yet earth-
shaking developments has even the least bit of a "continuation of the thing that is happening" flavor, so when one
considers them, one cannot help but wonder why we are so
enthralled by these "more of the same" predictions when
they are, in the present, not very enlightening and, in the
long run, invariably wrong.

A brief look at prophecy in the oil industry, which has
characteristically been of the most straightforward linear variety, will provide at least the beginning of the answer to
this last question, and should also serve as the beginning of
the answer to a more general question: Why do we persist
in accepting prophecies that are more intricate than the
"more of the same" variety but just as unenlightening and
ultimately just as false?

For the last two decades the oil industry has tried very
hard to predict the future price of oil in order to gauge what

sorts of revenues they could expect in the future, and thereby know how much money could be profitably invested for acquisition, exploration and development. During consecutive stages in this period of time, the forecasters in this industry have developed five different predictive consensuses.[2] We are still waiting to see how well the fifth of these will fare, but as far as the first four are concerned, they have all proven to be dead wrong.

The pre-1971 "more of the same" consensus predicted that oil prices would remain stable, with the expectation that prices would fluctuate by no more than mere pennies for the indefinite future. This predictive consensus was damaged by the rise of OPEC in 1971, and completely devastated by the oil embargo of 1973.

The second consensus, which lasted from 1974 to 1977, actually contained two variations, one of which originated in North America, and the other in Europe and Japan. In other words, there were two somewhat different "more of the same" predictions based on different experiences and perspectives of what "the same" really meant. The point is, however, that they were both in the same ballpark and, in the end, they both proved to be wrong. The difference between them, however, is revealing about how this kind of forecasting really works and what it means. The North American version was more optimistic than its Euro-Japanese counterpart. The reason for this is that it relied on related predictions that effective technological fixes in the form of economical substitutes for oil from shale and coal tar would be developed in a reasonable amount of time. The Europeans and Japanese, however, were more pessimistic about the prospects of beating the cartel in the future through technological innovation or by any other means. Yet in spite of this divergence, both versions of this particular predictive consensus complied with Orwell's characterization of "a continuation of the thing that is happening." As Cambridge Energy Research Associates have observed: "North American optimism was based on confidence in technology and experience of abundant resources, while Europe's pessimism was rooted in a history of resource constraints. Europeans had not only lived through shortages during World War II but had also experienced an 'energy crisis' in the late 1940s.

The Japanese were even more conscious of their resource dependence and vulnerability than the Europeans. Economic and resource 'dependence' was a new experience for North Americans, and more likely to be regarded as an aberration. For Europeans, it was the normal state of affairs. For the Japanese, it was a fact of life."[3]

In the end, however, both versions of this predictive consensus failed to anticipate the true strength of OPEC in pushing up prices. Therefore, both of these predictions were shattered by facts, and in 1977 the North American and Euro-Japanese oil price forecasts once again completely merged to project a huge price rise based on an oil crunch which was to occur around 1985. It did not occur around 1985, but occurred instead in 1979 with the fall of the Shah of Iran and the Iranian Revolution.

New predictions were again required, so in 1980 a fourth predictive consensus was developed which foretold that prices would continue to rise sharply for an indefinite period with "OPEC in the driver's seat." This consensus was also shattered in 1982 when an unexpected oil glut began to develop in the global oil market, effectively eroding OPEC's strength and pushing down prices, which finally collapsed in 1986.

Each of the first four predictive consensuses of the last two decades was shattered in turn by unpredicted events and was consequently replaced by the next. There is no reason to expect that the fate of the fifth, and present, predictive consensus, which prophesies OPEC's comeback sometime in the next four years, will be any different. If it does turn out to be correct, however, this will not be the result of its being more accurate; it will be because it is more vague and contingent than the others.†

The above analysis is not meant as a wholesale condemnation of forecasting in the oil industry. On one level, one cannot help but empathize with oil industry executives who feel they must rely on such forecasts to make their investment decisions. During the four-year period between 1980 and

† At the time this book is going to press, oil prices are again rapidly rising, but not because of an OPEC comeback, as the most recent consensus predicted, but because of the Persian Gulf crisis. What long-term effect this conflict will have on oil prices is, of course, unpredictable.

1983, 375 public oil and gas companies spent $227 billion to acquire properties and conduct exploration and development.[4] The expenditure of such large sums of money is nerve-wracking, to say the least, and, though industry executives have learned that price predictions are invariably wrong, they use them anyway.

They use them anyway because they feel the need to use *something*. The function of this type of prediction, in light of its persistent failure, is ultimately rather political if we look at it in the context of the corporate culture in which it plays its part. In the large modern corporation, prediction often serves the function of legitimating decisions; and the power of this function, and its consequences, should not be underestimated. Decisions must be justified, they must be based on *something,* preferably on something rational. But if something rational is not available—and this is more often the case than is usually admitted—then they must be based on something that at least *appears* to be rational. And, because of the nature of corporate culture, through a process of information exchange and corroboration, all predictions, that is, all appearances of rationality, fairly rapidly become one; they all converge into consensuses like the ones I described above.

The best position in corporate culture, especially with respect to prediction, is, of course, to be right when everyone else is wrong; from this may come the greatest rewards and the greatest amount of satisfaction. Second best is to be right along with everyone else. But if one is going to be wrong, then it is better to be wrong in the same way that everyone else is wrong rather than in a different way; at least then, when the moment of reckoning comes, this shows that you are capable of consulting with and listening to your colleagues, and everyone can feel foolish together, in a collegial fashion. It is not for nothing that one Canadian oil price forecaster has said, "Oil price forecasters make a flock of sheep look like independent thinkers."[5]

Beyond its questionable ability to forge unfounded consensuses and justify corporate decisions, there might appear to be little, if anything, to concern us about the role that price forecasting plays in the oil industry. In a sense, this type of forecasting should not even be called prophecy, or even prediction, for it is no more than a form of monitoring. Much like weather forecasting, another form of monitoring which uses a time frame that extends only slightly forward from the present, it may sometimes be mildly useful; often it is not. If all prediction were to be viewed from this perspective, there would be little to say about it. But this perspective is far too narrow to explain the deeper role of modern prophecy. The fact of the matter is, that a great deal of futurology—be it in the form of prediction, forecasting, or scenario writing—far from being no worse than mere speculation that basically harms only the speculators involved, often plays a destructive role in the world by justifying harmful political decisions.

It is one thing for the shareholders in the major oil companies to periodically squander what is presumably discretionary wealth in making speculations based on predictions of the future prices of oil. But consider the all too typical case of a country like Mexico. Mexico has engaged in a similar sort of oil price speculation and has in recent history planned a great deal of its development on the expectation of revenues based on these same predictions. Mexico nationalized its oil industry in 1938 under the leadership of then President Lázaro Cárdenas, but the speculation did not really begin until the mid-1970s, when President José López Portillo decided to strongly tie the economic development of the entire country almost exclusively to the development of newly discovered vast oil reserves. He thereby made economic development heavily dependent almost solely on the accuracy of predictions of future oil prices. In the ensuing period, not only did buoyant predictions legitimate a lack of discipline in labor, and among corporate and bureaucratic spenders, but, more generally, the kind of thinking that stemmed from embracing such predictions encouraged the development of a lopsided supply- or resource-based economy. Expectations of future oil revenues also legitimated national borrowing of over $100 billion during this period; of course the banks were as culpable as the government in financing all of these deals. When these predictions proved to be false, the 1986 collapse in prices resulted in a drop in government revenues of no less than 25 percent! In the wake of this calamity, the plans for economic development that were being promoted in 1988 from some political quarters in Mexico advocated measures no less drastic than the repudiation of large parts of the national debt.[6]

Mexico's basing its development policy on oil price predictions, in spite of their historical unreliability, is not unusual, since this is what macro-economic theory encourages one to do. But prediction of one sort or another is almost always at the heart of policy, and not just economic policy. Most policies—aside from the kind which are no more than mere posturing—are designed to bring about or respond to future developments: either a bad outcome is to be avoided or mitigated, or a good one is to be attained. It is not at all uncommon for a well articulated policy paper, based on a hopeful or fearful prediction and laden with a vast quantity of ideological blustering, to set the tone for debate and influence policy direction for a generation or more. And because the rhetoric of prediction is so powerful, it can often effectively close off the possibility of truly open debate for an entire era.

In modern times, grandiose and sweeping predictions have even served as the justification for policies affecting other countries and other people. For example, strenuous ideological prophecy was used to justify American territorial expansionism starting in the middle of the nineteenth century, some of which, incidentally, had a powerful impact on Mexico. In 1845 the American editor and author John L. O'Sullivan wrote an article in the *United States Magazine and Democratic Review* in which he predicted that in a hundred years time, that is by 1945, the population of the United States would grow to 250 million or more. Here, in a piece appropriately called "Annexation," he coined the powerful and famous prophetic term "manifest destiny" to legitimate the expansionist policy that he felt was justified by his prediction; he argued that it was the "fulfillment of our manifest destiny to overspread the continent allotted by Providence for the free development of our yearly multiplying millions."[7] O'Sullivan's prediction, with its disregard for the rights of native populations and other sovereignties, is a good example of a prophecy that has been sundered from any moral basis, or, perhaps more accurately, the extent to which morality, and even God, were reduced to the precepts of what O'Sullivan liked to think were natural laws. Later, appealing at once to the laws of both God and science, he wrote: "Texas has been absorbed into the Union in the inevitable fulfillment of the general law which is rolling our population westward; the connexion of which with that ratio of growth in population which is destined within a hundred years to swell our number to the enormous population of *two hundred and fifty millions* (if not more), is too evident to leave us in doubt of the manifest design of Providence in regard to the occupation of this continent." (emphasis in original)[8]

To late-twentieth-century ears, which are used to hearing policy pronouncements with questionable motivations and consequences made in more obscure and equivocal language, O'Sullivan's words are truly searing. Yet even more remarkable than this is the rest of the ideological baggage which accompanied this prophetic rhetoric. It was not enough that the population should grow and occupy the continent: all of the extra room, in this influential visionary's mind, was destined only for one kind of American, the white Anglo-Saxon. He wrote: "In the case of California . . . the Anglo-Saxon foot is already on its borders. Already the advance guard of the irresistible army of Anglo-Saxon emigration has begun to pour down upon it, armed with the plough and the rifle."[9] Not surprisingly, then, another part of O'Sullivan's vision was that, if and when America's slaves should be emancipated, they should also be deported to South and Central America so as not to pollute the Anglo-Saxon stock that was destined to populate the northern hemisphere. O'Sullivan stated:

> . . . It is undeniably much gained for the cause of the eventual voluntary abolition of slavery, that it should have been thus drained off towards the only outlet which appeared to furnish much probability of the ultimate disappearance of the Negro race from our borders. The Spanish-Indian-American populations of Mexico, Central America and South America, afford the only receptacle capable of absorbing that race whenever we shall be prepared to slough it off—to emancipate it from slavery and

(simultaneously necessary) to remove it from the midst of our own. Themselves already of mixed and confused blood, and free from the "prejudices" which among us so insuperably forbid the social amalgamation which can alone elevate the Negro race out of virtually servile degradation, even though legally free, the regions occupied by those populations must strongly attract the black race in that direction; and as soon as the destined hour of emancipation shall arrive will relieve the question of one of its worst difficulties, if not absolutely the greatest.[10]

One cannot overestimate the force of this prophetic propaganda. The doctrine of manifest destiny was used as an argument of legitimation for expansionism at first only by Democrats, but eventually the policy crossed party lines and was later also used by Whigs and Republicans. It was used for half a century to justify the annexation of Texas, California and Oregon, and ultimately repeated in debates about Alaska, Guam and Cuba. And there is no question, had the opportunity arisen, that it would also have been used to legitimate the annexation of Canada, because, according to O'Sullivan's prophecy, this was to be the last step before a vast and purely Anglo-Saxon North America would be able to defy the rest of the world. But obsession with grandiose future outcomes based on presently promulgated policies was certainly not a passing mood in the development of American political culture. As in other great nations, prophecy has been the spur that has driven on politicians with grandiose world views.

In the second half of this century, probably no politician has been as obsessed with and conscious of the future as Henry Kissinger. One of his former colleagues at Harvard has therefore remarked that the former secretary of state "can always be counted upon to utter commonplaces in the tone of prophetic revelation."[11] And, remembering his tenure as national security adviser and secretary of state under President Nixon, another American historian has observed that Kissinger's career during this period was based largely on a prophetic style of manipulation and deception.[12] Perhaps these judgments are somewhat harsh, but during a political career that has now spanned more than thirty years, prophecy has certainly been one of the hallmarks of Kissinger's rhetoric, and the role of the prophet seems to have long been part of his own self-image. In his very first book, as if penning the stage directions for his own controversial career, Kissinger wrote: "The statesman is . . . like one of the heroes of classical drama who has had a vision of the future but who cannot transmit it directly to his fellow man and who cannot validate its 'truth.' "[13]

Recently—perhaps sobered by the contentiousness of his career, but also, apparently, smitten by the recurrently popular ethic of managerialism—Kissinger wrote, in an article about Soviet-American arms negotiations, that "statesmanship consists, in large part, of foreseeing and managing the *inevitable*." (emphasis added)[14] Such a statement may be very compelling on the surface, but exactly what does it mean?

The ethic of inevitability, which is so attractive to politicians like O'Sullivan and Kissinger, is perhaps the greatest rhetorical device used by prophetic politicians. However, unlike O'Sullivan, one thing that Kissinger certainly did not spell out in his article—and what present-day prophets who finally do get down to such bald terms seldom do spell out— is why a certain course of events or actions should be *inevitable*. And what is more important is that those, like Kissinger, who choose to speak with a prophetic voice in our time seldom say why a particular way of managing a certain development is preferable to any other. Management and inevitability are attractive to prophets because they have a neutral tone. But nothing is inevitable, and management is not a neutral activity: it does not merely order things, it makes them happen. And usually, when management works as it is intended to, it makes things happen in a very certain way.

The sense of the inevitable, which is so strong in the pronouncements of policy-making prophets like O'Sullivan in the last century and Kissinger in ours, does not work in the same way for everyone. Historians who, with the benefit of hindsight, can try to be objective seldom, if ever, make the assertion that a certain course of events was inevitable.† But more important, though the rhetoric of inevitability may sound prescient in the mouth of the prophet, ultimately it is part of the rhetoric of cynicism and/or defeatism; yet it is a powerful device for closing and stifling debate, and can be used to legitimate the most questionable self-interested long-range goals or projects.

Needless to say, Kissinger and many other politicians use prophecy this way. Indeed, the last part of the article from which his pronouncement of inevitability was quoted is full of point-by-point prescriptions based on what he believed the Reagan administration should do to respond to certain proposals which Mr. Gorbachev had then put forth with respect to arms control in light of the American strategic defense initiative. Aside from the fact that some of Kissinger's prescriptions were based on questionable assumptions, in the end they were all rather constrictive. They constrained the entire debate about Star Wars to the leaden framework of cold war thinking which Kissinger himself had so long labored to promote. This is typical. Talk of an inevitable future always aborts most open discussion of real options, and at the same time narrowly defines both the range of choice and the type of activity in which it is said one can engage to solve the problems at hand.

It is distressing that so much future-thought is so full of a sense of the inevitable because there is an enormous amount of evidence, from the variety of arrangements and developments ongoing around the world, to indicate that there is a great deal of scope for people, as individuals and as nations, to shape their own destinies without deferring to so-called inevitabilities. The variety of life-styles, cultures, social structures and economies that exist even under similar conditions is so great that one cannot help, when one takes thought, but balk at easy talk of the inevitable.

† But many futurologists are so enamored of the notion of inevitability that they use it even in their occasional analysis of the past as well as of the future. For example, in the typically vulgar way in which futurologists analyze history, Stanley Lesse, a prominent medical futurologist, writes, "Historic records show that cultures that fail to heed the challenges of social and technologic shift *inevitably* sink into a morass of darkness and *inevitable* oblivion." (emphasis added) (Stanley Lesse, *The Future of the Health Sciences*, New York: Irvington Publishers, 1981, p. 13.)

However, inevitability is not the only rhetorical device used by our modern-day prophets. Often complementing the ethic of inevitability in prophetic rhetoric has been another of *boldness,* as if, once one is sure of what the future will be, the best behavior is to dash right for it. Some futurologists have even made a virtue out of the boldest kinds of forecasts, as if there is virtue in the forecast itself and bolder implies braver and therefore better. In fact Jerrold Maxmen, an American health futurologist, has gone so far as to assert: "While some forecasters appear to lack imagination, others actually seem to fear it . . . even though *all of the necessary facts are available,* the would-be prophet cannot see that they point to an inescapable conclusion. . . . This unwillingness to accept the *inevitable consequences of available facts* is what so often leads to excessively conservative forecasts." (emphasis added)[15]

One certainly could not accuse the Mexican government of relying on conservative forecasts when it based its entire lopsided and overheated economic development on traditionally unreliable predictions of the future price of oil. But in recent times there is perhaps no more troubling reminder of the questionability of radical economic interventions based on bold but mistaken forecasts than the adverse economic consequences which have followed in the United States as a result of the economic policies—perhaps one should say economic adventurism—of the Reagan administration.

A great deal has been written about Reaganomics from the perspective of economic theory. The theory of supply-side economics, which was the driving force behind Reagan's massive intervention in the American economy, was dignified by its promoters as being a subtle economic theory, but vilified by its detractors as "voodoo economics." But whatever else one may say about it, in the end Reagan's version of supply-side economics was little more than a mess of bad predictions. It predicted that tax cuts would put more money into the pockets of consumers and corporations. It predicted that the consumers would then save, spend, or invest this extra money: savings would provide capital for investment while at the same time spending would create demand and stimulate the economy. It also predicted that corporations would invest their own tax savings and the tax savings of individuals (which they could readily borrow from banks) in ventures that would create jobs. Jobs would be created not only for the middle classes, but also for the lower classes through a mechanism known as "trickle-down." And finally, the theory of supply-side economics predicted that, in the end, all of this favorable economic activity would generate additional tax revenue which would make up for the shortfall created by the cuts and pay for increased defense spending, which was being promoted at the same time.

It is now painfully obvious that only one of the above predictions has come true: when the government cut taxes some consumers, particularly those in the higher tax brackets, and many corporations did indeed have more money to dispose of—and the government had less. Since *control* is the underlying assumption of such future-minded interventions, it is notable that this last eventuality was the only part of the future scenario which the government, by its own decision-making and behavior, could and did control. By now it is all too familiar how the many decisions, large and small, that the government could *not* predict or control were made; these are the decisions that have created the present adverse economic situation in the United States and, because of America's pivotal role in the world economy, ultimately in the whole world.

During the 1980s in the United States investment and savings actually went down, and though there was a great deal of spending in certain sectors of the economy and in certain geographical regions, its form was not terribly encouraging. Car and home purchases went down during the 1980s because these particular items kept going out of the reach of more and more consumers in spite of the much touted prosperity. Many taxpayers who received rebates, and consumers in general, spent their extra cash on foreign goods thus stimulating not the economy of the United States so much as those of Japan and West Germany, and thereby contributing to the increase in the American balance of payments deficit. Others invested in non-stimulating items like real estate and art. All too many corporations, in turn, decided to spend their extra cash not on ventures which would create long-term employment, but on non-stimulating take-overs; the effect was to create some jobs, many of them temporary in the financial services industry which works on these deals, but also to destroy many long-term or permanent jobs in others. At the same time corporations doing the takeovers created for themselves a great deal of long-term, often unmanageable debt. However, given the climate which the Reagan administration created by cutting taxes and boosting defense spending, why should consumers and corporations necessarily have acted differently? Why, outside of acting in their own interests, should any of the players in the economic game have acted in such a way as to make Reagan's predictions of good economic outcomes into self-fulfilling prophecies?

In the end, the point about Reagan's economic predictions is that they were too simplistic to be believable; they were based on a caricature of how the American economy works, not on a profound understanding. They were based, in other words, on the manipulation of a single simple variable, not on a broad-based concerted and complex effort. In free societies people and corporations make their own decisions and serve their own ends. No matter what the economic theories may be predicting that they should be doing at any given time, they will behave according to their own complex purposes. It is the sum of individual decisions, large and small, which make a world—not a grand theory like supply-side economics which predicts it will be thus and so. Why should the decisions of the people of an extremely heterogeneous and individualistic nation like the United States conform to the shape of a U-curve (the famous Laffer curve which justified the Reaganomic predictions), an S-curve, or any other overly simple way of predicting extremely complex behavior? It is remarkable how many predictions are made even by our most "sophisticated" prophets on the basis of mechanistic and monolithic views of the nature of society and of the nature of individual and collective decision-making. And yet it was these groundless economic predictions that made the Reagan administration's decision to cut taxes and increase spending seem credible and legitimate at the time that it was made.

In the end, the supply-side forecasting of the Reagan

administration simply legitimated what has turned out to be an enormous and destructive intervention in the American economy. It is true that this intervention was not the only factor to cause the decline which has become noticeable at the end of the 1980s—when Reagan began to implement his economic policies, many of the factors that have been contributing to this decline were already in place. However, Reagan's policies did hasten it and make it critical—and much more intractable—when more sensible policies, policies that did not rely on an abstract, remote and mechanistic theory, could have delayed, averted, or perhaps even reversed these trends.

But the point of all these observations is not merely that the predictions upon which supply-side economics was based have proven in the long run to be wrong, and that serious harms have accrued as a consequence of acting on them. This scheme was wrong from the very first day: not only was it wrong as a prediction, it also acted as a false promise. The American people and government were put into a false position and thereby encouraged to behave badly by, among other things, spending money which they did not have, and which they groundlessly expected to have only at some time in the future: they were encouraged to live dishonestly.† It is true that it took awhile for the effect of this type of dishonest living to become abundantly clear, but the effect was there from the first day that the government, facing a shortfall in tax revenue because of the cuts it had imposed, had to borrow the money from the bank, that is, from American and foreign savers. Of course Americans have a strong streak of common sense and are not more inherently dishonest than any other people, but Reagan's predictions acted as a sort of spell. During this period, Americans thought that they were living honestly by accumulating debt, but they were in fact deluding themselves. They were deluding themselves because they had been lied to by means of the false prophecy of the Reaganomic economists. This is the nature of the false position that America now finds itself in due to heeding the false promises inherent in the Reaganomic predictions.

† In this context it is important to note that the American spending spree on foreign goods was actually encouraged by another bit of falseness, that is, the Reagan administration's policy of propping the U.S. dollar above its natural level.

While it may be true that a people always get the government they deserve, it is also true that the government they get shapes the behavior of the people they represent. The folly of the American people during this period reflects not so much their fecklessness as the power of prediction to corrupt people by suspending their common sense and incredulity and encouraging them to behave poorly.

Many Americans are now feeling very sober about their economy and its long-term prospects now that the much-vaunted future has arrived. During the 1980s the national debt rose to 180 percent of GNP compared to 137 percent during the three decades before that. Foreigners also own a vast number of financial and tangible assets in the United States which they have bought with their surplus trade dollars. The stability of the American economy now depends as much on the common sense and goodwill of foreigners as on the virtues of Americans. In recent years, in spite of the proven bankruptcy of grand economic theories to predict major developments, Americans are still trying to control their economy by prediction. Since inflation is a recurrent bugbear, influential economists are constantly predicting that it can be controlled through engineered recessions. For example, in 1988, Albert Wojnilower, a forecaster who works as a senior economic adviser at First Boston Corporation advocated the following prescription: "After six or seven years of expansion it seems to me we will be doing quite well if there's a recession in the second half of 1989. The recession lasts about a year, and unemployment goes to eight, nine, ten percent and then goes down again. I don't believe recessions are therapeutic, but sometimes they are unavoidable."[16] Wojnilower and other financiers, like Peter Peterson, who wrote a celebrated article on this topic in the *Atlantic,* seem to believe, as Henry Kissinger does, that they can both foresee the inevitable and manage it. The inevitable, in this case, is runaway inflation; managing it means an engineered recession. Wojnilower believes recession is the only way to control the inflation which he predicts will get out of hand as long as unemployment remains low and too many people have money in their pockets. Prophets like Wojnilower who foresee inevitabilities always have prescriptions for managing them in mind. In this case they want to *manage* the so-called inevitability of inflation by raising interest rates to create a *controlled* recession that will dampen inflation.

The narrowness of Wojnilower's vision is quite obvious. Why is inflation inevitable? Theoretically, inflation is the result of too many dollars chasing after too few goods. Our experience with inflation in the early 1980s suggests that there is more to inflation than this theory will allow, but insofar as this theory is correct, Wojnilower has chosen to look at only one side of this equation: the many dollars in people's pockets chasing after goods. What about the availability of goods? The fact of the matter is that America in particular and the world in general are now, just as these predictions of inflation are being made, experiencing a surplus of most goods, including those in greatest demand: most minerals, including oil, in the absence of a crisis like the one presently taking place in the Persian Gulf, food and textiles. So why raise interest rates to avoid the inflation that is by no means inevitable? Once one gets past the rhetoric of inevitability there are, of course, alternative courses to an engineered recession that the United States could pursue. William Greider has argued that, alternatively, America should try to get out of its economic difficulties by creating a policy that promotes growth, not contraction. America could thus pay its debts by creating new wealth and not through the austerity which will adversely harm the most helpless members of society.

Given the scope of action which can be taken in response to economic problems, it is disheartening to recall that while America was working itself into a tight corner by following Reagan's false economic prophets, Prime Minister Thatcher of England was also insisting to her fellow countrymen—while ever increasing numbers of them, especially outside of the London region, were being driven by her economic policies onto the rolls of the unemployed—that "There is no other way." When a leader says "such and such a course is inevitable," or, "there is no other choice," they mean to sound high-minded: "this suffering is necessary, and is to be endured for the sake of a better future for all"; or, "this

situation is in the nature of things, part of the world order."
Yet such an attitude is tyrannical.

Many actions which are taken by governments and large
corporations and justified on the basis of predictions of future
conditions are tyrannical. First, any adaptation in the present
time made in anticipation of conditions which are predicted
for the future is bound to contribute towards making these
predictions into self-fulfilling prophecies. How could it be
otherwise? To cite a now somewhat tired example from the
height of the auto-industrial period, if one builds superhigh-
ways on the basis of the prediction of increased demand for
them, automobile manufacturers will find it easier to sell cars
because of the ongoing expansion of the highway system and
demand will indeed increase. This is all very well if that is
the direction a nation wants to go and undoubtedly many
nations, even in this "age of information," would not mind
having a robust auto-industrial economy. However, in the
case of an economy that is willing to accept an increased rate
of unemployment rather than an increased demand for cars,
the legitimating nature of prediction becomes reprehensible.
Yet many governments, with the telling exceptions of Sweden, Japan, Austria and a few others, act as if there is no
choice but to adapt to this "inevitable" future.[17]

To illustrate this point in greater detail I will briefly
describe some developments which have occurred during the
last fifteen years or so in the economies of Sweden and Denmark. These developments demonstrate how effective societal wilfulness, as opposed to accepting inevitabilities or
pursuing grand schemes, can be in shaping national destiny.[18]

In 1973, at the beginning of the recessionistic period
which we are still in, the social policy-makers of both Sweden
and Denmark made divergent decisions about how to deal
with the projected "inevitable" rise in the tide of youth unemployment, and took divergent actions to implement them.
The Swedish government, always believing rising unemployment to be unacceptable, decided, in spite of the worldwide economic downturn, to try to retard and minimize
unemployment as much as possible by continuing to
strengthen what economists call an employment policy. In
the depth of this recession, the American economist Robert

Kuttner described the measures taken by the Swedish government to minimize unemployment: "The parent labor board spends about 12 billion Swedish crowns a year, or some 2 percent of Sweden's GNP, creating jobs. The board not only sponsors relief work; it subsidizes retraining and relocation costs for the unemployed, and runs the workshops for the handicapped. It can even stockpile goods in order to help manufacturers through short-term economic downturns, and it can invest capital in new ventures."[19]

The government of Denmark, on the other hand, has been unwilling—some would argue, unable—to tamper with the labor market. It decided instead only to maintain existing programs designed to mitigate the adverse effects of unemployment, and therefore maintained its rich variety of social and economic support programs which fall under the rubric of what is commonly called a welfare policy.

By 1983, ten years after these countries headed along their divergent roads, Denmark's unemployment rate had grown to 10.4 percent while that same year Sweden, during the worst part of the recession, experienced 3.4 percent unemployment compared to a European average of over 10 percent. The costs of implementing both types of approaches has been, and continues to be, much the same. The real difference between these two divergent social and economic policies lies not in costs but in consequences for the people involved and, like all really existential differences, is therefore immeasurable. Presumably the Danish government felt unable to respond to the rising tide of unemployment in any other way, but during this period the people of Denmark, having arrived at the future which their government believed to be acceptable for them, have been voting with their feet by emigrating in greater numbers.

By planning a welfare as opposed to an employment policy, Denmark and many other western countries have painted themselves into an existential corner. A society with a higher rate of unemployment has become the norm for these countries: programs are entrenched, patterns have been set, money that might have been committed for job maintenance and creation has instead been committed to transfer payments. And now, several years later, the scope for maneuvering is rather less. The world economy and individual national economies are no longer very forgiving. Of all of the bad planning that goes on in this world, the kind that is most debilitating in the long run is the kind that the late Professor Herbert Marcuse of Brandeis University had in mind when he said that planning limits choice.[20] Preemptively limiting choice in planning is equivalent to the ethic of inevitability in prediction. The kind of planning that Marcuse had in mind was reflected in Reagan's economic policy in the sense that it squeezed America into an economic corner in which economic choices are now limited and/or made by foreigners. It should be contrasted with the kind of planning that Sweden has chosen to do, the kind that enriches the context which makes development possible and thereby maintains or even expands the realm of choice. After all, should Sweden now decide, for reasons that are almost impossible to imagine, to go the route of subsidizing leisure rather than employment opportunities, it can much more easily do so than can Denmark change its course.[21]

Reagan's debilitating—it is yet too early to say whether it will turn out to be disastrous—economic planning highlights another way in which the future, as ultimate realm of simple solution to complex and difficult problem, is used to falsely enhance the present.[22] Any behavior, no matter how reckless, can be justified in the present if a future solution is posited. Present accumulation of massive debt has been said to be acceptable—as long as prosperity is predicted so that, presumably, future generations can repay the debt with spare cash; use of nuclear reactors in the present is also supposed to be all right—as long as it is supposed that in the future there will be a solution to the problem of waste disposal. In this way, the unknown and unknowable are used by one generation to betray the next. This development, so characteristic of our time, is profoundly disturbing and rather ironic because planning for the well-being of the future generation used to be considered one of the virtues of the present generation. Today, this process is all too often perverted so that the future generation is systematically betrayed by the present one.

One certainly could not accuse Reagan of having used conservative forecasting in legitimating his supply-side economic plan; in fact he even tried to make a virtue of the radical nature of his interventions in the American economy while predicting the boldest and best outcomes. But whether his motives were based on foolishness, as some of his detractors have argued, or cynicism, as the more outspoken ones have held, it is tragic that in making his moves Reagan did not make the important distinction between bravery and recklessness. Aristotle pointed out in his *Ethics* that it is recklessness that is the opposite of cowardice, whereas bravery, the real virtue in all of this, is the golden mean between these two extremes. What the reckless forecasting of the Reagan administration has taught us during the last decade is that it is the ability to distinguish between recklessness and bravery that is the true mark of the statesman today, not a sense of the inevitable, as politicians like Kissinger would have us believe.

The virtue of statesmanship is not to "foresee the inevitable and manage it" as Kissinger has contended—and certainly not with false and self-serving predictions. The virtue of statesmanship is to bring out the best in people by creating a political culture, like that of Sweden, that makes them act responsibly. Acting responsibly always means taking into account the bigger picture; acting in the present and acting in a consistent, disciplined and sustained way. Greider's suggestion that America solve her fiscal problems through expanded growth is certainly more attractive from the perspective of the vulnerable unemployable than is Wojnilower's prescription of a recession. But both rapid growth and rapid contraction are dangerous courses because they are hard to control: the former can lead to a so-called overheated economy and runaway inflation, while the latter can spiral down to long-term depression. Neither is as desirable as the kind of stability that comes from consistent, responsible behavior in the present. This responsibility has nothing to do with ideology. Sweden and Japan, which both have a political culture which is geared towards making the population act responsibly, are on different sides of the political spectrum, the former being more to the Left, while

the latter is more to the Right. It is the coherence of their
culture and not wilful abandonment to grand schemes for
the future that is guiding them forward.

Talk of the inevitable by our prophets is both insidious
and powerful, and when abused, as it usually is, is tyrannical.
When we hear it, we would do well to ask ourselves: What
does the promoter of a particular inevitable scenario have
at stake in having it realized? What do they have to gain?
And, perhaps more importantly, because there is no such
thing as a neutral future, what do other, undoubtedly more
helpless members of our society, have to lose?

The tyranny of prophecy very often lies in the fact that
it inspires us, as Orwell has said, to act out of fear or a desire
for power (in economics this is called greed). It therefore
brings out the worst in us. And although such prophecy may
not always be a wilful act of manipulation per se, it acts as
though it is, inspiring us to abandon our common sense and
our best virtues for those which the false and self-serving
prediction tell us will help us to succeed or survive. Aristotle
wrote in his *Politics* that, on the contrary, government leadership should be such that it brings out the best in people.
Irresponsible prophecy brings out the worst: it brings out
the exploitative forces of greed, abandonment and neglect.
And, ultimately, tyrannical prophecy leads to the denial of
individual meaning and fulfilment, because if one acts so as
to make such prophecies self-fulfilling, one is acting to bring
about the fulfilment of the prophet, not of oneself.

In this century prophecy has been playing on our anxiety
about the future in all sorts of ways. Twenty to twenty-five
years ago prophecy was, for the second time this century,
in what sociologists would call its charismatic stage. In the
United States, popular futurologists like Herman Kahn, Alvin Toffler and Buckminster Fuller were at the height of
their popularity and had managed to capture both the public,
private, individual and corporate imaginations. Toffler
played on our fears by telling us how difficult it would be to
cope in an ever more rapidly changing world; Fuller played
on our hopes by telling us we could solve all of our problems
by clever design; and Kahn played on our nerves by talking
about nuclear war in the most bloodless, academic way. In

France, Bertrand de Jouvenal had established the journal called *Futuribles,* in which he began to publish a sort of Michelin Guide to the future—places to go, places to avoid—in the form of speculative essays. Futurologist bureaucrats like Ervin Laszlo and Amadou-Mahtar M'Bow (the latter was later to be disgraced) were rapidly working their way up through the well-funded international agencies; futurist societies were springing up all over the world and holding conventions from Oslo to Tokyo. In spite of a plethora of serious problems and conflicts, the world was generally a much more genuinely optimistic place then, and futurology was, in a way, part of the optimism that pervaded it. But though it was a part of this optimism, it certainly was not the basis for it.

Though its profile at present may be somewhat lower than it was then, futurology is now more pervasive than ever. And modern prophecy has also entered a new phase, which sometimes makes its effects more subtle. Like all charismatic movements, it has finally become institutionalized and rationalized, has become a given, a presence, an essential part of our corporate and bureaucratic life and culture, as well as of our personal lives.

Our world is full of advisers that function much the same way as the government task force for which I worked, but often in ways that are not nearly so bureaucratically equivocal. We have all heard by now of the thousands of newsletters published by business forecasters. Some of these are a form of monitoring and serve as a security blanket, but many have encouraged serious hiccups in the stock market in recent years, and some even contributed to the panic that led to the crash of 1987. When the next crash comes, they will undoubtedly also help it along. More important, however, is the fact that many analyses of the stock market crash of October 1987 have concluded that it was caused by the instability created by "futures" trading. If the stock market is at all rational some of its rationality has been based on its operation in real time, that is present time, with all of the necessary corrective feedback loops this entails. Futures trading, which in America has largely been fueled by the more speculative traders who are based in Chicago, has only served to unground and undermine a system that is often excessively abstracted and little enough grounded in reality.†

Beyond the minor industry of purveying "privileged" knowledge about the future in the form of newsletters, most large private corporations now use futurologists as consultants, or even have them on permanent staff. Futurologists are to be found advising the highest levels of government, including heads of state, all over the world, both East and West. Futurologists are "in," they are now, like the court astrologers of old, an integral part of our culture. They are no longer the irrepressible starry-eyed children they were in the 1960s. They are seasoned consultants and bureaucrats, plying the leaden seas of the so-called rationalism that today encroaches upon every nook and cranny of our culture and society. Our anxiety about the future has naturally enhanced the position of our prophetic politicians, and of our futurologists and forecasters—they have the map of the future, they will tell us how to get there.

All of this frenzied prophetic activity is carried out in the name of progress and necessity, or inevitability. George Orwell has remarked about progress: "If each epoch is as a matter of course better than the last, then any crime or folly that pushes the historical process forward can be justified. Between, roughly, 1750 and 1930 one could be forgiven for imagining that progress of a solid, measurable kind was taking place. Latterly this has become more and more difficult . . ."[23] We have certainly seen enough crimes and folly committed in our time for the sake of the future in the name of progress and its handmaiden, inevitability. In this chapter alone I have mentioned dispossession of land, transfer of

---

† Futures trading is typical of novel schemes that give advantage to interest groups but are rationalized as being in the public interest. Many revolutions are like this, but in the case of futures trading the victims are blamed for not being able to master the computer technology that makes this trading possible. In a critique of futures trading in *The New Republic,* James Cramer has noted "the current debate always begins with the inevitability of a product that is less than a decade old, and instead gets diverted to remedies about how to live with increased volatility that futures cause." But he rightly maintains that "the debate isn't about technology, it's about capital. If the investors in stocks had the same amount of buying or selling power as the users of the computers, and if the users of computers had to be bound by the rules against bear raids, we would be proud to embrace the new technology. But that's not the case." (James J. Cramer, "Basket Case," in *The New Republic,* November 13, 1989.)

wealth from the poor to the rich, borrowing beyond means and forced unemployment. The prophecies upon which all of these policies were based were false, not only intellectually but, more important, morally. That is why we can properly speak of the tyranny of prophecy.

It may be difficult to say which prophecies are false and may do us harm but it is possible to do so if we take thought; usually it takes more courage than wisdom to figure it out. Most false prophecies fly in the face of common sense, common decency, or both. They ask us either to prepare for something that will not happen; not prepare for something that is bound to happen in the expectation of miraculous (read technological) redemption; persist in something that is foolish, fatally flawed; or neglect something good and worthwhile because we are told we will not need it in the future. And one does not need an elaborate fantasy in order to escape reality: the simplest lie will do if it serves the purpose of deflecting our attention from it. Even the overwhelming costs of failed economic predictions do not seem to bring home to us the general weakness of economic theory. After giving a long account of failed economic development plans in both the Third World and the West that have relied on false economic predictions, Jane Jacobs observed that: "Failures can help set us straight if we attend to what they tell us about realities. But observation of realities has never, to put it mildly, been one of the strengths of economic development theory."[24] If you are going to escape the responsibility of reality, what does it matter what ship you use? The ship can be the most prosaic thing in the world. A simple linear projection, which is the substance, even today, of a vast amount of forecasting, with all of its apparent simplicity, sterility, and lack of emotion, will serve well as a lie.

So why do we follow our prophets? We can understand some of the irrational reasons simply by looking at the origins and meaning of trends. It is impossible to say where these eruptions we call trends actually come from, but it would be wrong to assume that they necessarily come from the best part of our nature, and undoubtedly they often come from quirky, perverse or even pathological aspects of our subconscious, aspects which want to be exalted or to play. Therefore we should take to heart Orwell's caution against bowing down to the conqueror of the moment, not only because, as he himself observes, at the moment of conquest it is impossible to gauge how far or how fast he will go, but also because the conqueror, that is, the present trend, may not be such an admirable thing in the first place.

Every period produces trends which tend to have a certain tone or flavor; in our time, this flavor tends to be rationalistic. I say rationalistic rather than rational because the technological juggernaut that drives most modern trends pertains only to a part of reason, its tendency to reduce problems to their simplest components, its reductionist aspect, rather than to the whole thing.

It has been said that most modern visions are caricatures of reality. This is true because it is in the nature of caricature both to oversimplify and to represent an exaggerated aspect of a larger reality as the whole thing. (What greater caricature of reality is there than the straight line epitomized by the linear projection that is so dear to the futurist's heart.) In the nineteenth century, humorists like the Frenchman Albert Robida used caricature to satirize modern trends. It is a sign of the humorlessness of our time that we take these future-minded caricatures seriously.

The danger in following our modern visionaries and thereby contributing to the fulfilment of their prophecies is two-fold. If we fail to fulfill their visions, we will have wasted a great deal of money, time and energy in trying to realize them. If we succeed, however, then we diminish our humanity precisely to the degree that we do succeed by squeezing it into one corner of our souls, that corner which I have just called rationalistic.

Actually, the part of our nature which drives trends while wearing the mask of reason appeals to highly irrational elements. Orwell has rightly ascribed the elements of fear and worship of power to modern futurity but more generally, the psychology of trend-chasing is mob or horde psychology. All of these irrational elements are laid bare in the trends which erupt in the fashion industry. Here we can also see the self-interested and exploitative roles played by the prophets of that industry, who are commonly and shamelessly called trend-setters. When we see individuals suspending their judgment and deluding themselves in order to squeeze or bend their natures in the service of following fashion trends, we rightfully find the spectacle pathetic, but we little appreciate the degree to which this same nature-bending phenomenon occurs in our institutions, in politics and in business.

Modern prophecy taps into every aspect of the modern consciousness: how we think about most of our problems, the psychological and ideological trappings of our souls. And the influential false prophets of our time are like bad psychotherapists who go into practice because of an endless and unresolved fascination with their own neurosis, and encourage their patients to ceaselessly play with theirs rather than face reality and take responsibility for their lives. Therefore the study of modern prophecy is not only a study of what we are becoming, but of what we are. In the next two chapters I will explore this psychological and ideological soul, and in the following four, my case studies, I will show how this plays itself out in vital and particularly vulnerable areas of our existence, how we defend ourselves, how we replace ourselves, how we preserve ourselves, and how we treat the world of nature. In the final chapters I will offer alternative ways of approaching the problem of the future, of what we are going to become.

NOTES

1. René Dubos, *Beast or Angel: Choices that Make Us Human* (New York: Scribner, 1974), pp. 119, 122.
2. The following analysis is drawn from Cambridge Energy Research Associates (CERA) and Arthur Andersen & Co., *The Future of Oil Prices: The Perils of Prophecy* (Cambridge and Houston, 1984).
3. CERA et al., p. 13.
4. Arthur Andersen & Co., *Oil & Gas Reserve Disclosures: Survey of 375 Public Companies, 1980–1983* (Houston, 1984), cited in CERA et al., pp. 1–2.
5. CERA et al., p. 8.
6. See Daniel Yergin, "Taming the Dinosaur," in *The New Republic* (July 4, 1988), pp. 17–20.
   Of course Mexico has not been the only nation in our time that has based its plans for economic development on simple-minded projections; after all, simple-minded projections are the primary product of macro-economic theory in our times. No one has summarized the all too familiar panorama of foolishness better than Jane Jacobs, who observed: "Khrushchev, visiting the United Na-

tions, banged his shoe on the table and foretold a Soviet economy that by 1975 would overtake America's and thereafter proceed to 'bury' the West. In the United States, Presidents Kennedy and Johnson and their advisers not only assumed, as most Americans did, that the country's high productivity and economic supremacy were assured far into the future; they also assumed that the fiscal measures they were using to fine-tune the economy were going to eliminate even its jiggles: no more depressions, and soon no more recessions." She continues: "Poor countries on the fringes of Europe were anticipating great prosperity when it came their turn to join the European community and share in supplying its huge, integrated and safely wealthy markets. . . . People and rulers in backward countries, including those that had just won independence from colonial rule or were struggling to do so, expected professionally drawn up development schemes to engineer prosperity and progress for them too. Their expectations were fully shared in countries financing development schemes with loans or gifts." But what was the result of these grandiose predictions and the expectations they created? "We think of the experiments of particle physicists and space explorers as being extraordinarily expensive, and so they are. But the costs are as nothing compared with the incomprehensibly huge resources that banks, industries, governments and international institutions like the World Bank, the International Monetary Fund and the United Nations have poured into tests of macro-economic theory." (Jane Jacobs, *Cities and the Wealth of Nations: Principles of Economic Life*, London: Viking, 1985, pp. 3–6.)

7. John L. O'Sullivan, "Annexation," in *United States Magazine and Democratic Review* (July–August 1845), p. 5.
8. O'Sullivan, p. 7.
9. O'Sullivan, p. 9.
10. O'Sullivan, p. 7.
11. Richard Pipes, "Why the Soviet Union Thinks It Could Fight and Win a Nuclear War," in *Commentary* (July 1977), p. 24.
12. Frederick Siegel, *Troubled Journey* (New York: Hill and Wang, 1984).
13. Henry Kissinger, *A World Restored: Metternich, Castlereagh and the Problems of Peace, 1821–1822* (Boston: Houghton Mifflin, 1973).
14. Henry Kissinger, "My Reply to Mr. Gorbachev," London *Observer,* (September 8, 1985). Kissinger has a great deal at stake in the present arms-control negotiations since, as I will demonstrate in Chapter Four, his earlier prescriptions, based on his own predictions, significantly contributed to the nuclear arms build-up. His view of the statesman as forecaster/manager is in sharp contrast to that of Hannah Arendt who has written, on the contrary, that "Proudhon's passing remark, 'The fecundity of the unexpected far exceeds the statesman's prudence,' is fortunately still true. It exceeds even more obviously the expert's calculations." (*On Violence.*)
15. Jerrold Maxmen, *The Post-Physician Era: Medicine in the Twenty-first Century* (New York: John Wiley & Sons, 1976), p. 10.
16. Cited by William Greider in "The Shadow Debate on the American Economy," in *Rolling Stone* (July 14–28, 1988), p. 86.
17. In this context I cannot help but recall that towards the end of the last recession when I was working as a consultant to my strategic planning task force in the Government of Ontario, one of the big issues that came up then was how the Education Ministry should respond to the prediction of ever increasing rates of unemployment, especially among youth. Since one of the functions of the education system is to prepare youth for the world of work, my task force felt that it was in a quandary as to how to plan for this much touted eventuality. One solution that some members of the group toyed with was that we may have to change our education system to prepare youth for "involuntary leisure" rather

than for work. And it should be borne in mind that in adopting this strategy, or at least, for the moment, paying lip service to it, the task force was following the lead of the Council of Europe which around that time was also publishing papers advocating similar policies, in response, apparently, to the alarming rise of youth gangs in many European cities.

18. The following account is drawn from Robert Kuttner, "Trials of Two Welfare States," in *The Atlantic Monthly* (November 1983), pp. 14–20.

19. Kuttner, p. 16.

20. Herbert Marcuse, *Eros and Civilization: A Philosophical Inquiry into Freud* (Boston: Beacon Press, 1966).

21. Even in Sweden, where the government has adopted a policy of trying to avoid unemployment rather than one which more or less accepts it as inevitable as in the case of Denmark and Canada, one finds futurological thinking in a similar, though more insidious, vein. In addressing the unemployment problem in a recent publication, a committee of futurologists in the Swedish Secretariat for Futures Studies came to the conclusion that, "In order for this [future workplace] equation to balance in terms of employment, working hours will have to be reduced and *some continued increase will be required in the public sector . . .* full employment without a reduction of working hours *and an enlargement of the public sector* does not appear to be a realistic target." (emphasis added) (Secretariat for Futures Studies, *Time to Care*, Oxford: Pergamon Press, 1984, p. 240.) Reduce the length of the work week—fine. But why should the public sector be the one to take up the slack? Instead of planning to play the role of employer of last resort, why should not the government of Sweden, with probably the most sophisticated job creating and retraining apparatus in the world, not create conditions so that the private sector, rather than the public one, take up the slack in the fight against rising unemployment? However the irony of members of the public sector advocating a future expansion of their own area of the economy seems to have entirely escaped this committee of planners and futurologists. This is the sort of thinking that exists behind "managing the inevitable"—and this is the sort of thing that often passes for planning today.

22. In a celebrated article that analyzes many of the time bombs that have been put in place in America because of a dishonest regard for the future, Peter G. Peterson has written: "We have, in addition, saddled ourselves with an informal debt of nearly $10 trillion in unfunded liabilities in Social Security, Medicare, and federal pensions. That astronomical figure is the difference between the benefits today's workers are now scheduled to receive and the future taxes today's workers are slated to pay for them. It amounts to a hidden tax of $100,000 on every American worker, and its toll will be exacted on our children." (Peter G. Peterson, "The Morning After," in *The Atlantic Monthly*, October 1987, p. 60.)

23. George Orwell, "Catastrophic Gradualism," in *Collected Essays, Journalism and Letters* (New York: Harcourt Brace Jovanovich, 1968), Volume 4, p. 17.

24. Jacobs, *Cities and the Wealth of Nations*, p. 7.

No plausible claim to intellectuality can possibly be made in the near future without an intimate dependence upon this new instrument [the computer]. Those intellectuals who persist in their indifference, not to say snobbery, will find themselves stranded in a quaint museum of the intellect, forced to live petulantly, and rather irrelevantly, on the charity of those who understand the real dimensions of the revolution and can deal with the new world it will bring about.

—EDWARD FEIGENBAUM

THE PSYCHOLOGY OF FUTUROLOGY

Susan Sontag once made an astute comment about photography that might well have been made about futurology, a field with which photography has a great deal in common: "Photography, which has so many narcissistic uses, is also a powerful instrument for depersonalizing our relation to the world; and the two uses are complementary. Like a pair of binoculars with no right or wrong end, the camera makes exotic things near, intimate; and familiar things small, abstract, strange, much farther away. It offers, in one easy, habit-forming activity, both participation and alienation in our own lives and those of others—allowing us to participate, while confirming alienation."[1] Sontag's observation might be disturbing for those who instinctively look at pictures with an uncritical eye, because it robs photography of much of its commonly presumed innocence, an innocence which is reflected in such popular sayings as "the camera never lies," and "one picture is worth a thousand words." But by questioning photography's superficial innocence Sontag has also shed light on the photographer's social role, ascribing a more active status, as "participator" and "alienator," than is usually attributed to him.

Sontag's insight is also disturbing in other ways that are relevant to both photography and prophecy. In a sense, she has asserted a social critic's version of Heisenberg's famous dictum that there is no such thing as pure observation because observation is itself a kind of *interference* or *intrusion;* the very act of observing changes the observer and/or the observed even while it is being performed. However, if observation is an *act* rather than a *happening,* then it is a moral act. It is moral because it entails both perspective and posture; it defines not only where the observer stands but how, by positioning himself, he would like to look at the world, and how he would like to make the world appear to himself and to others to whom he might be describing it. Unless it has no particular interest to you, you seldom simply look at something: you eye it, or you watch it at a safe distance, or you peek at it, or peer at it, or stare it down. You may even try, by your very act of observation, either to control or avoid it. In all observation there may be elements of directness, honesty, clarity, but there may also be elements of avoidance, condescension, worship.

The futurologist has much in common with the photographer because his enterprise is also highly selective and deeply interpretive by nature. And, insofar as present reality is so rich that it can never adequately be captured by observation, how much less so can future reality? All predictions, all "observations" of the future, are superficial, are snapshots *by nature and by necessity.* Consequently, they have built into them not only the limitations of distant perspective, but also opportunities for deception—of others as well as of oneself. Even where goodwill exists, these opportunities arise from unavoidable selectivity; in the absence of goodwill they arise from wilful or foolish misconstruction. Predictions, like snapshots, also have the ability to depersonalize the world because they are characteristically so abstract and general, and in this abstraction is contained a great deal of moral lassitude. It is all right, it seems, to predict a recession or rising interest rates, even if the act of prediction helps to bring these things about, because the harm that they cause is abstract, not meant to harm any particular person's future.

To a certain extent the biases and limitations of forecasting are also true of the social sciences in general. However, in the social sciences one can occasionally temper the distance; one can alter one's perspective by attempting to draw closer; one can drop theory and orthodox methodology by going out into the field to try to get an unmediated taste of raw reality. For example, if an economist observing the economy of the United States in the late 1980s were confused by the distant perspective given by aggregate statistics (statistics that do not reveal the particulars of its inner workings but post a number of seemingly healthy indicators like low unemployment, low inflation and relatively low interest rates), he might try to unpack this perspective by taking a closer look at certain details. If he did so he might find, for example, that the unemployment rate was deceptive because one-eighth of all employed persons were employed only part-time; or, if he looked at other data to try to determine the meaning of having a job he might learn that, in spite of high employment, an increasing number of those who had recently entered the job market had given up hope of ever owning their own homes. But futurology cannot make use of the kind of self-correction that comes from drawing closer, because its distance from its subject matter is part of its method, is part and parcel of the field itself. Futurologists are trapped in a distant observational outpost of their own contrivance. If they attempt to shorten the distance by shortening the time frame in which their predictions are made, they take the life out of them; their prophecy becomes less interesting because, as it is framed closer to the present time, it begins to lose the right to call itself prophecy. (What is so terribly prophetic about predicting that you are going to have lunch with a certain friend next week?) Furthermore, as one shortens the time frame even further, one is finally really working in the present, and one is reduced, ultimately, to monitoring it. Of course, studies of the present can be made to appear to be studies of the future—and very often they are—but only by being dressed up in futuristic blather. The true social scientist can alter his perspective by drawing closer because what he has ultimately fixed in his mind is reality;

the futurologist cannot draw closer even if he wishes to do so because what he has fixed in his mind is imaginary, it does not yet and may never exist.

Photography, at its worst, is undoubtedly superficial. But unlike photography, futurology, even at its best, does not have the redeeming feature of at least potentially being able to leave a somewhat honest record. While the photographer's psychological makeup includes, as Sontag has remarked, the elements of participation and alienation, the futurologist's includes distancing, avoidance, self-delusion and deception. In this sense, both photography and futurology are active participants in the cult of superficiality. They both freeze a minute part of the real or imaginary world, turn it into an icon and invite us not to question it but to pay homage—or even to worship it.

From the above remarks it should be clear that there is more to the psychology of prophecy than the cowardice and worship of power which Orwell found so striking. But the best way to get a deeper and more broadly based psychological understanding of why so much folly manages to maintain such a strong hold on our lives is to examine a few prophets in action to observe both what they do and why their appeal works. I will begin with one who is fairly contemporary but not current, so that it will be possible also to apply to him the "test of time."

Anyone who is interested in computers, especially if they are also interested in the field of artificial intelligence, should know something about the work of the logician Alan Turing, who, in the 1930s and 1940s, was one of this field's great theorists. In fact, like Einstein in the field of physics, Turing provided a great deal of direction and much of the theory which many scientists have spent their entire careers exploring. However, while Einstein was perfectly willing to let the chips fall where they may in the proving or disproving of his theories, Turing chose to assume the role of propagandist for his views, and what is particularly interesting about his role as a propagandist is that he played it by assuming the part of the prophet.

In 1950 one of the big burning questions in the field of artificial intelligence (AI) was "Can computers think?"—a question that still interests people today. In that year, Turing wrote a famous article called "Computing Machinery and Intelligence" in which he addressed this question in such an intriguing and compelling way that it set the tone of the discussion for most people who have raised it from that time to the present day. What is interesting about Turing's answer was that though the question was posed in the present tense, he chose to play the role of prophet and answer it for future time.

Since Turing was one of the most eminent logicians of our time it is not surprising that his argument appears on the surface to be completely logical; I will have to quote him at length to convey the logical flavor of his argument.[2] He started this paper by dismissing the question "Can computers think?" as too ambiguous to be meaningful. Instead he offered an alternative approach that worked as follows:

> I propose to consider the question "Can machines think?" This should begin with definitions of the meaning of the terms "machine" and "think." The definitions might be framed so as to reflect so far as possible the normal use of the words, but this attitude is dangerous. If the meaning of the words "machine" and "think" are to be found by examining how they are commonly used it is difficult to escape the conclusion that the meaning and the answer to the question, "Can machines think?" is to be sought in a statistical survey such as a Gallup poll. But this is absurd. Instead of attempting such a definition I shall replace the question by another, which is closely related to it and is expressed in relatively unambiguous words.[3]

Notice that Turing did not say why a question should be considered to be meaningless just because it is ambiguous. Is the question, "Do you love me?" which is always at least a little ambiguous, also therefore always meaningless? But let us follow his argument a little further to see what he proposes to be a more meaningful and appropriate question. Turing went on to deal with the question of whether machines can think in the following way:

The new form of the problem can be described in terms of a game which we call the "imitation game." It is played with three people, a man (A), a woman (B), and an interrogator (C) who may be of either sex. The interrogator stays in a room apart from the other two. The object of the game for the interrogator is to determine which of the other two is the man and which is the woman. He knows them by labels X and Y, and at the end of the game he says either "X is A and Y is B" or "X is B and Y is A." The interrogator is allowed to put questions to A and B thus:

C: "Will X please tell me the length of his or her hair?" Now suppose X is actually A, then A must answer. It is A's object in the game to try to cause C to make the wrong identification. His answer might therefore be:

"My hair is shingled, and the longest strands are about nine inches long."

In order that tones of voice may not help the interrogator the answers should be written, or better still, typewritten. The ideal arrangement is to have a teleprinter communicating between the two rooms. Alternatively the questions and answers can be repeated by an intermediary. The object of the game for the third player (B) is to help the interrogator. The best strategy for her is probably to give truthful answers. She can add such things as "I am the woman, don't listen to him!" to her answers, but it will avail nothing as the man can make similar remarks.

We now ask the question, "What will happen when a machine takes the part of A in the game?" Will the interrogator decide wrongly as often when the game is played like this as he does when the game is played between a man and a woman? These questions replace our original, "Can machines think?"[4]

From the above quotation it should be fairly clear that, as a psychologist, Alan Turing was a particular type of behav-

iorist, the kind that attributes a great deal of meaning to
appearances, that is, to the external manifestations of psychological states. Therefore to him, on a certain level, people
and computers could both be conveniently regarded as black
boxes. To behaviorists it does not matter what goes on inside
the box—we do not, perhaps cannot, know anyway—as long
as what comes out is the same. Thinking—whatever it may
actually be—and the imitation of thinking are, for all intents
and purposes, the same thing by virtue of the fact that they
produce the same result: a word or phrase, a symbol, a
gesture, or an act.

For forty years now practitioners in the field of artificial
intelligence have been trying to develop programs that, for
different purposes and on different occasions, would enable
computers to play the imitation game so well that what they
"say," that is, their output, might not be easily distinguish-
able from what a thinking human being might say under the
same circumstances. Presumably this great project will be
completed when a program is produced that will enable a
computer to play the imitation game on all occasions and
for every purpose. At that point, computers into which this
program is loaded will "think" even better than humans
because—it is a commonplace by now—whatever it is that
computers in fact do, they do it faster and with more data
than do human beings.

Some scientists say this will never happen, others that
it is just a matter of time. Who is right is not important here,
and, in any case, unprovable one way or the other at present.
What is important, however, is that Turing hedged his bets
and assumed a fallback position on this issue, and here is
where he played the part of the futurologist. Later in this
same article he wrote: "I believe that in about fifty years'
time it will be possible to program computers, with a storage
capacity of about 10^9, to make them play the imitation game
so well that an average interrogator will not have more than
70 percent chance of making the right identification after five
minutes of questioning. The original question, 'Can machines think?' I believe to be too meaningless to deserve
discussion. Nevertheless I believe that at the end of the century *the use of words and general educated opinion* will have
altered so much that one will be able to speak of machines

thinking without expecting to be contradicted." (emphasis added)[5]

This passage is worth examining closely because it reveals not only how Turing operated as a futurologist, but also how futurologists characteristically think about the issues of the future. The first thing that is noteworthy about it is simply that Turing chose to play the role of oracle, and that this could not help but be a rather self-serving thing to do under the circumstances. After all, Turing was in a field that had by 1950 already shown great promise of growth. It is the tendency of people in such fields to be their own promoters, and what better way to do this than by playing the role of prophet, by predicting that at some point in the not too distant future your field will be bigger and better than it is at present.[6] If enough people believe you and get involved in your project on the basis of this belief, your prophecy is bound to be self-fulfilling for this reason alone.

Second, Turing predicted that the battle over whether or not computers think will be won at the end of the century in one way or another, if not by facts, then by "the use of words." But notice that by making this prediction Turing was directly contradicting what he had said in the first passage we looked at when he stated: "If the meaning of the words 'machine' and 'think' are to be found by examining *how they are commonly used* it is difficult to escape the conclusion that the meaning and the answer to the question, 'Can machines think?' is to be sought in a statistical survey such as a Gallup poll. But this is absurd." (emphasis added) By making his prediction in these terms, Turing revealed here that, at least for some of its adherents, there is a hidden agenda behind the artificial intelligence movement, and that that agenda is to win, if nothing else, than the war with words by somehow or other changing the way people use them. Naturally, this moved the artificial intelligence project out of the realm of science alone and into the realm of politics. Notice too that although Turing was opposed to referring to common usage as a test for answering the question "Can computers think?" *at present,* he thought it would be perfectly all right to use this test *in the future* by which time, presumably, usage would have changed along with "general educated opinion." Characteristically, however, he did not say what he meant by educated opinion. In short, all of the ambiguity which he found so objectionable in dealing with this problem in *the present* would be perfectly acceptable in *the future,* especially because by then the artificial intelligence movement would have "general educated opinion" on its side.

Although words, if they are not used to make lies, do reflect reality, their relationship to reality is somewhat loose, and in a sense at any given moment in time we always have to create meaning anew with them. Generally speaking a prediction has little or no meaning if it relies for its fulfilment on a change in the deepest meaning of any of its key terms. For example, suppose that I, a man of modest means, were to predict that in twenty years time I would be a billionaire, meaning a man of extraordinary wealth. Suppose, too, that although in relative terms my wealth did not in fact increase during that period of time, the inflationary pace was such that at the end of it my assets were in fact worth a billion dollars. Technically speaking, with respect only to the superficial sense of its terms, the prophecy would be fulfilled but it would be a meaningless fulfilment. Similarly, and more to the point about prophecies about thinking, a hundred years ago the term literate had a meaning very different from the one we know now. In the late nineteenth century a literate person was one who not only could technically read and write but was also well-read, that is, a "literate" person then was what we might call a "cultured" person now. The accuracy of any prediction about literacy made at that time about the present would have to be judged in terms of the great shift in meaning of the term over the years. There is a substantive as well as a formal meaning to words and any prediction that does not pay attention to the substantive meaning of words is not so much a prediction of the real world but only about a change in the use of words, which can be brought about by propaganda as well as by a change in reality.

Ironically, almost forty years after Turing published this paper, in spite of the enormous amount of work that has been done by the vast army of researchers, theoreticians and programmers in the artificial intelligence movement to engineer hardware and write programs that enable computers to play the imitation game with increasing ability in certain controlled situations, very few people, except, perhaps, those working in the field of artificial intelligence, still find it appropriate to ask the question, "Can computers think?" But in historic movements sometimes one can only appreciate the true depth of irony with the benefit of hindsight. What I have in mind now is that by making these statements Turing was, perhaps unintentionally, setting the stage for Edward Feigenbaum, a present-day prophet of the artificial intelligence movement who has added a new twist to the debate by going so far as to define "educated," or at least "intellectual," in terms of computer literacy.

In 1983, thirty-three years after Turing's famous article was published, computers were definitely *in*. Artificial intelligence scientists are part of the establishment, software production and marketing are big businesses, and Feigenbaum, a Stanford University computer scientist and entrepreneur of AI software, in the inimitable style of the cult-prophet, writes that "no plausible claim to intellectuality can possibly be made in the near future without an intimate dependence upon this new instrument [the computer]." He then goes on to predict that "those intellectuals who persist in their indifference, not to say snobbery, will find themselves stranded in a quaint museum of the intellect, forced to live petulantly, and rather irrelevantly, on the charity of those who understand the real dimensions of the revolution and can *deal with* the new world it will bring about." (emphasis added)[7]

According to Feigenbaum, Turing's prophecy is so much on the way to being admirably fulfilled that, if we are to accept what he asserts, it is no longer the machines who are on trial but people—scoffers and disbelievers, those who have not bought into the new system and the new norms. Whether or not computers can think is no longer an issue for Feigenbaum. For him, the big question now is, "Can people who are computer-illiterate claim to be intellectuals?"

This is the gist of Feigenbaum's contention, but more absurd than its thrust is its tone. It is not enough merely to use these machines, we must become "intimately dependent" on them, and, if we do not, then our lives will become not merely peripheral, out of the mainstream, but "irrelevant." But most important, for all of the wonders these machines create, the world of the future will emphatically not become more benign, because we will not only have to live in it, we will have to *deal with it*. Feigenbaum's prediction contains the kind of smugness that characterized the worst kind of Victorian Darwinism, in which the dictum "survival of the fittest" was uttered not merely as a scientific principle, but as a war-cry. It proclaimed, and prophets like Feigenbaum continue to proclaim to this day, that only the fittest will survive—and the prophets, of course, are pleased to count themselves among their number.

But getting back to Turing, adopting ambiguity only when it suited his purposes was not the only rhetorical device he used when he played the role of prophet. A more important one was his willingness, when it suited his purposes, to oversimplify, sometimes even trivialize a problem and/or its related solution. Consider Turing's proposed test for determining whether computers will be able to think in the future. If the turn-of-the-century computer will, by imitation, have a "70 percent chance" of fooling the "average interrogator" for "five minutes," it will win the game, and all disbelievers will presumably be forced to conclude that computers can indeed think.

Why five minutes? Aristotle, who was also a behaviorist in the sense that he believed you could gain ethical knowledge only through experience of your own behavior, asked another difficult question in his *Nichomachean Ethics* nearly 2,500 years ago. He asked, "How can you tell if a person is happy?" but rather than the five-minute test, he applied another, rather more strenuous one. Aristotle, reflecting an ethic that was already long-standing in Greece by his time, asserted that we should not assume a person to be happy by observing his behavior for a period of less than the whole of his lifetime. He applied the lifetime rule by saying, in effect, that happiness is one of those things that cannot be defined by a brief experience, but only by a whole lifetime of activity and feeling.

The difference between Aristotle and Turing is not

merely one of degree—it is much more fundamental than that. It is the difference in their respective approaches to understanding the world. Turing, as a prophet trying to capture a complex reality, is very much the photographer. Clearly, for Turing, thinking is sort of a happening, a snapshot event. On the basis of this onetime event we are to presume that it can be sustained for a lifetime—or, at least it is the same as if it could be. Whereas to Aristotle happiness is a process, the appropriate evaluation and definition of which entails a lifetime of observation and deliberation. Turing, by projecting a very complex problem into the future, was able also to trivialize it by making it remote—so that his solution, his clever, trivial little test, might seem adequate to it.

The technique of trivializing a problem by projecting it into the future and then offering a trivial solution for understanding and resolving it is very common among futurologists of both the optimistic and pessimistic variety (although the latter, naturally, do not always get down to "solutions"). Trivialization is the futurologist's equivalent of the photographer's alienation. Of course it is sometimes also used in the present in order to give a sense of certainty where one does not really exist, as when physicians, for instance, will say a cancer has been cured if it goes into remission for five years, in spite of the fact that certain cancers are known to have incubation periods of more than twenty years. If your cancer returns after five years and, say, one month, then you are still said to have been *cured*—but, nevertheless, somehow or other you have it again.

Another good example of the trivialized solution to a previously trivialized problem comes from Professor Archie Bowen, a futurologist at Carleton University in Ottawa. Bowen has predicted the demise of middle managers by the year 2000 using the following foolish reasoning: "Today's manager, as such, I don't believe will exist in the year 2000. In fact, managers tend to feel that their jobs are relatively safe through this [computer] revolution. It's a comforting feeling. It's the comforting feeling that you might have if you were at the foot of an avalanche and you were looking the other way and didn't see it coming at you. *The role of*

*the manager is merely to manipulate information and make
decisions.* In most cases that function, as we have discussed
earlier, is ideally suited to the computer and has already
been taken over by the computer." (emphasis added)[8] From
Professor Bowen's account it appears as if the chief require-
ment for using the futurologist's trivialization technique is
ignorance about what one is talking about. For instance, the
case could also be made—and quite persuasively nowadays—
that university professors, like Professor Bowen himself, also
play the role of middle managers in their own corporations.
However, in spite of his eagerness to do so with other professions, it is difficult to imagine Professor Bowen predicting
his own demise, that is, the demise of his own profession,
or trivializing his own work as being no more than "merely
manipulating information" and/or "merely making decisions."

Edward Feigenbaum also uses the trivialization trick
later in the same book when he predicts the future uses of
the computer in society. For example, suppose a problem
of the future will be loneliness and anxiety among the elderly? In that case, predicts Feigenbaum, we will simply
provide them with robot companions. Here is one of his
visions:

The geriatric robot is wonderful. It isn't hanging
about in the hopes of inheriting your money—nor
of course will it slip you a little something to speed
the inevitable. It isn't hanging about because it can't
find work elsewhere. It's there because it's yours.
It doesn't just bathe you and feed you and wheel
you out into the sun when you crave fresh air and
a change of scene, though of course it does all of
those things. The very best thing about the geriatric
robot is that it *listens.* "Tell me again," it says,
"about how wonderful/dreadful your children are
to you. Tell me again that fascinating tale of the
coup of '63. Tell me again . . ." And it means it.
It never gets tired of hearing those stories, just as
you never get tired of telling them. It knows your
favorites, and those are its favorites too. Never

> mind that this all ought to be done by human care-
> takers; humans grow bored, get greedy, want va-
> riety. (emphasis in original)[9]

But perhaps, upon reading this passage, the reader is thinking that this vision is not really so objectionable if one allows
that Feigenbaum, from his own perspective, is probably describing a desperate remedy for a desperate situation.
Though a human rather than a machine solution might be
ideal, in the case of care of the elderly, given present values
and trends, the human solution may no longer be feasible,
and therefore we should perhaps not be too critical of the
machine alternative. One might take some comfort in thinking that this was the reasoning behind Feigenbaum's predic-
tion/proposal and that his attempts to make it sound
attractive by praising its virtues are desperate attempts to
make the unsavory seem palatable; but one would be mistaken in doing so. Feigenbaum's solution, far from being a
desperate one, is actually characteristic of the psychology of
futurology; it is an *ideal* solution, the solution of *choice*. It
is corroborated by Richard Wolkomir, another American
futurologist, in his account of the role that robot pets or pals
will have in the future lives of all classes and categories of
humans, not just the elderly:

> If people already have trouble differentiating be-
> tween their relationships with people and a ma-
> chine, over the next decade or so, as we develop
> computers with ultrahigh-speed parallel processing,
> people may find conversations with a robot indis-
> tinguishable from talks with people . . . they may
> even find the machines to be preferable.
>   Here we are, hardly settled into our electronic
> cottages, and already the age of electronic pals is
> upon us. Androbot's Nolan Bushnell painted a
> comforting picture of future friendships when he
> introduced his diminutive (three foot tall) home
> robot. While you wiggle a video-game joystick,
> making your aluminum sidekick dance a jig, it will
> speak to you, sing your favorite songs, or whisper

Shakespearean sonnets in your ear—the very model
of a learned and entertaining soul mate. As Bush-
nell told reporters when he announced his new robot protégé: "We're talking about a someone, not
a something—a friend that would greet you after a
long day at the office."[10]

The question, of course, is not whether these machines, as
they are envisioned by futurologists and computer scientists
playing the role of prophet, will ever be perfected. Only time
will tell. The real point is, given the enormous confidence
these prophets have in the potential of this evolving technology to do and be just about anything, that their visions
are dominated by a certain tone: technology will only be
used in one way and not another; it will be used to pander
to our whims and vanity and not to promote the development
of our virtues. One can only assume that this tone reflects
the personalities of these prophets themselves because they
so ardently promote it, to the exclusion of countless feasible
others.

Feigenbaum, Wolkomir and many other modern prophets who belong to what might be called the "techno-romantic" school of futurology seem to be enamored not merely
of the technical fix, the technical solution to a human problem, but of a very particular type of technical fix, one which
places individual autonomy and control above social interaction. The point about the celebrated future with machines
that they describe above is not only that these devices will
be hypothetically accessible to all, but that they will entail
a sort of automated enshrinement of their owners' egos; in
this way they will, in a sense, fulfil certain individual needs,
but always in a banal sort of way. The issue that seems to
be of paramount importance to these futurologists is how to
achieve individual mastery of personal, isolated environments, and how to put the individual who owns the machine
at the commanding center of the environment in which he
lives. The type of mastery which they advocate, the only
type, it would appear, that seems feasible to their minds, is
a sort of petty mastery, like personalized stereo carried to
ever greater degrees. In the scenarios that they paint for us,

having one's personal whims and conceits satisfied is more important than having to deal with contrariness in others, or having to rub up against personalities that are different from one's own. In a word, these are future scenarios in which psychological avoidance is the name of the game.

No one has summarized the psychological makeup of the techno-romantic school of futurology better than Stewart Brand in his description of the research endeavors of the Media Lab at MIT, where, he reports, engineers actually claim to be going about the business of "inventing the future." Every research project is being designed to cater to the characteristic futurologist personality that craves isolation and control. Writes Brand: "Everything mentioned involves communications, empowers the individual, employs computers . . . and makes a flashy demonstration."[11] There is that sexy term "empower"; it is used so much today that you cannot help but wonder if it still has any meaning. Yet it must have some meaning because, if nothing else, it evokes the all too common psychological states of frustration and helplessness and implies a remedy for them. It is interesting, however, that although for millennia power has always had mixed connotations, implying a potential for both good and evil, the way the term is used here and the way it is now generally bandied about, it seems to imply that we are to believe that empowerment will always be an absolute good. Is it always good to empower your feet by driving everywhere in your car? or to empower your hand by putting a gun in it? What Brand's glorification of individual empowerment does not address are the issues of when, to what degree, and under what circumstances we should become empowered. If you examine their projects for solving social problems, the techno-romanticist solutions seem to imply that we should empower the banal side of our natures and thereby further shelter ourselves from the unpleasant aspects of reality; in effect, we should become more narcissistic, self-flattering, closed-minded. It is hard to imagine how humans who controlled their personal and business relationships by constantly interacting with machines this way could possibly develop their personalities or even their minds.

Yet, ultimately, it would be inaccurate to say that these

futurologists are completely oblivious to the darker side of human nature; their vision is not only to control the enemy from without, who often happen to be other ordinary humans, but also the one inside of us. However, as usual, the technique that they advocate for achieving this control is a mechanical one—automated decision-making, so that the individual may abdicate responsibility for his or her existence.

Roy Mason, another American futurologist, has published a scenario in which he depicts a day in the life of a family that will live in the super-automated house of the future, based on a prototype located outside of Orlando, Florida, called the Xanadu House. The most striking quality about the scenario he describes in this prophecy is that the house computer not only panders to the narrow vision and whims of its occupants, like the toys that Feigenbaum and Wolkomir describe so admiringly above, but that it even appropriates a great deal of simple day-to-day decision-making from its inhabitants. For example, the "master" of the house, as he is called in Mason's vision, decides to order a meal from the automated kitchen, but it happens to contain cholesterol and therefore may be harmful to his health. So the computer vetoes his request in this endearing little early morning breakfast scene:

> Johnny dashes into the kitchen just as his father is finishing his first cup of coffee. After hearty "good mornings," both go to the computer dietitian and punch in their breakfast orders for the autochef. Johnny's order of hot cakes, orange juice, and milk goes through with no trouble, but John Sr.'s scrambled eggs, bacon, and toast are quickly nixed for their high cholesterol count. He is forced to settle for an English muffin, orange juice, and another cup of coffee.[12]

And so, early in the morning in this ideally automated home of the future, the computer gets to play culinary tyrant with the "master" of the house—presumably, of course, for his own good. Actually, things are not quite as bad as that. Everyone knows that computers only do what they are programmed to do, and so Mason, unlike some other futurologists†—has also envisioned an override mechanism. Using this mechanism when ordering the evening meal, the master does manage to get a piece of chocolate cake, in spite of the computer's better judgment.

Mason's entire article reeks of a dim, if not dim-witted, view of human nature. In fact, one finds no humans in this story at all, only caricatures. Their foibles are petty—father and son are both reluctant to get out of bed, mother needs to be coaxed with "a gentle massage like thousands of tiny fingers"—and so are their strengths. If the characters in Mason's prediction of future domestic life remind one of anything, it is of comic strip characters like Dagwood and Blondie: the energetic, moderately intelligent woman who quietly craves a small amount of affection and/or attention; the reluctant but ultimately goodwilled and able father whose weakness is for food, not sex; and the children, a crude version of their parents. These people are safe to read about and, presumably, would be safe to live with if one could ever find them in the real world. The minor wrinkles in their personalities can readily be ironed out with clever appliances.

In writing of their visions, Feigenbaum, Wolkomir and Mason are basically acting as existential cheerleaders for the automated world they feel comfortable contemplating, and in which they would like us all to live in the future. But Mason's vision also points to an inevitable consequence of extreme mechanization and automated decision-making: the loss of individual freedom, including the freedom to make decisions and to make mistakes. And this last twist is not

† A speculation from the *Omni Future Almanac* is not nearly so equivocal about the virtues of automated decision-making. In fact it justifies this process in terms of utilitarian principles and "computer rights" of all things. Here is what the *Almanac* has to say about this issue: "The decision-making power of computers will become so awesome that a Computer Responsibility Act may have to be passed in the United States. A possible scenario: In 2035, some seven hundred fifty publicly assisted housing unit residents, deemed expendable by a civic energy balance maintenance computer, will be frozen in their homes. Many of the elderly will die. Upon examination and investigation, the computer will respond that its evaluation revealed that the community was better served by letting the individuals freeze than by saving energy in any other fashion. Resulting protests from computers over the dismantling of the offending machine may lead to negotiations on computer responsibility for such actions. The establishment of a computer court for dealing with ethical problems will be the result." (Robert Weil [ed.], *Omni Future Almanac*, London: Sidgwick & Jackson, 1982, p. 32.)

merely a novel idea which this author lacked the decency to remove, it is an essential part of the psychology of futurology.

The French futurologist François Hetman has given a name to this aspect of future-think. He calls it "comprehensive guarantism," and not only does he think it is a reasonable thing to expect that everyone will want nothing more than to live in an environment of maximum comfort and ego-gratification, but he also thinks it logical that they will be willing to give up freedom for the sake.[13] In an article written in 1962 called "Well-being and Freedom in 1970," Hetman predicted that the demand for well-being will increasingly take the form of a categorical absolute. He also went on to predict that it will be logical for people to sacrifice a great deal, including their freedom, for a maximum amount of comfort and safety. In his vision of the future, the greatest ideal, in a pablum-seeking society, will be risk-free existence, insurance against anything and everything that is the least bit threatening or unpleasant. It follows that the greatest "risk," death, is also on the list of things that futurologists believe can be "avoided"—provided, of course, that one is willing to give up *a certain amount of freedom*.

This last theme was taken up with a vengeance by American futurologist Grant Fjermedal in a book which he published in 1987 called *The Tomorrow Makers: A Brave New World of Living Brain Machines*. From the title of this book it is easy to guess that the research he did for it consisted of interviews not with physicians and microbiologists, the traditional purveyors of immortality, but with computer-scientists. The project that these scientists are working on is to devise the techniques, software and hardware to make it possible to transfer the "contents" of the human brain into a computer, make several copies of "the file," put them into robot bodies and thus make the human subjects both "immortal" and "multipresent" at the same time. Here is the process, called "downloading," as it is described in an interview by Fjermedal with Hans Moravec, a senior research scientist at Carnegie-Mellon University.

> "That computer sitting next to you in the operating room would in effect be your new brain. As each

area of your brain was analyzed and simulated, the accuracy of the simulation would be tested as you pressed a button to shift between the area of the brain just copied and the simulation. When you couldn't tell the difference between the original and the copy, the surgeon would transfer the simulation of your brain into the new, computerized one and repeat the process on the next areas of your biological brain. Though you have not lost consciousness or even your train of thought, your mind— some would say soul—has been removed from the brain and transferred to a machine," Moravec said. "In a final step your old body is disconnected. The computer is installed in a shiny new one, in the style, color, and material of your choice."[14]

If one ponders closely what Moravec is saying here, the arrogance of this vision is truly extraordinary, even considering that we are dealing here with a vision of the future (after all, even visions of the future have to have some continuity with the present). Here, of course, we have Turing revisited, but this time we have the imitation game in spades. Even supposing, for the sake of argument, that one of these clever surgeon robots could be constructed, how long will the person on the operating table be given to decide whether the "copy," the imitation of himself which is being constructed in an electronically-fitted box beside him, really is the same as the original, that is, really is the same as himself? Will we be asked to settle for a snapshot of reality in this case, too? Will "five minutes" do for this imitation game? Consider also some of the enormous assumptions behind this quest: first, that the mind or "soul" is actually located in the brain and only in that part of the body; and second, that the structure of the brain, if it could indeed be thoroughly analyzed, would be similar to and compatible with computer logic and circuitry, and could therefore be assimilated to it. As far as the second assumption is concerned, if anything can safely be said to be the case, the accumulating evidence seems to demonstrate that computer and brain structure are actually very different. Though we still know very little about this area, recent studies suggest that memory is located in the brain in a non-specific way, that is, memory that is lost by cutting out one part of the brain may later be regained in another. We do not yet know how this comes to be in human brains, but this simply does not happen with computer discs, as anyone who has had data erased from the memory of his or her computer will willingly testify. And yet the vision and project continue, as if these scientists could possibly know what they are doing!

Having read this account, the reader may also be wondering what will become of the human brain—and bodies!—after the downloading is completed. When Fjermedal asked Moravec about this he replied in a cavalier way: "You just don't bother waking it up again if the copying went successfully. . . . It's so messy. Humans have got so many problems that you might just want to have it retired. You don't take your junker car out if you've got a new one." This disdain for the body is rather common among the technologically moonstruck type of futurists. Professor Marvin Minsky of MIT, who is also working on aspects of this project, echoes sentiments similar to Moravec's later in the same article: "Why not avoid getting sick and things like that? . . . It's hard to see anything against it. I think people will get fed up with bodies after a while. Then you'll have another population problem. You'll have all the people of the past as well as all of the new ones."†

Disdain for the body is not a new thing in either eastern or western philosophy, but in the latter it was probably given its first articulate expression by Plato in his dialogue called the *Phaedo*. When reading the interviews in Fjermedal's article I could not help but remember similar remarks written by Plato in his dialogue about Socrates's last hours. The heart

---

† Perhaps through working with machines for so long Minsky seems to have developed a serious antipathy to living creatures. In 1980 he wrote, "Today, a successful biological science is based on energetics and information processing; no notion of 'alive' appears in the theory, nor do we miss it." (See Marvin Minsky, "Decentralized Minds," in *Behavioral and Brain Sciences* [1980] 3, p. 439.) In a way it might be nice if this absurd notion were true, then biological researchers could stop experimenting with live animals and the animal rights activists would no longer have to worry about this problem! Minsky is a future hypist par excellence. Later in the same article, to prove a fantastic point, he plays the part of the future historian and quotes, as evidence, an as-yet-unpublished journal of the future. Recognizing the absurdity of this kind of rhetoric he quickly concedes it to be a joke—but uses it again a few paragraphs later, this time without the concession.

of the passage that Fjermedal's article reminded me of goes
like this:

> Surely the soul can best reflect when it is free of all
> distractions such as hearing or sight or pain or plea-
> sure of any kind—that is, when it ignores the body
> and becomes as far as possible independent, avoid-
> ing all physical contacts and associations as much
> as it can, in its search for reality.
>   That is so.
>   Then here too—in despising the body and
> avoiding it, and endeavoring to become indepen-
> dent—the philosopher's soul is ahead of all the
> rest.[15]

Of course the ancient Greeks had no computers or thoughts
of downloading in the sense that Moravec and Minsky mean
it, but in the *Phaedo,* as in the world of these futurists,
discarding the body is the preliminary step for achieving
immortality, because they believed, or tried—as far as their
at times fanatical addiction to pure reason would let them—
to believe in the immortality of the soul. For them the body
only obstructs the quest for immortality and creates discom-
fort, distraction, and distortions. The soul can be pure only
when freed from the body, like the "soul" that these prophets predict will one day be constructed in the memory section
of a computer.†

Since these present-day computer-scientist futurologists
do not appear to believe in the immortality of the soul outside
of its transfer into a computer, it follows that for them the
height of tragedy would be to miss the boat for this technological type of immortality. Gerald Sussman, another MIT
professor who is also working on aspects of the downloading
project, has expressed this tragic sense in the following

---

† It is remarkable that some of the ancient Greek philosophers as well as these
modern futurologist counterparts had so little appreciation for the positive aspects
of inhabiting a human body: the sensuous nature of good health, the heightened
consciousness stemming from the pleasures of the body, the contentment brought
about by physical contact, hard work, and physical exertion. Obviously, this is the
philosophy of old men whose bodies, through the debilitation of age, have progressively become a burden to them.

words: "Everyone would like to be immortal. I don't think
the time is quite right but it's close. I'm afraid, unfortunately,
that I'm in the last generation to die."

Disdain for the human body and the desire to mechanize
it are particularly characteristic of present-day futurology.
However, in spite of its roots in antiquity, this attitude is a
real departure from the spirit of the end of the last century
and the first half of this one. The cultural antecedents for
futurist magazines like *Omni* were the hobbyist magazines
like *Popular Mechanics* and *Electronics Illustrated,* which
began to develop mass appeal and following just before
World War I. Aside from offering a few do-it-yourself plans
for the home tinkerer, their content, like that of their modern
counterparts, was a mixture of science-fiction, popularized
science and a panorama of curious discoveries from around
the world. But in those days, Darwin's theory of evolution
was still a very strong part of the popular imagination and
so the progress of civilization was typically correlated with
the belief that the human body would continue to evolve to
an ever higher level. Ideally, supermachine and superman
were seen as being complementary and, in a way, evolving
together.

More to the point, however, these magazines were honestly aimed at average individuals who wanted to improve
their lot in life. Their advertising content tells the whole
story. Along with ads for correspondence courses in refrig-
erator- and radio-repairing—the vocations of the future of
that time—were ones offering Charles Atlas's famous course
for turning 97-pound-weaklings into "he-men." There is still
some of that, of course, in the present-day ads for exercise
machines and vitamins, but today's futurist magazines have
a more narcissistic flavor than did their predecessors. But
more significantly, in the area of mental activity, which is
supposed to be so important in the present "age of information," most of the responsibility is abdicated to the machines, which are pictured as already having achieved
supremacy in this area. In short, in the present-day vision
of the future, the coevolution of humans with machines
seems to have stopped with, ironically, the humans having
been left behind.

There are any number of ironies in the visions of our

modern-day prophets but this is particularly true of the work of the artificial intelligence movement. Not surprisingly, many members of the artificial intelligence movement are also futurologists, and it is certainly from the work of this movement that many futurologists draw their inspiration. The affinity between futurologists and the "artificial intelligentsia" is only natural: they are both in the business of trying to reduce life problems to what they consider to be their essences, that is, to manageable bits. Futurologists do this by projection and computer scientists do it by imitation. In the world of science, as well as in the world of art, there is certainly room for both of these techniques—but they both entail a particular danger. The danger is in what might be lost in the process, that problems that are projected and objects that are imitated will be trivialized in the process. It takes a great deal of discipline and honesty to avoid this trivialization.

Joseph Weizenbaum, a distinguished MIT computer-scientist, is of a different ilk from those we have so far encountered. He is one member of the artificial intelligence movement who does have this discipline and consequently never makes more of what he has constructed than he rightfully should. But even this is not perfectly safe because his followers, who are less intelligent and less honest than he is, have seriously misconstrued his work. In his book, *Computer Power and Human Reason,* he laments just such an incident in his career.[16] A number of years ago he devised a program which he called ELIZA that could make a computer imitate a psychoanalyst, much in the manner of Turing's description at the beginning of his famous paper. Weizenbaum's purpose in writing this program, however, was to demonstrate the absurdity of such a device, to show how simplistic and inflexible it would be. But his reviewers thought it was wonderful—not an ironic gesture but a serious enterprise. It was widely praised and imitated and, even to this day, there is a demonstration of it for children at the Lawrence Hall of Science in Berkeley to show how clever computers can be at imitating psychiatrists. But the demonstration does not even mention Weizenbaum's intentions in constructing the program, his reservations about its potential misuse, or his misgivings about what it actually does

do. This is how hungry we are today to trivialize our problems, even to our children, to reduce them to the nth degree
in order to be able to claim mastery over them, no matter
how petty that mastery may be, and it is this hunger for
mastery on which our prophets play.

If one had to summarize the psychology of these futurologists, one would have to say that their main motivational
force seems to be a quest for a petty sort of mastery. By
projecting problems into the future and thus making them
remote, they can then be made to appear masterable, or at
least manageable, if by no other means than, as Turing has
taught us, by the mere manipulation of words. The quest of
modern prophets is also for a paltry kind of control: of others, that is, commandable machines that have taken the place
of people, and of the self, when responsibility is delegated
to machines so that decisions can be made automatically,
without any self-struggle. Of course, generally speaking,
mastery and control are not in and of themselves bad things.
But we are not talking here about Rostropovich playing the
cello. Rostropovich's mastery of the cello does not contain
the element of mastery through alienation that seems to be
so central to the psychology of so many futurologists, and it
is certainly not geared towards enhancing his creature
comfort.

The complementary tendency—to at once glorify small,
tentative, or at least very limited accomplishments and trivialize even the greatest of challenges—is a strong one in
futurology. Some might say it is a characteristic of optimists,
but it is also a quality of fools. It is the foolishness of the
child who, intoxicated by the initial easy but dramatic accomplishments of, say, beginning to learn a musical instrument or mastering any other serious skill, deludes himself
into thinking that really significant mastery will come just as
easily, just as quickly, and just as dramatically as these eu-
phoric beginnings. Though such foolishness may be tolera-
ble, and even becoming, in children, it is troubling, if not
pathetic, in adults.

This is well illustrated in the vision which is presently
being promoted by Stewart Brand. It is worth recalling that
Brand used to be a sort of cult figure in the late 1960s and

early 1970s. In 1968 Brand founded and edited a popular review of "tools for living" called the *Whole Earth Catalog.* It reviewed tools and technical manuals for gardening, farming, land use, shelter, light industry and craft. It also reviewed alternative communities and life-styles, all the sorts of things that we now call "New Age." It was a great coffee-table and bookstore-browsing book, and also served as a sourcebook for the "back to the earth" movement, which was then going strong.

Brand's review was also a source book for budding futurologists. It opened with a paean to Buckminster Fuller, reviewing all of his books and also those of other, more esoteric futurists. There was an obvious link between Fuller and the reviews of tools: Brand believed, as did Fuller, in salvation through design, that well-designed tools would make the future world a better place. Brand's catalogues characteristically addressed the minor problem of access to tools, but made short shrift of the major problem of how they are to be used.

It is easy to understand how Brand and Fuller were drawn by the paradigm of design: it is nothing if not seductive. Well-designed tools, furnishings, houses are often very life-enhancing, and anyone who has ever mastered anything knows that mastery is enhanced with proper tools. But ultimately the paradigm is very limited: how many tinkerers do we know who have exquisite tools yet hardly know how to use them, or conversely, can work wonders with inadequate tools, can make a cardboard cello sing and build a house with found material and basic hand-tools. Yet Brand really was thinking that these tools would of themselves create a more masterful future. In *The Media Lab: Inventing the Future at MIT,* his 1987 paean to tools-cum-vision of the future, he reveals the persistence of this belief and tells how, during a brief period in which his vision of the future seemed to him to have gone blank, far from inducing him to reassess its premises, this development simply threw him into an existential black hole: "Back in 1968 when I started an access-to-tools compendium called the *Whole Earth Catalog,* and for a few years following, I'd had a clear feeling for the 'future' and what to do about it. By the time I'd done half a dozen versions of the book, ending with a *Whole Earth*

Software Catalog in 1985, I had no idea whatever about futures and was operating strictly on reflex."[17]

Brand sadly came to the realization that he could not live with uncertainty about what the future held in store. So what did he do about it? He went to MIT for a few months to review the fanciest computer-enhanced communications tools on the planet and wrote a book about them. Yet, in his mind, this book is no mere review of tool development in progress; it is, in his own words, "about two media labs. It is about the specific five-story pile of equipment, academics, and ideas in eastern Massachusetts, and it is about the worldwide media laboratory in which *we are all likely to be experimenters for the rest of our lives.*" (emphasis added)[18]

It is difficult to say exactly what Brand means by this abstract and impersonal proclamation because, like most futurologists using high-falutin phrases, he characteristically does not explain what it means in his book. But what a nice egalitarian sounding phrase it is—until one considers its implications by trying to personalize it a bit. If we are *all,* in fact, experimenters in this lab, then who will be sweeping the floor and dishing out food in the cafeteria? After all, even in this age of inexpensive electronic equipment, this is a privileged existence that Brand is describing. Whose future was he really talking about? On the other hand, it is difficult to imagine what this vision might even mean. Would these tools, which can produce things like a customized newspaper, a customized television station and a robot secretary which knew its boss's whims and fancies, really be accessible to everyone? And if they were, should we regard them as the lowest common denominator, the highest common denominator, or the essence of our future egalitarian life on earth? Will we all really be working and playing with sophisticated communications devices for the rest of our lives? Will these devices really help us through our days; through our eating, bathing and sleeping; through our search for love, work, power; through our avoidance of love, work, power? All of us? Including, for instance, those who are now entering the work force in the fastest expanding sector, euphemistically called the hospitality industry, which is offering low-paying, low-tech jobs like waitressing, short-order cooking and dishwashing? All of us?

Brand at least managed to banish his uncertainty about the future and come up with an image he himself could easily live with on his tugboat in San Francisco Bay. After leaving MIT he wrote with great relief: "The Media Lab provided, finally, what I went for—a clear feeling of the future and some ideas about what to do about it."[19] And yet there is no statement in the entire book that explains what this "clear feeling of the future" really is, never mind what to do about it. What it *appears* to be, however, is a vision of the future as the realm where we will be able to objectify and depersonalize our existences. As it turns out, however, this is not a new vision for Brand, but an old one. A number of years ago Brand wrote: "To get a hand on your future you've got to get outside yourself, because only from outside can you see your space-time environment whole. One way is to identify out into another culture, Indian or whatever. . . . Another is to take Philip Wagner's trip into fascinated objectivity about earthly doings."[20] Fascinated objectivity: there certainly are many examples of this in Brand's book. Even in the last chapter, when he finally does make an attempt to sober up from his cheerleading mode, he writes about our future robot secretaries: "Programming these machines to match one's habits and preferences can be tiresome, but it's also usefully revealing. It forces you to be conscious about everything you would like the machine to do, which can be an opportunity to change habits while your mind is on them. Once the machines are programmed, you can be unconscious again and do what they're knowing, probably more, better, and easier than before . . ."[21] Whatever "fascinated objectivity" may be, one of the great feats that one will be able to accomplish in this future way of being will be to treat one's habits as if they are as easily programmable as a computer. This vision is certainly embarrassing to those of us who have trouble keeping even New Year's resolutions in the dreary present in which we are now living! But Brand is not merely talking about everyday personal habits which are fundamentally enough a part of character to be very difficult to change; he envisions no limits to how far design will be able to go to make us better future people. Later he writes in the same spirit: "Designing *ethical* robots is a long and interesting problem. We have enough trouble designing

ethical human beings. Maybe practicing on robots will help."
(emphasis in original)[22]

It must be very comforting to live on a tugboat in San
Francisco Bay and think that one is going to share a common
future, a common destiny, with a younger person who is
starting out their working life as a short-order cook, simply
on the basis that you may both—but on very different levels
and in very different ways—be using the same computer-
enhanced telecommunications system. But a telecommunications system is not a laboratory, and using it does not make
one an experimenter—unless, of course, one trivializes the
work of scientific experimentation. By espousing the pseudo-
egalitarianism which is implied by his electronic vision—the
computer as the great equalizer, the six-gun of the future—
Brand is, in the end, avoiding the real issue of how fundamentally different is the relationship of different classes of
users to technology, present, past and future.[23]

In the end, Brand's book tells us a great deal more about
the psychology of futurologists by what it leaves out than by
what it says, by its failure to address in any way the messy
developments of the present that, if allowed to continue, are
bound to play themselves out by creating future problems.
All of the mess is avoided just so that Brand can have a neat
and flashy tool-rich future to relate to.

Ironically, avoidance is a dominant element in the psychology of futurologists, just as, Susan Sontag has reminded us,
alienation is for photographers. After all, as the futurologists
gaze into the future they are not social actors or even, properly speaking, social observers of the scenes which they envision. Rather, given the unavoidably severe limits to their
perspective, they are basically social voyeurs, much as photographers sometimes are. But photographers at their best
are artists, trying to intrigue and suggest the possibilities of
life. Futurologists are not nearly so honest or modest. As
far as futurologists are concerned, it would be more accurate
to say that they are easily titillated by what they see—or
think they see—and in turn share their vision by trying to
titillate the rest of us. Because of the element of avoidance
in their posture, because they can never get close to what
they are pointing at, they do not have to be responsible to

it and can always perform their dramatic posing and pro-posing at a safe distance.

It is often said of voyeurs that theirs is an act of offense and aggression. In a way this is true, but it is also true that theirs is an act of defense and avoidance. It is easy for voyeurs to glorify what they see because with their little peeps they can never truly understand it, they can never achieve the often unglorious but truly substantive understanding—and responsibility—which comes from real contact.

In the end, of course, it is not an optimistic but rather a dim view of humanity that is reflected in the visions of a great number of futurologists, even those who like to number themselves among the optimists of the world. Most utopians of the past, from Thomas More on down, have tried to envision future conditions which would ennoble the soul. It is a sad comment on our modern-day visionaries that they are advocating future conditions in which the soul—their own as well as those of others—will be systematically avoided.

NOTES

1. Susan Sontag, *On Photography* (New York: Farrar, Straus and Giroux, 1973), p. 167.
2. Because it is one of the main themes of this book, the following analysis focuses narrowly on some propagandist elements that unfortunately made their way into Turing's thinking, but Turing's thought has already been seriously critiqued along a number of other lines by philosophers of science. Perhaps the most prominent, but not necessarily the most subtle, of these was launched in 1980 by John Searle who argued that computers have syntax, that is, the ability to follow rules, but not semantics, the ability to understand what they mean. Along a similar line see also S.G. Shanker, "Wittgenstein versus Turing on the Nature of Church's Thesis," *Notre Dame Journal of Formal Logic* (1987), vol. 28, no. 4, pp. 615–649, which highlights some important discrepancies between Turing's mathematics and the philosophical conclusions he attempted to draw from it, and "The Dawning of (Machine) Intelligence," *Philosophica* (1988), no. 2, pp. 95–144, which elucidates the roots of Turing's philosophy of knowledge in behavioral psychology and demonstrates the mutually reinforcing errors in both which have been carried forward by cognitive science. In another vein, see Nicholas Georgescu-Roegen, *The Entropy Law and the Economic Process* (Cambridge, Mass.: Harvard University Press, 1971), especially pp. 1–94, which argues that it is impossible to express certain kinds of concepts in mathematical terms and therefore impossible for computers to "understand" them.
3. Alan Turing, "Computing Machinery and Intelligence," in Alan Ross Anderson, *Minds and Machines* (Englewood Cliffs, N.J.: Prentice-Hall, 1964), p. 4.
4. Turing, p. 5.

5. Turing, pp. 13–14.

6. A more recent example of self-promoting propaganda cum futurology in a "newer" field can be found in E.O. Wilson's preface to his book *Sociobiology,* in which he writes: "The conventional wisdom also speaks of ethology, which is the naturalistic study of whole patterns of animal behavior, and its companion enterprise, comparative psychology, as the central, unifying fields of behavior biology. They are not; both are destined to be cannibalized by neurophysiology and sensory physiology from one end and sociobiology and behavioral ecology from the other . . . I hope not too many scholars in ethology and psychology will be offended by this vision of the future of behavioral biology. It seems to be indicated both by the extrapolation of current events and by consideration of the logical relationship behavioral biology holds with the remainder of science. The future, it seems clear, cannot be with the ad hoc terminology, crude models, and curve fitting that characterize most of contemporary ethology and comparative psychology. Whole patterns of animal behavior will inevitably be explained within the framework, first, of integrative neurophysiology, which classifies neurons and reconstructs their circuitry, and, second, of sensory physiology, which seeks to characterize the cellular transducers at the molecular level." (E.O. Wilson, *Sociobiology,* Cambridge, Mass.: Harvard University Press, 1976, p. 6).

7. Edward Feigenbaum and Pamela McCorduck, *The Fifth Generation: Artificial Intelligence and Japan's Computer Challenge to the World* (London: Pan Books, 1984).

8. "The Future of Work: The Future Office" (videorecording), Toronto: TV Ontario, 1982.

9. Feigenbaum, p. 193.

10. Richard Wolkomir, "Robots at Home," in *Omni* (April 1983), p. 76.

11. Stewart Brand, *The Media Lab: Inventing the Future at MIT* (New York: Viking, 1987), p. 4.

12. Roy Mason, "A Day at Xanadu," in *Futurist* (February 1984), p. 20.

13. François Hetman, "Bien-être et liberté en 1970," in *Bulletin S.E.D.E.I.S.*, no. 811, *Futuribles* (February 10, 1962), no. 24.

14. Grant Fjermedal, "Surrogate Brains," in *Omni* (October 1986), p. 38.

15. Plato, *Phaedo* 65, c-d (trans. Hugh Tredennick), in *The Collected Dialogues of Plato* (Princeton, N.J.: Princeton University Press, 1961).

16. Joseph Weizenbaum, *Computer Power and Human Reason: From Judgement to Calculation* (Harmondsworth, England: Penguin, 1984).

17. Brand, p. xi.

18. Brand, p. xiii.

19. Brand, p. xvi.

20. Stewart Brand (ed.), *The Updated Last Whole Earth Catalog* (New York: Portola Institute, 1974), p. 9.

21. Brand, *The Media Lab,* p. 254.

22. Brand, p. 258.

23. See Edmund Sullivan, "The Computer as Equalizer," Ontario Ministry of Education, 1983.

Many have dreamed up republics and principalities which have never in truth been known to exist; the gulf between how one should live and how one does live is so wide that a man who neglects what is actually done for what should be done paves the way to self-destruction rather than self-preservation.
—MACHIAVELLI

3

THE IDEOLOGY OF FUTUROLOGY

Given his usually ponderous persona, it may surprise some readers to learn that no less prominent a politician than Winston Churchill was, in his time, smitten by the futurist bug. In 1932, while he was sitting as a member of the British Parliament and after he had already served a term as chancellor of the exchequer, he wrote a prophetic article which he published, of all places, in the hobbyist magazine *Popular Mechanics*. Here he speculated about what the world would be like fifty years from that time. Whatever its merits as prediction—it happens to have the usual unremarkable track record which characterizes "more of the same" projections— what is really interesting about Churchill's article is the fact that he packed a great deal of ideological baggage in with his futurology.

Near the beginning of this piece he took a couple of gratuitous swipes at the Soviet Communists; this is hardly surprising. More revealing than this assault is a vision that comes at the end of the article in which he predicts that man will eventually be able to produce test-tube babies. This, of course, was not such a remarkable prediction in itself, given the fact that, although the DNA code had not yet been cracked, man had forever been speculating about and searching for the essence of life in the laboratory, and the field of embryology had, even by that time, already yielded many of the precursors in thought and technique for achieving the feat of growing and manipulating fetuses *in vitro*. However, what was significant about Churchill's vision were some of its details: he imagined that the development of techniques for producing test-tube babies would naturally be accompanied by a program of what we would today call genetic engineering, but Churchill's genetic engineering was for very questionable purposes.

After setting the scene by making an ambiguous allusion to *R.U.R.*, a fantasy play about the invention of robots which was very popular at the time—were we to regard humans whose coming into being had been tampered with by their predecessors on earth as mere robots?—he wrote, "There seems little doubt that it will be possible to carry out the entire cycle which now leads to the birth of a child, in artificial surroundings. . . . Interference with the mental development of such beings, expert suggestion and treatment in the earlier years, *would produce beings specialized to thought or toil*." (emphasis added).[1] For Churchill, the prospect of future techniques for growing fetuses in the laboratory presented opportunities for intervention, but intervention of a certain kind, the kind of intervention that would not ameliorate, but rather would enhance the class differences which were, and to a great extent still are, so characteristic of English society. Never mind the evolutionary questionability of engendering humans who, like toy poodles, were to be genetically diddled into overspecialized niches. Never mind, either, the social and moral questionability of such interventions.

Churchill is not the only forecaster to use prophecy to make an ideological argument about class. Unfortunately it is a tradition of long standing. In 1798 the English economist Thomas Malthus published a famous treatise called *An Essay on the Principle of Population as it Affects the Future Improvement of Society*. In this pamphlet Malthus predicted what would today be commonly called a "doom and gloom" scenario of the "time-bomb" variety, much like the "limits to growth" type of predictions that were produced in the early 1970s by the Club of Rome. Malthus prophesied that, since the population, when unchecked, increases in geometric ratio (that is, like compound interest), whereas the food supply only increases in arithmetic ratio (like simple interest), the people of England would eventually starve. Malthus's pamphlet had many of the qualities of modern futurology. It relied on simple projection and on a mathematical model based on very questionable assumptions— Why should the population always continue to grow unchecked? Why should the rate of food production not increase more rapidly than it happened to be at the time the author was writing?—all of which were eventually proven to be unfounded. But more importantly, there was an explicit prescription contained in Malthus's prediction: that the lower classes restrain their rate of reproduction. It is now conventional wisdom among historians that this prescription vindicated the prejudices of the dominant elite of the society in which Malthus lived who wanted to blame the poor for their misery rather than take some of the responsibility for this situation on themselves.[2] This futurology was therefore imbued with self-righteous moralizing of a threatened elite.

Yet the ideological bias of such projected visions is not unusual in futurology; in fact, a close scrutiny of the prophecy business shows it to be extremely common. Ideology is not merely a by-product of certain kinds of prophetic vision. On the contrary, prophecy is a basic tool of ideology, Left or Right, East or West. In fact, attempts by one ideological camp to exert influence by "outprophesying" the other have been prominent centerpieces in ideological propaganda wars throughout recorded history; and of course the ultimate prophetic act in any ideological camp is naturally to predict its triumph over all others.

You do not have to go very far to demonstrate this: if you follow the now fading propaganda war between the competing ideologies of East and West, you can easily find some fascinating, and ultimately very revealing, skirmishes. For example, a few years ago the Soviet futurologist Georgi Shakhnazarov published a cutting diatribe in which he lam-

basted western futurology for being—bourgeois, of course—
but also, among other things, *unscientific.* According to
Shakhnazarov: "Futurology originated in the West as a specific academic discipline to provide an immediate alternative
to the Marxist-Leninist, communist ideas about the future
society. It was no natural offspring born at a point where a
new branch of science hives off from the general body of
knowledge. It was rather a peculiar hybrid artificially produced by the bourgeois social sciences . . . to meet a gen-
erously rewarded demand. Unlike any genuine science that
arrives at the truth at the end of the road, futurology has an
anteriorly posited result to which it must suit the facts."[3] It
may have gone largely unnoticed in the West—this certainly
was not a major Soviet propaganda offensive—but neither
was Shakhnazarov's diatribe a mere idle volley from the
Soviet propaganda machine. Why did he write it, and who
was he really addressing? After all, why should this Soviet
propagandist care whether western futurology is good, bad
or indifferent?

To understand why this was an issue for Shakhnazarov
and for his communist masters, it is necessary to consider
his work in context. Until recently, in the Soviet Union the
ideological machine was constantly working to legitimate
the state of political domination that existed there and in the
eastern bloc in general. The mere existence in the West of
a futurology which claimed to be scientific was bound to rub
against the Soviet ideological grain because futurology, of a
special sort, was a centerpiece of the Soviet ideological campaign. And because this Communist ideology had its roots
in Marxist political thought, futurology held a central position since even before the Russian revolution.

In writing this diatribe Shakhnazarov was working, in a
vulgar and rather technocratic sort of way, along two prominent lines in the tradition of Marxist political criticism. The
first is the persistent claim by Marxist theory that it is notable,
almost unique, for being *scientific.* And related to this claim
is another to the effect that Marx's thought contains powerful
insight into the nature of the world order—and insight which
emphatically includes a great deal of foresight. This second
strain is often referred to as the visionary or utopian aspect
of his thinking.

A little elaboration will help to explain how this relates to the concerns of this book. Very early in his writings Marx developed a specialized and very purposeful use of the word *scientific*. Marx used the term in various contexts often to contrast his own thought with that of other philosophers and social theorists. In Marx's critique, *science*, that is, his own work, was deemed to be more rational, more in touch with the true nature of things and with the logic inherent in that nature, than the "impoverished" philosophy of other theorists. By making this distinction Marx was both making a political move, in that he was trying to empower his own thought by elevating it above all others, and following the tradition which has been so powerful and persistent ever since the Enlightenment, the deification and worship of reason. So it was in this special, exclusive sense that Shakhnazarov was arguing that western futurology is not *scientific*. In the end, the implication in Shakhnazarov's book is that, since western futurology is not Marxist, almost by definition it cannot therefore possibly be *scientific*.[4]

As far as Marx's claim to special insight into the evolution of civilization is concerned, the story is similar. Marx's world view relied heavily on his penetrating analyses of economic, historical and political events, all of which he used in order to explain the evolving social, economic, and political order. He drew on his historical studies and analyses of current events to make broad predictions of future developments, all within the framework of the logical progression which he claimed he was uniquely able to discern. This way of thinking was particularly evident in his theory of revolution. One of the important features of Marx's theory of revolution was that it would proceed everywhere in logical, predictable stages. It is impossible to do Marx's usually rather thickety thinking justice here but, roughly speaking, in his scheme a stage of extreme discontent and contradiction was to be followed by another stage of violent overthrow of the existent regime; this was to be followed by a stage of legitimate domination called "dictatorship of the proletariat" during which new conditions and new social and economic relationships would be established; and this stage was ultimately to be followed by no political domination whatsoever, Marx's version of utopia, in which government of the sort we know now would no longer be necessary because of the so-called "withering" of the state into civil society. What is critical here, however, and what makes Marxist prophecy no different from many strains to be found in the West, is that this last stage exists always at some unknown point in the future and justifies the injustices, inconveniences and inequities which must be borne between now and then. Everything—including, in Marx's scheme, capitalism—is preparation for that stage. Everything points logically and *scientifically* in that direction. This was used to justify the recent state of affairs in the Soviet Union which entailed, among other things, constrained elections, domination of the state and individuals in the society by a single party, an elaborate policing system and all of the other all too familiar things that flow from Marx's prophecy. In short, the ruling party justified its domination not only on the basis of the status quo and its purported egalitarianism, but also, significantly, on the basis of insight—insight into the ultimate long-term good of the nation which was largely based on foresight into the future.

In this world view the non-Communist world remains full of contradictions because it has not yet reached its Communist phase. Not only is it full of inequity and injustice, but it remains subject to the irrationalities of capitalism usually epitomized by the surges and flutterings of the business cycle. However, upon surveying western futurology, Shakhnazarov's problem was that the largest and most prominent part of it also claims to be systematic and scientific in its analysis of world events, and also plays that game of political image management which specializes in evoking the future. In light of this fact, and in light of the ideological competition between East and West, which was based in large part on delineating *differences* between the two camps, the existence of the growing field of futurology in the West since the end of World War II, therefore, logically represented a threat. This threat was not to the physical Soviet state, of course, but to something very basic nevertheless: the Soviet persona, its very identity, which claimed, through its Marxist origins, to have a monopoly on scientific prophecy. If you consider the matter in this light, it is obvious that futurology would be one of those items to which the Soviets would have wanted to claim exclusive rights. The reasons are similar to those that motivated Marx to claim exclusive rights to the use of *science* in his political theory and, it must be added, similar to those that have led to the exclusive claim to political freedom which has so often been made for the West. Under these circumstances, therefore, how could the Soviet Union regard the rise of a so-called scientific futurology of the West with indifference?

Marxism is not the only ideology that relies heavily on a vision of the future. A well articulated vision of the future is the natural centerpiece of most ideological systems, especially those on the farther ends of the political spectrum. The reason this is so is that the extreme ideologies all envision the playing out of a great drama over time, and the final climax (the extreme ideologies always seem to go in for dramatic climaxes)—be it the "withering" of the state if it is an ideology of the Left, or some sort of breathtaking apocalypse in which the world will be destroyed and/or renewed if it is one on the Right—is always played out at some, usually unspecified, period in the future. A good example in recent years of the ideological right wing's use of prophecy to legitimate policy was the remark made by Reagan's former secretary of the interior, James Watt, who, when questioned about his department's policy to lease federal wilderness land for commercial development and exploitation, remarked that he saw no problem with deforestation because it would create a clearer view for the Messiah when He returned to redeem the earth in His Second Coming.

Politicians, who often view themselves as major actors in these great dramas, are always inordinately concerned with the final act. If they feel they have been major players in important decisions, they invariably want to have their judgment vindicated by the future; if they feel they are great leaders, they want future time to indicate that they knew exactly where to lead their people, even if their regime entails great hardship.† But more fundamentally, politics being

---

† When political leadership entails great hardship for the population, this must always be justified by an attractive or at least worthwhile future outcome, in which case the hardship is equated with making sacrifices for future generations. However, such leadership means that the leader be alienated from the people insofar as he does not share their burdens.

the tenuous business that it is, they are very concerned about their own personal futures. If they feel that they are an important part of the present status quo, they want to continue to be an important part of the status quo that is to come; they want to reproduce the present political order in such a way that no matter what else happens they will retain an important role in the political order of the future.

These different sorts of obsession with the future have long been a favorite preoccupation of politicians; in fact it is no exaggeration to say that at certain times they have been treated by politicians as a kind of religion. In the first century B.C the Roman senate would not make a move without first consulting the book of the Sibyl, a famous collection of prophecies made by a woman from Cumae. When this collection was destroyed by a fire in the Capitol in 83 B.C. the senators were unwilling to make any decisions until it had been replaced. It became so much a part of the established order that a group of conspirators led by Lentulus felt obliged to manufacture a set of rival ones, forgeries, to refute the official prophecies, much as opposition parties today publish rival policy papers and make rival predictions to discredit the official ones published by the government of the party in power to promote their own views. For the Roman senate, the publication of opposing prophecies was no small matter: these rival predictions were so threatening that Augustus had two thousand copies destroyed in 12 B.C Similarly, in Wales in 1406, laws were framed against "false prophecy" because there had been a great deal of divination that was said to be against the state. Today, of course, futurology think tanks like the Rand Corporation serve as the source of and repository for our current set of Sibylline papers. They are not, however, produced by an inspired woman— or inspired men for that matter. They are churned out by technocrats using the whole array of modern quantitative and qualitative projection techniques. But in the consciousness of the politicians who consult them, these papers serve the same function as the Sibylline papers did in Rome; they are, quite literally, a part of their secular religious practice.

Getting back to Shakhnazarov, though, of course he was right about western futurology. It is assuredly not a science. But it is no less of a science than was the futurology of the Soviet Union. In a sense, Shakhnazarov's diatribe was a modern-day symbolic equivalent of Augustus burning the rival prophecies of the Lentulus camp. But what is more important than this is that the *claim* to be scientific or systematic is a characteristic feature of much of the futurology of both East and West. It wears the mantle of science even though it cannot properly be said to be a real science itself. And we should bear in mind that this is no mere affectation; it serves several indispensable functions. First, not only does it distinguish futurology from the most questionable forms of forecasting like astrology, extrasensory perception and all of the other more esoteric forms of divination which flood our existential airwaves, but this characteristic use of scientism also serves the functions both of lending legitimacy to the tenuous business of prediction and of obscuring its hidden agenda. In short, the scientism of futurology serves as a mask for its inherent ideology.

This kind of legitimation is crucial to futurology's wellbeing. Since the predictions and prescriptions which futurologists make must somehow be made credible in the eyes of their audiences, it follows that a very good way to accomplish this has been to somehow associate their activity with science. Notwithstanding the growing skepticism and doubts about its uses, science retains the cachet of mastery and legitimacy. It remains deeply entrenched in our civil religion that scientists both know the nature of things and can effectively act on the world to make things happen. Not surprisingly, therefore, many futurists have gone very far in order to establish an association with science. They use scientific methods and techniques—whether or not it is meaningful or appropriate to do so—and above all they use a great deal of scientific or pseudo-scientific language. Even the term "futurology," which was coined by the German sociologist Ossip Flechtheim in 1942, serves the purpose of creating this association.[5]

We came across an example of the use of pseudo-scientific jargon in the last chapter when I introduced futurologist François Hetman's term, "comprehensive guarantism (*garantisme intégrale*)." Consider it again: clumsy, pretentious, and murky, but definitely containing an air of scientific *savoir faire*. Why use this phrase when one could just as easily, and far more clearly, have said something like "complete insurance"? The answer becomes immediately obvious as soon as you consider the phrase in context. This phrase is used to modify the word "existence." How could anyone use the whole phrase, "complete insurance against existence" without feeling foolish? Hence, "comprehensive guarantism."

Though perhaps they are no worse than futurologists from other countries, French futurologists have long been notable for inventing jargon. In the early nineteenth century the French utopian socialist Charles Fourier was particularly imaginative and colorful in this game. He liked to argue by what he called "analogy" and predicted that, in the harmonized world of the future, "anti-lions" would tame the world of nature, "anti-crocodiles" would shrink its domain and there would be a creature called a "great hen" which was to lay enough eggs to pay off the English national debt in six months. Would that there were a few such "great hens" around in our time, that is, Charles Fourier's future!

In order to give the reader a better taste of what is entailed in this game, here are a few more examples of the kinds of pseudo-scientific words and phrases that futurists regularly use. They are not nearly as colorful as Fourier's, but they make up for this by being a great deal more pretentious and absurd. It is impossible to resist making a few comments about them.

Futuro-Epistemology-Conceptology-Engineering. The Japanese futurist Yujiro Hayashi coined this phrase at a conference in 1967 in order to help the convenors classify their research of the future. It breaks down to the following three categories: *Futuro-epistemology* is the study of conditions under which one can gain an objective understanding of the future. *Futuro-conceptology,* on the other hand, is the conscious activity of mapping out desirable futures. And *futuro-engineering* describes a practical activity: applied research on means for implementing desirable futures. The first term seems to describe an impossibility. Under what conditions could one possibly gain an "objective" understanding of that which does not yet exist? Most scientists have enough trouble getting an "objective" understanding of things that are in front of their noses! But if you are going to lay claim to being scientific you have to claim to be objective, hence *futuro-epistemology*. The second term describes a prescriptive activity which, however, pretends to be derived from the nature of things. It suggests that the process of mapping out desirable futures is value free and scientific rather than being full of moral considerations. Whose desirable futures do these futurists have in mind? If the term meant negotiating or building consensus around desirable futures, then it might be acceptable as a political challenge, but mapping in this context is an evasion in the form of a pseudo-scientism. As to the third term, once one gets past the considerable hump of introducing an agenda of desirables, as one does in the second term, the means for getting them would fall into the realm of practical problem solving, engineering.[6]

Symbiosis. Here a common scientific word is appropriated and used in a characteristically uncommon and inappropriate way as follows: "It is clear that over the past century our relationship with it [the telephone] has grown more complex. Today we have a sort of symbiotic relationship with telephones. In tomorrow's society, the symbiosis, for better or worse will be even stronger." According to the *Oxford English Dictionary,* symbiosis is "the permanent union between organisms each of which depends for its existence on the other as the fungus and alga composing lichen." It is clear that either the author did not really understand the word—after all, telephones are not organisms, so what can it possibly mean to say they depend on humans—or, more likely, that he decided, by a mere wave of the futurologist's lexicographic wand, to elevate these appliances to the level of organisms in order to enhance his forecasting by glamorously associating it with the environmental movement. The hidden message: if you use your fancy telephone a great deal you will be developing a natural relationship with it and perhaps contributing to ecological stability.[7]

Ephemeralization. Probably Buckminster Fuller's most famous idea was that by using clever design we can do more with less. The word *ephemeralization,* which is supposed to describe that process, is obscure enough on the surface, but it is even harder to understand when he uses it in context, as in the following: "The progressive doing of more with less

per each and every reinvested resource unit of energy M
(matter), energy R (radiation) and I (intellect). Wealth is
intellect harnessed in animate energy, tooled anticipatorily
to automatically produce the forward metabolic regeneration
of humanity. Ephemeralization is scientifically identifiable
with anti-entropy; it is a product of the metaphysical conservation being more effective and coherent than physical
entropy." Once you work out the pseudo-scientific babble,
it should be clear that Buckminster Fuller, like many futurologists, belongs to the school of economic thinking that
holds that material scarcity, as opposed to human nature, is
the real economic problem. This passage is part of a larger
argument that says that clever design will optimize the use
of resources and eliminate scarcity, and thus eliminate the
need for politics, a tool that humans have invented to deal
with the issue of distribution under the conditions of scarcity.
What Fuller is really implying in the above passage is that
if we solve our technical problems, our human problems will
simply fall into place.[8]

Basic Long-term Multifold Trend. Futurologist Herman
Kahn made the less than profound observation that certain
major trends are complex, interrelated and likely to continue
for the long-term. He used this phrase as a sort of conceptual
net into which to place these trends so he could, in a sense,
call them his own. Included on his list are: worldwide industrialization and modernization; population growth; increasing the tempo of change; increasing capability of mass
destruction; and accumulation of scientific and technical
knowledge. Here we have a combination of stating the obvious without bringing any additional insight to it, and masking this by combining one's terms in an unfamiliar package.
Kahn was a supreme master of packaging—was there ever
a time when cultural change did not have to do with complex
and interrelated events and phenomena?[9]

Disintermediation. Emerson would have used the term
"self-reliance" instead, and we would all have immediately
known what he meant. This other word, *disintermediation,*
was invented by futurist Paul Hawken to describe a hiccup
of a trend which occurred in most of the advanced industrial
nations in the late 1970s and at the beginning of the 1980s.
He noticed that during this period of high interest rates many

investors were switching from stocks to bonds because of their higher rate of return. Because one can buy bonds directly at a bank without a broker, he shortsightedly saw this development as a trend to eliminate the middle-person, and cleverly called this process *disintermediation*. Meanwhile, a few years later, the stock market is bullish and not only are stockbrokers very much back in business, but banks are charging more for services and the financial services industry is growing rapidly. But before, during, and after this hiccup many people, mainly women, have continued to sew at home and thereby disintermediate the manufacturers of clothing—without even knowing they are in the business of disintermediation.[10]

These are but a handful of innumerable examples but, aside from giving the uninitiated reader a taste of what this business is all about, it should make my point abundantly clear. In spite of their pretension, once you master them, most of the ideas expressed by these terms are remarkably simple-minded. It is easy to see why futurologists desperately need the ballast of scientism in order to be taken seriously. In the end, their quasi-scientific terms are little more than fancy, obscure and sometimes wrong and/or inaccurate ways of naming very ordinary things.

The process of naming things, or the parts of them, in order to try to understand them is an activity which is as old as science itself. But when we name things with unnecessarily esoteric language, we do something more than simply try to understand them; we try to own them, we appropriate mastery of these things for ourselves alone and for the members of the group with whom we share this special language. This is unquestionably a political act because any group which can claim mastery over something that most people would also like to understand and control is in this way exercising dominance over them. In the last decade or so this fact has at least been recognized in the field of medicine, by many patients and some doctors, and so, thankfully, we now have a small movement to simplify medical terminology.

The question of domination brings us squarely into the realm of politics. The French sociologist Alain Gras has argued that futurology is basically a technique of political domination, and that it is intimately linked with the policy of ruling elites because its hidden agenda is the reproduction of domination.[11] It may not be fair to say this of all of futurology, but it is disconcerting how often themes of dominance and elitism emerge in this field. In the last chapter we had a taste of this in Edward Feigenbaum's raving about the rising class of computer technocrats—he calls them "intellectuals"—who will presumably come to dominate the life of the mind. Likewise Buckminster Fuller, who is usually more sober than Feigenbaum, nevertheless glories in talking about his influence on the decision-makers of the world.[12] Daniel Bell, on the other hand, has self-righteously proclaimed that the mandate of his group of futurologists, the Commission on the Year 2000, was to "widen the sphere of moral choices," while at the same time he has prescribed that the range of actors who should make these choices should be kept narrow and should consist primarily of intellectuals, the class of which he happens to be a part.[13] But no one has gloated more than Herman Kahn about the privileged position held by these advisers to the future-makers of this world. He has even prided himself on being duplicitous in his role of court astrologer, saying one thing to the general public and another to the powers that be:

> Two different perspectives can be used in future studies . . . [they] can be labeled *descriptive* (or *predictive*) and *normative* . . . descriptive forecasting is basically passive, merely attempting to record what the world will be like so that we may react to it.
>
> The normative perspective emphasizes changing the future in a desired fashion, making more likely *the good* and/or less likely *the bad*. . . . However, although descriptive forecasting may be useful in many fields where the outcome cannot be affected by choices today, decision makers are primarily concerned with normative forecasting. In practice, it is not possible to separate the two types completely. There are obvious constraints and limits on the ambition of any individual or institution that must be descriptively forecast before any normative forecast can be made. When working on

individual projects for agencies or organizations we put our primary emphasis on the "normative" approach, trying to delineate what options are open to decision makers and what can be the implications of their decisions; but when addressing a more general audience, as in this book, we emphasize the "descriptive" face of futurology, although normative aspects are certainly present. (emphasis added)[14]

One thing that can be said for Kahn is that his elitist pretensions were perfectly consistent with his normative vision of the world of the future. In an earlier book, it is remarkable how many techniques for population control are included in a neat list of one hundred—futurologists love to deal in round numbers—expected developments. These include:

Other new and possibly pervasive techniques for surveillance, monitoring, and control of individuals and organizations.

New and more reliable "educational" and propaganda techniques for affecting human behavior—public and private.

New and relatively effective counterinsurgency techniques (and perhaps also insurgency techniques).

Other genetic control or influence over the "basic constitution of an individual."[15]

Futurology is also used by corporate elites, not only to try to control the outside world, the *environment* as it is frequently called, but for control within the corporation and in infighting and competitions within the corporation itself. Two Dutch futurologists, Henk Becker and Joseph van Doorn, have observed that "futures research has become important for successful negotiations. A policy maker either uses the results of a futures research project to beat his opponents, or his opponents attack him by using futures research and he needs to have this kind of research available to hit back." They also remark that "futures studies must transform uncertainty into risk as much as possible. The dynamics and complexity of the social systems which the policy maker wants to control demand analytical instruments that are able to consider the relative (unpredictability) of the developments involved."[16] Even in our business corporations, which pride themselves on governing themselves strictly on the basis of rationality, there is no rhetoric more powerful than the often irrational rhetoric of prophecy, nor any better tool for self-promotion or the promotion of one's favorite policy ideas. And even when the acknowledged unpredictability of the outside world finally does leave corporation executives feeling uneasy, their anxiety can always be assuaged by prophetic placebos.

Another sense in which futurology acts in the service of social control was suggested by Ivan Illich, who has argued that futurology promotes cultural convergence along technocratic lines. He has observed that "most of the research now going on about the future tends to advocate further increases in the institutionalization of values."[17] Given the technocratic consciousness which so heavily permeates futurological thinking, this would almost be inevitable. As I demonstrated earlier in my analysis of prediction in the oil industry, wherever else one might find diversity and individuality of thought and values, it is not in this realm. In fact, all too often one comes across an outright hostility to a diversity of values, or even to values per se. Tohru Motooka, head of the Japanese Fifth Generation project, has asserted: "[Fifth Generation computers] will take the place of man in the areas of physical labor, and, through the intellectualization of these advanced computers, totally new applied fields will be developed, social productivity will be increased, and *distortions in values will be eliminated.*" (emphasis added)[18] Both the "institutionalization of values" and the "elimination of distortions" in them reflect a rhetoric for which modern prophecy is always striving—the rhetoric of consensus, that cool-headed and benign posturing so valued in politics and economics because it leaves no room for dissent or criticism. Although the prophet often assumes a harsh, stern face when he is issuing a warning, his mask of preference is the serene face in which ideology always prefers to appear in public, the unassailably benevolent and impenetrable face of the rhetoric of consensus.

But the consequence of institutionalizing values, or, as Tohru Moto-oka would have it, eliminating distortions in them, is that the number of what may generally be regarded as "reasonable" courses of action is seemingly diminished. More than this, if you take the narrowing of reasonable choices together with the narrowing of the numbers of actors that can make these choices—both being trends that futurology promotes—you have a simple recipe for elitist domination. There is a saying among strategic planners in the private sector that captures this idea nicely. It has a marked predatory flavor which goes, "plan or be planned for."[19] If you do not make plans and get others to go along, then you will have to go along with the plans that they make for their own benefit and for *you.* If this sounds like a form of corporate Darwinism, it should. Many of Darwin's more elitist followers in the late nineteenth century were ardent futurologists. They believed in hastening the process of natural selection through selective breeding in the interests of the upper classes, much the same as Churchill predicted we would do through genetic engineering. They believed too in what another author has called "the arrival rather than the survival of the species."[20]

In this context, the scientism of futurology serves another function: it neutralizes the opposition which may exist in the mind of a public with different values by appealing to transcendent values, the values of science. What are these values? The Greeks of antiquity equated science, which was then part of philosophy, with the pursuit of the truth, and equated truth, in turn, with the good. This idea, easy to believe then and attractive even now, has been perpetuated to this day. It accounts for part of the prestige of science, even though most of it is based on its power rather than its association with virtue. But if there ever was an easy relationship between truth and good, it has been lost from science today. It is a commonplace that scientific knowledge can be used for either good or evil. There is nothing inherent in logic or reason that leads to goodness or virtue—we are all familiar by now with the adage that the same process that made Ford efficient at building cars made Hitler efficient at killing people. However, today many scientists skirt this issue by saying that science is beyond good and evil—a stance that is probably what led the German philosopher Jürgen Habermas to remark that "technocratic consciousness reflects not the sundering of an ethical situation, but the repression of 'ethics' as such as a category of life."[21] Again, there is no better rhetoric than the prophet's favorite rhetoric of consensus for repressing ethics. All ethical issues are immediately repressed as soon as consensus is assumed.

One of Buckminster Fuller's last books, *Critical Path*, even tried to make a virtue of the sundering of ethics. He begins it with the incredible assertion, "It is the author's working assumption that the words *good* and *bad* are meaningless." This statement he justifies by the following childish line of reasoning: "This is based on science and not on opinion. In 1922 physicists discovered a fundamental complementarity of disparate individual phenomena to be operative in physical Universe. This was fundamentally amplified with the subsequent discovery of the always-and-only-different, always-coexisting proton and neutron which, with their always-coexistent electrons, positrons, neutrinos, and antineutrinos, are eternally intertransformable." (emphasis in original)[22] Fuller's method of sundering ethics is to neutralize them by using the simple but silly device of an analogy to chemistry. In his analogy, good and evil are treated like chemicals, acid and base, which combine and lose their original properties and identity when simply placed together in the same vial. Much of the book from which this quotation was taken is also devoted to touting his own simple-minded ideas about how to save humanity through efficient design (see *ephemeralization* on page 91). But all of this is placed in the context of a dispassionate "scientific" view of the world as a sort of test-tube experiment—perhaps it works, perhaps not. God exists in this world (indeed Fuller refers to Him as if they have a special relationship) but Fuller would have us believe that God is indifferent to the outcome of the experiment.

However, if you usher values out the front door, they have a peculiar habit of sneaking in again through the rear, and naturally they make a reappearance even in Fuller's scheme. Though God is indifferent, Fuller reminds us that we must be *truthful* if we are to make it in this world, especially when we are programming computers: "The nearest each of us can come to God is by loving the truth. If we don't program the computer truthfully with all the truth and nothing but the truth, we won't get the answers that allow us to 'make it.' "[23] Even setting aside the anthropomorphism of such a statement, what could Fuller possibly have meant by entreating us to be *truthful* when we program computers? Surely he meant nothing as trivial as entering our symbols and figures as precisely as we can. That would be the kind of imperative to direct perhaps at schoolchildren, and Fuller's concerns seem to go well beyond that. His exhortation reminds one of a memorable passage in Hannah Arendt's famous essay on truth-telling called "Lying in Politics." I shall quote it at length because it makes some penetrating points about what truth-telling might mean, and why it is antithetical to the field of futurology.

Unlike the natural scientist, who deals with matters that, whatever their origin, are not man-made or man-enacted, and that therefore can be observed, understood, and eventually even changed only through the most meticulous loyalty to factual, given reality, the historian, as well as the politician, deals with human affairs that owe their existence to man's capacity for action, and that means to man's relative freedom from things as they are. Men who act, to the extent that they feel themselves to be the masters of their own futures, will forever be tempted to make themselves masters of the past, too. Insofar as they have the appetite for action and are also in love with theories, they will hardly have the natural scientist's patience to wait until theories and hypothetical explanations are verified or denied by facts. Instead, they will be tempted to fit their reality—which, after all, was man-made to begin with and thus could have been otherwise—into their theory, thereby mentally getting rid of its disconcerting *contingency*. Reason's aversion to contingency is very strong; it was Hegel, the father of grandiose history schemes, who held that "philosophical contemplation has no other intention than to eliminate the accidental." Indeed, much of the

modern arsenal of political theory—the game theories and systems analyses, the scenarios written
for imagined "audiences" and the careful enumer-
ation of, usually, three "options"—A, B, C—
whereby A and C represent the opposite extremes
and B the "logical" middle-of-the-road solution of
the problem—has its source in this deep-seated
aversion. The fallacy of such thinking begins with
forcing the choices into mutually exclusive dilem-
mas; reality never presents us with anything so neat
as premises for logical conclusions. The kind of
thinking that presents both A and C as undesirable,
and therefore settles on B, hardly serves any other
purpose than to divert the mind and blunt the judgment from the multitude of real possibilities. What
these problem-solvers have in common with down-
to-earth liars is the attempt to get rid of facts and
the confidence that this should be possible because
of the inherent contingency of facts. (emphasis in
original)[24]

Arendt's implied point—that the same sort of mentality that
will make a person a certain kind of historian will also make
him or her a typical futurologist—is not just fanciful. Although historians can try to maintain their integrity by at
least trying to be faithful to the always too elusive "facts"
which make up their palette, both professions concern themselves with a theoretical mastery of action and of events over
time. Amazingly, some futurologists even regard themselves
as historians of a sort. Therefore, Daniel Bell, who is considered the intellectual's futurologist, has made the all too
clever assertion that while historians are concerned with *retrospective history,* futurologists are concerned with something he calls *prospective history.* In coining the phrase
prospective history to describe what futurologists do, Bell
seemed to be trying to legitimate futurology, which was then
a newer and more vulnerable field, by associating it with
conventional history. In his foreword to futurologist Burnham Beckwith's book, *The Next Five Hundred Years,* Bell
wrote: "While it may be startling to think of looking ahead
five hundred years, one realizes that the great historians have

always taken periods of several hundred years to identify
and explain the major social processes which lay behind the
course of civilizations and empires. It took several hundred
years for Christianity to become accepted in the Western
world. Five hundred years is a period one takes, as Gibbon
did, to deal with the decline of the Roman Empire. Five
hundred years is a normal unit in the history of ancient Egypt
and certainly of classical China. What Professor Beckwith is
doing is writing *prospective* rather than *retrospective* history.
This is his claim to novelty." (emphasis in original)[25] Novelty
is the futurologist's favorite word. Yet there is nothing novel
about Bell's analogy at all—it is simply absurd. Here we
have the clever gazer into time: at one moment he sets his
time-telescope to gaze at a point five centuries earlier; then
he merely flips it around one hundred and eighty degrees
and gazes at events that will occur five centuries later. In
fact, Bell's characterization of the futurologist's profession
brings to mind a discussion that Alice had on the other side
of the looking glass:

"The rule is, jam to-morrow and jam yesterday—
but never jam *today*."

"It *must* come sometimes to "jam today," Alice objected.

"No, it can't," said the Queen. "It's jam every
other day: Today isn't any other day, you know."

"I don't understand you," said Alice. "It's
dreadfully confusing!"

"That's the effect of living backwards," the
Queen said kindly: "it always makes one a little
giddy at first—"

"Living backwards!" Alice repeated in great
astonishment. "I never heard of such a thing!"

"—but there's one great advantage in it, that
one's memory works both ways."

"I'm sure *mine* only works one way," Alice
remarked. "I can't remember things before they
happen."

"It's a poor sort of memory that only works
backwards," the Queen remarked.

"What sort of things do *you* remember best?"
Alice ventured to ask.

"Oh, things that happened the week after
next," the Queen replied in a careless tone.[26]

In a sense, Arendt's description of the historian's or politician's relationship with facts, with reality, is even more apt
for the futurologist than for the historian, because when it
comes to facts, futurologists have the freest hand of all—
who, after all, shall come from the future to testify against
them?—and the rhetoric of "consensus" can be employed
by them with greater impunity than by anyone else. When
futurologists paint their little inventories of "likely scenarios," one never finds them advocating one that, in the context which they are addressing, would likely be regarded as
extreme. In this respect, they give the appearance of being
as reasonable as Aristotle, who exhorts the man who would
be happy to steer his course along "the golden mean." Aristotle, however, respected individuality and the contingency
of facts enough to assert that this mean will be different for
each and every person.

Of all of the futurologists around today, perhaps none
has demonstrated a more childlike aversion to the contingency of facts than Yoneji Masuda in his vision of a future
society which he calls "Computopia." All of the age-old
ideals of a humanistic utopian society exist in his vision,
except, unfortunately, for the humans themselves, in any
form which even the optimists among us would easily recognize. Masuda's Computopia is a future society in which
the use of computers would be maximized, not only for the
purposes of saving labor and increasing productivity, but
also to "enhance" social relations and decision-making.
For example, political negotiating, and, ultimately, political
decision-making would regularly, daily, be made by refer-
enda using universalized computer networking. In Masuda's
vision, somehow or other the mere permeation of society
with computer technology would bring out the best in everyone. But should a poor soul falter or change his mind, there
is still always coercion to bring him in line, and Masuda, like
Kahn, paints this all too human trait into his vision in a self-
righteous and paternalistic way:

Let us consider some examples of this type of group futurization. One such might be venture businesses with a *new type of management organization.* A number of people who share the same business goal, might, for example, get together and set up a business venture. With shared risk, each would become responsible, in the activities of the enterprise, for one's own particular field. One might undertake the responsibility of providing capital; another might contribute specialized knowledge and experience. Each would have equal rights of participants in management; income from the enterprise would be distributed according to the agreement between all members, and each would agree to share the responsibility in case of loss.

Notice that up to this point he is merely describing, with the aid of a moderate amount of jargon, the type of arrangement that might be made even at present in a limited partnership agreement. It is ever the futurologist's way to project mundane present-day phenomena into the future and mystify them by dressing them up in fancy language. But then what follows after this is good old-fashioned domination:

In this type of venture all positions would be decided by the agreement of all participants which means that even the chosen president would be subject to the authority of the whole group, and failure to improve the performance of the enterprise would mean dismissal from such office. And if, for example, it was found that working for the enterprise conflicted with one's individual futurization, leaving the enterprise freely would be the only option. To carry out the responsibilities undertaken for a fixed period with the agreement of all would be the prime duty of such a person, *who would not be able to quit before the term of office ended.* (emphasis added)[27]

I ended the last chapter by observing that the psychology of futurology largely entails a sort of petty mastery of the self which finally boils down to self-avoidance. In the ideology of futurology mastery is extended also to others; predicting the future is part of the process, also, of trying to dominate it. Language is the key tool in all of this because with language one can do anything: with words anything is possible, and in the realm of action, language is always in the vanguard, is always forward-looking, is always supreme.

But finally, even in the context of this mastery of others, we also find *avoidance* to be the persistent theme in the ideology of futurology: not avoidance of the self so much—the individual hardly comes into the picture here at all—but of the disconcerting facts and values that do not fit neatly into the self-promoting future picture. The Soviet Union, which used to make a fetish of its own peculiar kind of futurology, has been avoiding facts and values in its culture for decades with some extremely detrimental economic and social effects that are only now being faced squarely. Futurehype in the West is more subtle than the Marxist variety, and certainly not as institutionalized, but it has had, and continues to have, adverse effects in all sorts of areas of our culture (some of which will be examined in the next section of this book).

It is always questionable to subordinate present realities to theories about the future because such theories can never properly be tested by facts. But when, as is often the case with prediction, the theories turn out to be projects for self-promotion, or the promotion of an elite or interest group, we have a recipe for ineffectiveness at best, disaster at worst.

As the reader will learn in Chapter Four on futurehype in the military, ideology is not just a matter of words with no consequences. All of the fiercest trappings of ideology are vested, in the end, in the military, and the way they are played out there can decide the fate of a civilization in an extraordinarily short period of time.

NOTES

1. Winston Churchill, "Fifty Years Hence," in *Popular Mechanics* (March 1932), p. 397.
2. See, for example, Annie Vinokur, "Malthusian Ideology and the Crises of the Welfare State," in Turner, Michael, ed. *Malthus and His Time* (New York, St.

Martins Press, 1986). Also, John M. Sherwood, "Engels, Marx, Malthus, and the Machine," *American Historical Review*, (1985), vol. 90, no. 4.

3. Georgi Shakhnazarov, *Futurology Fiasco: A Critical Study of Non-Marxist Concepts of How Society Develops* (Moscow: Progress Publishers, 1982), p. 7. See also, I. Bestushev-Lada, "Bourgeois 'Futurology' and the Future of Mankind," in A. Toffler (ed.), *The Futurists* (New York: Random House, 1972).

4. Marx's scientific pretenses run through the greater part of his work—in fact they were so important to him that Engels saw fit to mention them (though not as *pretenses,* of course) in his graveside eulogy. Perhaps Marx's most famous and powerful statement of the *inevitable* nature of future developments is contained in his Preface to *Capital* where he wrote: "Intrinsically it is not a question of higher or lower degree of development of social antagonisms that result from the laws of capitalist production. It is a question of these laws themselves, or these tendencies *working with iron necessity towards inevitable results.* The country that is more developed industrially only shows, to the less developed, the image of its own future." (emphasis added) Likewise, his most famous utopian vision is to be found in *The German Ideology,* whereas the idea of the necessity for a transitional phase of "revolutionary dictatorship of the proletariat" is spelled out in *Critique of the Gotha Program.* Marx was not the only nineteenth-century utopian who sought to harness raw power to effect his transformation to utopia—but his advocacy of a centralized, party-dominated power made him part company with other nineteenth-century socialists, particularly the anarchists who found this idea repugnant and anathema to their own more individualistic ideals.

5. Along with his critique of futurology, George Orwell is also notable for having written about the politics of language, how language is used to obscure ideology. We are all familiar with how he did this in his fiction, but one of his most famous essays was also on this subject. In "Politics and the English Language" he wrote: "It [the English language] becomes ugly and inaccurate because our thoughts are foolish, but the slovenliness of our language makes it easier for us to have foolish thoughts. Modern English, especially written English, is full of bad habits which spread by imitation and which can be avoided if one is willing to take the necessary trouble. If one gets rid of these habits one can think more clearly, and to think clearly is a necessary first step towards political regeneration." ("Politics and the English Language," in *In Front of Your Nose,* New York: Harcourt Brace Jovanovich, 1968, p. 128.) The heart of Orwell's argument was that politicians often use difficult or unclear language in order to obscure the meaning of what they have to say since, were they to say it clearly, it would be obvious to anyone who was paying close attention that what they were hearing was "a mass of lies, evasions, folly, hatred and schizophrenia," to use his inimitable expression.

6. Yujiro Hayashi, "The Direction and Orientation of Futurology as a Science," International Future Research Congress, Oslo, September 12–15, 1967.

7. Ben Bova, "Future Phones," in *Omni* (February 1985).

8. R. Buckminster Fuller, "Comprehensive Design Strategy," in *World Resources Inventory,* Southern Illinois University, December 5, 1967.

9. Herman Kahn and Anthony J. Wiener, *The Year 2000* (New York: Macmillan, 1967).

10. Paul Hawken, *The Next Economy* (New York: Henry Holt and Co., 1984). Alvin Toffler invented a term called "prosumerism" to define the same concept in *The Third Wave* (London: Pan Books, 1981). Fortunately they have not yet had a dispute about concept ownership.

11. Alain Gras, *La Futurologie* (Paris: Collection Clefs, 1976), p. 29.

12. R. Buckminster Fuller, *Utopia or Oblivion* (New York: Bantam Books, 1969).

13. Daniel Bell, *The Coming of Post-Industrial Society* (New York: Basic Books, 1973).
14. Herman Kahn and B. Bruce-Briggs, *Things to Come: Thinking about the 70s and 80s* (New York: Macmillan, 1972), pp. 244–245.
15. Herman Kahn and Anthony J. Wiener, *The Year 2000* (New York: Macmillan, 1967).
16. Henk A. Becker and Joseph W.M. van Doorn, "Scenarios in an Organizational Perspective," in *Futures* (December 1987), p. 670.
17. Ivan Illich, *Deschooling Society* (New York: Harper and Row, 1971), p. 2.
18. Cited by Joseph Weizenbaum in "The Computer in Your Future," *New York Review of Books* (October 27, 1983), p. 59.
19. See Russell Ackoff, *Creating the Corporate Future: Plan or Be Planned For* (New York: John Wiley & Sons, 1981).
20. W.H.G. Armytage, *Yesterday's Tomorrows* (London: Routledge and Kegan Paul, 1968), p. 49.
21. Jürgen Habermas, "Technology and Science as Ideology," in *Toward a Rational Society: Student Protest, Science and Politics* (Boston: Beacon Press, 1970), p. 113.
22. R. Buckminster Fuller, *Critical Path* (New York: St. Martin's Press, 1981), p. ix.
23. Fuller, p. xxxvii.
24. Hannah Arendt, "Lying in Politics," in *Crisis of the Republic* (New York: Harcourt Brace Jovanovich, 1972), pp. 11–12.
25. Daniel Bell, Foreword to Burnham Beckwith, *The Next Five Hundred Years* (New York: Exposition Press, 1967), pp. v–vi.
26. Lewis Carroll, *Through the Looking Glass and What Alice Found There* (London: Macmillan, 1927), pp. 99–100.
27. Yoneji Masuda, *Computopia: Information Society as Post-Industrial Society* (Bethesda, Md.: World Future Society, 1981), p. 138.

Our problem is not only to face the somber and grim elements of the future, but to keep them from obscuring it.
—ROBERT OPPENHEIMER

4

FUTUREHYPE IN THE MILITARY

War is such a risky business that, in a way, it is a wonder that it is ever undertaken. Of course there have always been defensive wars, and the motives for undertaking them are not too difficult to comprehend. But a remarkable number of wars throughout history have been started on the basis of the far more questionable and far less rationally compelling motives of nationalist fervor, the competition between ideologies, imperialistic ambitions and the imputed evil nature of the enemy. Because of the often dire consequences of war, it takes an extraordinary state of mind to contemplate, prepare for and undertake warmongering and war-making that is based on these motives alone. Even before the advent of the atomic age, it was possible, with great will and effort, to decimate an entire civilization and an entire epoch of building during the course of a relatively short war—now, it is easy.

Therefore it requires an extraordinary deadening of some parts of the mind and spirit and an inordinate enlivening of others to undertake war. To prudent people, who will first consult their common sense and comfort, this mind-set does not come easily, and sustaining it is no trivial matter. The individual's natural reluctance to go to war can be overcome only with compulsion, in the form of a draft, or with words, that is, with propaganda. In fact, in the business of war prophets are the most accomplished of all propagandists, the most powerful purveyors of the words that produce the mind-set that makes war possible. The power of these prophets is a consequence of their claim that they can predict what warriors most want to know: how things will turn out.

Throughout recorded history, warriors have been desperate for guidance about how their war undertakings will turn out, and prophecy has often been the only "advice" that has been forthcoming. In fact, the relationship between prediction and military affairs has always been so strong that it is safe to say that if futurology did not now exist, the military, in its characteristically determined way, would probably be trying to invent it.

In every age wars have been both started and conducted, at least partly, and sometimes even wholly, on the basis of prophecy. "Force is the midwife of Progress," wrote Marx, and in our century many revolutionary wars have been started on the basis of Marx's theory that violence is necessary to beget change. The two centuries of Crusades were also started in part because of the pervasive millennial prophecy about the coming end of the world that permeated tenth- to twelfth-century consciousness. The undertaking of these wars was more or less considered to be unfinished business that would hasten the return of the Messiah.

And when prophecy per se has not been one of the main factors that has helped to instigate a war, there has often been some grand political theory with a great prophecy built into it. One way of understanding the influential domino theory, the roots of which go back to the time of the Athenian Empire of the fifth century B.C., is to think of it as a prediction that if you lose one allegiance now you will inevitably lose all of the allegiances there are to lose at some point in the future. This is the kind of reasoning that Athens used to justify its imperial adventures of expansion and subjugation during the early stages of the Peloponnesian Wars when it had the upper hand.

The role of prediction in warfare was particularly evident in antiquity when the domino theory was first contrived, and when soothsayers, oracles and other sorts of prophets regularly played a prominent and often very public role in personal, social and political affairs. In fact, though war futurologists now sit in offices and sometimes work in large bureaucracies, in the ancient world warriors used to take their prophets out onto the battlefield with them—so they could then be appropriately held accountable for their advice right on the spot.

But thinking of the role played by prediction in the wars of antiquity brings to mind a certain irony: the first casualty of the Trojan War was not a man, not a warrior, but a woman—and she was a victim, not of the fighting, but of the prophecy that preceded it. The legend of King Agamemnon and his hapless daughter, Iphigenia, speaks volumes on the theme of prophecy in that war, and it also has a great deal to say about our own time: in many ways, it epitomizes the pathetic and pathological relationship between forecasting and fighting.

According to legend, before setting out for Troy all of the Greek ships assembled at Argos, the city in Sparta from which Helen had been taken by the Trojan prince, Paris. The Greek allies then proceeded to have their war council. However, just before they were about to set out for Troy, the seas began to storm without letup. Hindered and troubled by this development, Agamemnon, king of the Argives and leader of the expedition, consulted an oracle by the name of Calchas. This prophet said the storms were caused by the goddess Artemis and predicted that she would stop them and allow the ships to depart only if Agamemnon would sacrifice his daughter, Iphigenia, to her. This the king finally decided to do. On the pretext of marrying her to the hero Achilles, he summoned Iphigenia to the altar at the Bay of Aulis, where the ships had been assembled, and sacrificed his daughter to the goddess. The storms stopped and the ships set out for their famous and fateful war.

In considering the role of prophecy in human affairs,

this legend has all sorts of fascinating implications. Calchas's prophecy was typical of Greek predictions—and of many modern ones too—in that it was extremely ambiguous. Not only could it be interpreted in more ways than one, but it was cloaked in mysterious innuendo. After all, this prediction was not simply a set of marching orders: on the basis of the information which Calchas gave him, and faced with the prospect of having to slay his own daughter in order to go to war, Agamemnon could have decided that what Artemis was really trying to tell him by bringing on the storms was that the war was ill-advised and that he should call it off. That Artemis did not really want Iphigenia's life is suggested by the legend which says that, just before Agamemnon struck her, when he had averted his eyes so as not to have to see his knife pierce his daughter's neck, the goddess quickly substituted a deer in Iphigenia's place and spirited the girl away to the Island of Tauris, where she eventually established a cult with Iphigenia as high priestess. But in the end the king did choose to sacrifice his daughter so that he could go to war. Needless to say, this was not the first, nor would it by any means be the last time someone would decide to sacrifice a family member in order to be able to go off to fight one sort of war or another. The core of the legend still contains the idea that on the mere basis of an ambiguous prophecy a king was willing to sacrifice his daughter in order to be able to go to war.†

The Trojan War lasted ten years, and though the Greeks eventually won it there was an enormous amount of suffering on both sides of the battlefield and on the home fronts, not only for its duration but for a great many years afterwards. And yet, in spite of the havoc which they helped create, the oracles were continually consulted during the course of this long campaign, so unwilling were the warriors to rely on their own judgment.

Wars may be long or they may be short, but planning for them, which is now extremely dependent on forecasting,

---

† A similar legend, in inverted form, is found in the Bible. When Jephthah, a leader of the Israelites, was about to make battle with the Ammonites he made an oath to God that upon returning home he would sacrifice the first thing that he saw from his household if he won. Tragically, this turned out to be his daughter and the sacrifice was duly made (Judges 11).

is interminable. This has especially been true in heavily militarized states like the United States and the Soviet Union. Not only is planning carried on during the periods between the wars, but it continues at an ever more frantic pace during the conflict itself. During the course of a war, the desperate military mind hurls itself forward to the next battle. If hope is lacking, the warrior looks for it in the future; if things are already going well, he looks to the future for victory and more security. The whole point of this kind of thinking is, quite simply, to envision scenarios of future encounters with the enemy by asking some form of the following question: What will be the outcome if, at some point in the future on a certain battlefield, the men and arms at our disposal meet with those at the disposal of the enemy? From this question follows a related urgent question: What do we have to do now to ensure that things will go our way then? This kind of thinking is the beginning and the heart of all strategic and tactical thinking.

In a limited sense, up to the present era, forecasting has been a reasonable and worthwhile enterprise for the armies of the world. After all, the military specializes in "controlling" events, and where there is control, prophecy is more capable of self-fulfilment, and so prediction is more likely to be accurate. It is not difficult to make a case that what will happen to purposeful, disciplined and motivated men under arms is somewhat predictable. In a way, prediction is built into the nature of fighting. Engaging in battle is an exercise in forward motion: it is a desperate striving for a favorable future. Bullets, missiles and all types of military projectiles have points and direction; flesh and armor are permeable by these points; force, hardness, resistance, persistence and all of the basic variables of war are measurable factors. And, most important of all, on the occasion of battle men are acting on the basis of orders, on compulsion. Loyalty, devotion and *esprit de corps* are exacting taskmasters, and what these are lacking can often be made up for by fear and desperation. Independent thinking and random behavior, subversion and working at cross-purposes, though not unheard of, are not the norms of behavior for warriors. Ideally, and, to a great extent even practically, the purpose of the individual is therefore closely bound to, almost completely merged with, the purpose of the group and thus, ultimately, of the state. Under these circumstances, why not make predictions?

On the other hand, even in the ancient world, long before the advent of the present period of rapid and hectic technological innovation, at a time when one could more easily make the case that war-fighting variables were far fewer and more easily understood, we have examples of false prophecies based on gross miscalculations. One has only to recall the fierce pride and determination which attended the Athenian preparation for the campaign against Sicily in the Peloponnesian Wars to be chastened about listening to prophets. At that time, Athens was by all accounts, especially its own, the most culturally and technologically advanced city-state in Greece, and certainly the richest. The idea of starting an imperial war to expand its empire to include Sicily and ultimately all of Italy was therefore, at least in principle, not incredible when it was proposed. Predictions of the success of this campaign were accordingly made by ambitious Athenian warmongers of many political stripes. But in the end Athens was badly beaten by the Sicilians whose territory it invaded, and great numbers of Athenian soldiers were consequently drowned in a foreign harbor whose waters were colored red by their own blood.

Aside from the determination to fight off aggression, among the factors that contributed to the victory of the Sicilian city of Syracuse and its allies over Athens were innovations in naval technique and technology, innovations that were actually accomplished during the very course of battle. These innovations, along with the fierce Sicilian resistance, were factors the Athenian prophets had simply failed to predict. According to Thucydides, the historian of the Peloponnesian Wars, the innovations that the Syracusans effected were to shorten and reinforce the prows of their ships. They then set poles into them and used them for prow-to-prow charging and ramming against the Athenian ships. The Athenians' prows were weak since they were accustomed to coming alongside rather than fighting prow-to-prow.†

---

† On the other hand, to cite a recent example of a successful innovation on the part of an invader, the Israelis were very successful in using drones as decoys for the purpose of knocking out the Syrian surface-to-air-missiles in the war in Lebanon.

Naturally, the desirability of forecasting becomes even more compelling during periods of technical innovation, when new weapons and techniques are being introduced into the war-fighting equations. However, as we can see from the above example, when innovation is involved, forecasting may be even more questionable than it usually is because unknown variables are introduced into the equation in the form of untried and untested new techniques and technology. And, since neither side has a monopoly on this type of activity, results can go either way. Therefore, to the old questions—How many men will we have available when battle is engaged? With what weapons will we furnish them? How will we effect resupply and care for the wounded?—are added a second set of more imponderable ones. When will the new weapons be available? How well will they work? How long will it take to train our warriors to use them effectively? And, most important of all: How will they affect the outcome of the next encounter given an enemy who will also be very motivated to counter our innovations and perhaps even devise others of their own?

It is difficult for us to imagine today that the second set of questions relating to innovation are relatively new, but this is certainly the case. The written description of a future war has been a genre for over two hundred years, but early versions did not envision, and therefore did not even try to predict, the effects of technological innovation in weaponry. The very first description to appear in print was written by an anonymous author in England in 1763 and was called *The Reign of George VI, 1900–1925*.[1] Briefly speaking, it is no more than an idyll of conquest and pacification of Europe by a future King of England. But what is remarkable about it to our ears, which are so accustomed to hearing about new developments in weapons technology almost every day, is that in this prophecy all of the weapons and tactics of the eighteenth century were simply projected to the twentieth *with no change.*

To understand the mind-set that made this possible, we need to remember that this scenario was written before the onset of the Industrial Revolution: it simply did not occur to the author, conditioned by centuries of relatively little innovation in warfare, to imagine new and fantastic weapons coming into play to alter, perhaps decisively, the outcome of future battles. Therefore, in conjecturing about this future war, the second set of questions pertaining to innovation were not even asked.

Given the present rate of weapons innovation, it is impossible to imagine anyone today writing a "credible" scenario of a future war that did not include, did not in fact highlight, the decisive importance of some hitherto unused, perhaps even unheard of, wonderful new piece of weapons technology. The change in conditioning that makes the thinking of modern war futurologists so different from that of their ancestors of the mid-eighteenth century occurred gradually with the development of the Industrial Revolution from the late eighteenth to the late nineteenth century. But the new genre of future war scenarios, which depends so heavily on weapons innovation, was born rather dramatically when Sir George Chesney, then an undistinguished military engineer who was about to begin retirement, published a scenario called *The Battle of Dorking*. It first appeared in the May 1871 issue of *Blackwood's Magazine* and was later published as a book.

The Battle of Dorking was written at the dawn of the arms race based on innovative technology that began with the introduction of iron-clad ships and breech-loading artillery in the Franco-Prussian War of 1870 and has proceeded incessantly and at an ever more hectic pace ever since. It was the innovations of that war that inspired Chesney. Since the Franco-Prussian War had dramatically changed the power structure of Europe, Chesney's article, which envisioned a future war in which Germany would conquer England by using new fighting technology, was not merely a fanciful exercise. As the English historian I.F. Clarke has remarked, "*The Battle of Dorking* episode was much more than a major publishing event of 1871. It was undoubtedly the most remarkable propaganda piece that had appeared since the Junius Letters."[2]†

The whole purpose of this predictive scenario was to show how decisive arms innovation could be, and it worked

† The Junius letters were a series of anonymous letters which appeared in newspapers in England in the late eighteenth century and were famous because they typically assassinated the character of the leading political figures of the time.

more effectively than anyone, including the author, was able to anticipate. *The Battle of Dorking* was very widely discussed and immediately reprinted in several different languages all over Europe. Naturally it was rapidly followed by alternative scenarios that argued for more positive outcomes. These alternative scenarios had titles such as: *After the Battle of Dorking or What Became of the Invaders?*; *The Battle of the Ironclads*; *The Cruise of the Anti-torpedo*; *What Happened after the Battle of Dorking or The Battle of Tunbridge Wells*; *Mrs. Brown on the Battle of Dorking*; and, *Chapters from Future History*.

In short, Chesney's article set the psychological tone for the whole period of war speculation that followed. As Clarke has commented elsewhere: "These apprehensions of wars to come, by their very number, must have sharpened expectations if they did not modify strategy . . . it became common practice to describe imaginary defeats or victories in some future period in order to demonstrate the need for appropriate reforms in the armed forces, or to advertise the advantages of the measures and policies they recommended."[3] But beyond this psychological effect, it appears as if Chesney also demonstrated a number of other things by writing this article, some of them perhaps unintentionally. The main thing that he proved was what an extraordinary effect the combination of a new warfare technology and the existence of a long-standing "enemy"—in this case Germany—could have on the imagination of literate masses. With hindsight, it is easy for us to understand why the population of Europe, still reeling from the social and economic turmoil created by the Industrial Revolution, would be so greatly impressed by the prospect that similar dramatic developments might be repeated on the battlefield. But more than this, as Clarke observes, articles of this sort make such a profound impression because "they spring from the universal desire to see the enemy as contemptible, inferior and already defeated. . . . The greater the passion, the greater is the element of nationalistic fantasy. . . . Hope and fear, a desire to teach and to warn, are behind all these tales of future warfare."[4]

Furthermore, whether he intended it or not, Chesney also proved what a great vehicle for self-promotion being a prophet at the right time can be. Being an oracle during times of national anxiety is a great step on the road towards self-advancement, which in Chesney's case, not uniquely for a prophet, meant becoming a politician. A little over a year after he wrote *The Battle of Dorking* this obscure colonel, just returned to England and about to retire after a tour of duty in India, managed to get himself elected to the British House of Commons.

In our time, as in Chesney's, playing the role of oracle has similarly proven to be a good vehicle for promoting a political career. One only has to think back to the presidential debates between Richard Nixon and John Kennedy to call up images of two politicians trying to outprophesy one another. They both predicted—Kennedy, as it would turn out, with greater effect—that the Soviet Union would eventually outperform the United States both economically and militarily unless the United States acted quickly and decisively to accelerate her own development in these areas. The famous "missile gap," which would eventually turn out to be nonexistent, appears to have had the same effect in galvanizing the public in 1960 as did the "ironclad gap" in Chesney's *The Battle of Dorking* in 1871. However, since both candidates in the American election used much the same rhetoric, other factors came into play to decide its outcome.

In the early 1980s Robert McNamara, Kennedy's defense secretary, blamed the misperception upon which Kennedy had based his pre-election rhetoric on misinformation stemming from a competition between two camps in the military intelligence community—military intelligence is, of course, a prime commissioner and purveyor of military prophecy. He then went on to describe the profound effect, in the form of an arms build-up, that this misinformation ultimately had. McNamara said:

> Go back to 1960 when many in the U.S. believed there was a missile gap favoring the Soviets. With hindsight it became clear there wasn't any missile gap. But Kennedy had been told there was. What actually happened was this: In the summer of 1960, there were two elements in the U.S. intelligence community disagreeing on the relative levels of the

U.S. and Soviet strategic nuclear forces. . . . One
element greatly overstated the level of the Soviet
nuclear force vis-à-vis the other element. The first
element had data which they believed justified their
interpretation. When one looked over it, it became
clear the data didn't justify the conclusion. And
within two years of that time, the advantage in the
U.S. warhead inventory was so great vis-à-vis the
Soviets that the Air Force was saying that they felt
we had a first-strike capability and could, and
should, continue to have one. If the Air Force
thought that, imagine what the Soviets thought.
And assuming they thought that, how would you
expect them to react?[5]

They reacted, of course, by building up their own supply of
warheads and developing systems for delivering them.

McNamara's statement succinctly summarizes the ongoing dynamics of the arms race and the role that prediction
plays in the policy that has promoted it. Since the beginning
of the nuclear arms race in 1949, we have had several imputed "deterrent gaps" in the form of nonexistent "missile
gaps" and "bomber gaps," and, when the public got tired
of hearing about gaps, they were transformed, during the
Reagan administration, into "windows of vulnerability," *The
Battle of Dorking* mentality looms large behind every proclamation of a gap and, as in the case described by McNamara
above, the result of this propaganda is usually a massive
arms build-up. In attempting to "catch up" with the enemy
each side inevitably surpass them, either in quantity, quality,
or both. However, except for the launching of the first un-
manned satellite, an innovation in which the Soviet Union
took the lead for only one year, the United States has consistently led the Soviet Union in military innovation (see
Table). Reporting on the congressional testimony of Malcolm R. Currie, a past director of defense research and engineering, Robert Aldridge, a former high-level nuclear
weapons engineer who now spends all of his time as a disarmament activist, has described this nuclear weapons
rainbow-chasing in the following terms: "Currie's perspective conveniently slipped back and forth between present

Comparison of US-USSR
Technological Developments

	U.S.	U.S.S.R.
First deployed tactical nuclear weapons in Europe	1954	1957
First ICBM flight	1958	1957
First satellite in orbit	1958	1957
Acquired low penetrating bomber	1959	1975
Acquired supersonic bomber	1960	1975
Deployed solid propellant in missiles:		
SLBMs	1960	1977†
ICBMs	1962	1968
Placed satellites in geosynchronous orbit	1963	1974
Put MRVs on missiles:		
tested	1963	1968
operational	1964	1973
Put penetration aids (chaff and decoys) on missiles	1964	not to date
High speed reentry vehicles:		
tested	1968	1973
operational:	1970	1975
Put MIRVs on missiles:		
tested	1968	1973
operational:		
ICBMs	1970	1975
SBMs	1971	1978
Developed stellar inertial guidance (SIG)	1969–70	1972–73
Put on-board computers on missiles	1970	1975
Number of foreign military bases	hundreds	few

† Deployed 12 SS-N-17 SLBMs on one Yankee class submarine only.

From Robert Aldridge, *First Strike!*, 1983. The table illustrates the hectic pace of nuclear weapons innovation that has characterized the arms race for over thirty years. It is remarkable that the modern arms race began with the introduction of ironclads and breechloaders in the Franco-Prussian War which ended in 1871. The weapons have changed but the *Battle of Dorking* mentality which predicts victory in future wars through the introduction of new weapons technology has remained essentially the same.

and future tense to accommodate his preordained conclusions. When looking at the U.S. forces he spoke in the present tense of our inability to launch a preemptive first strike
in an open society. But when referring to the Soviets he
alluded to what may be possible at some future date and
used that as evidence that the Soviets are upsetting some
perceived stability in the nuclear balance. On this basis he
argued that we need even more sophisticated weapons,
thereby upsetting the current balance, in order to 'restore'
a balance that might be upset by the Soviets at some future
time."[6] How did we get into this rut of madly dashing towards
the future in order to close fictitious gaps? One has to go to
the beginning of the nuclear arms race to understand what
is going on here; one has to look at the development of an
illusion called "limited nuclear war."

After the United States dropped atomic bombs on Hiroshima
and Nagasaki, World War II came to an abrupt and dramatic
ending with the unconditional surrender of Japan. To most
observers the atomic bomb appeared, quite rightly, to be
the most revolutionary innovation in weapons technology in
the history of mankind. And, as had been true in the wake
of previous revolutionary developments, the prophets came
out in number predicting its consequences for future wars.†
The power of atomic bombs was so incredible that former
soldiers did not even attempt, as Chesney had done, to describe scenes on the battlefields of the future. Instead, they
focused on the aftermath of future wars, what the world
would be like after a war with "the bomb." They thus became
gloomy existentialists, brooding about the dark side of human nature and writing warnings in the form of depressing
post-war scenarios like Nevil Shute's *On the Beach* and Aldous Huxley's *Ape and Essence*. Unfortunately, given their
characteristically pragmatic bent, for a variety of reasons the

---

† After Alfred Nobel invented nitroglycerine in 1860 he predicted that, because
its effects were so devastating, this would mean the end of wars forever. Similarly,
in 1864 when lighter-than-air balloons were coming into their own, the famous
novelist Victor Hugo wrote to his friend Nadar, a celebrated balloonist, that this
meant the end of all war because balloons would effectively abolish all national
boundaries—as if the boundaries themselves were the cause of wars.

soldiers were obliged to leave policy formulation and imagining what future wars would be like to abstract thinkers in government and private agencies. As one American historian has observed: "Current U.S. Strategic theory was thus born of a marriage between the scientist and the accountant. The professional soldier was jilted."[7]

What did these "scientists and accountants" who wrote prophetic military policy papers come up with? In 1945, when the United States had a monopoly on the atomic bomb, the mainstream of prognostication of its effects on future wars was, quite simply, that it would abolish them entirely. The destructive capacity of these weapons was widely understood even then to be so great that only a few would be needed to inflict enormous damage and, no matter how many one side delivered, it was thought that the enemy would also manage to deliver the few that were necessary to inflict what military theorists euphemistically call "unacceptable damage." The conventional wisdom that followed from this understanding was that if these weapons of mass destruction could not be abolished entirely they should be maintained at equal levels on both sides in order to create a stalemate. This was the theory of mutual deterrence, plain and simple, that was strongly argued by a group of academics at Yale in a book called *The Absolute Weapon*. And this was also the vision of Robert Oppenheimer who, in a famous article for the November 24, 1945, edition of *Saturday Review,* predicted that "in a world of atomic weapons wars will cease."[8]

Oppenheimer's vision, and that of the Yale academics, was also publicly echoed during his first term by President Eisenhower, who promoted it with the slogan, "there is no alternative to peace." As it turned out, however, just as Augustus had to contend with a rival school of prophecy led by Lentulus (see Chapter Three), a rival school of thought about the future of war began to develop by the end of the 1940s.

P.B.S. Blackett, a distinguished British physicist, contributed a great deal to what might be called the "verbal taming" of atomic bombs in a book he published in 1949 called *Fear, War, and the Bomb.* In this book he compared atomic bombs with conventional bombs simply, and solely, on the basis of explosive power. Noting that the U.S. Strategic Bombing Survey which had been conducted shortly after the war had demonstrated that conventional bombing had had little effect until the very end, on either German war production or morale, he argued that atomic bombs, with comparable explosive power, would also not be decisive in winning future wars between the great powers. In short, he predicted that nuclear bombing would be survivable, and therefore nuclear wars of the future, like other kinds of war, would be winnable providing one were willing to persist and follow through with conventional methods of occupation.

The idea that nuclear war would not necessarily lead to Armageddon, could be limited and was, in fact, winnable, was taken up and promoted in America as a justification for planning limited nuclear wars in the future as an alternative to "peace with no alternative." Many so-called cold warriors promoted this idea in the mid-1950s, but probably the most notable among these were the members of a study group in the Council on Foreign Relations, a private citizens' advisory group, which included a variety of people from different fields, among them such prominent future politicians as McGeorge Bundy, Henry Kissinger and Paul Nitze.

Their work should be understood in context: 1956 was, of course, an election year and some Democrats were trying to make political hay, just as Kennedy would in his debate with Nixon four years later, by taking Eisenhower to task for being "soft on Communism." Typically, one of the things they talked about then was what would turn out to be a fictitious "bomber gap." And, that year, in the January and April issues of the Council's influential policy journal *Foreign Affairs*, Paul Nitze and Henry Kissinger published what would eventually become seminal articles promoting their ideas about how, under certain circumstances, we could plan on having *limited* nuclear wars in the future.†

Bearing in mind the ideological basis for the arms race, it should be noted that Kissinger's point of departure was

---

† Kissinger at this time had not yet chosen his final political affiliation and was yet to work, in a minor capacity, for President Kennedy before finally becoming a Republican. He joined the study group late in its deliberations and came on board for the purpose of writing up their ideas. The year after the seminal article he published what was essentially the final report of this study group, his book called *Nuclear Weapons and Foreign Policy*, which became a bestseller and bible for cold warriors.

an ideological one: he began by questioning Eisenhower's proclamation, "there is no alternative to peace," by calling it not a policy but a "dilemma." He then went on to set the stage for his alternative perspective with a bit of the prophet's characteristic mystification, noting that "It is paradoxical, however, that so much hope should concentrate on man's destructive capabilities."[9] And then he continued in the characteristic manner of the oracle, as Clarke says, to teach and to warn: "If the phrase 'there is no alternative to peace' were to become accepted doctrine, it could lead only to a paralysis of policy."[10]

Before examining Kissinger's prescriptions in greater detail, it is instructive, by way of contrast, to compare his argument thus far with the one made earlier by Oppenheimer and the authors of *The Absolute Weapon*. As far as Oppenheimer was concerned, atom bombs, by their very nature, were too destructive to be used for "limited" purposes in any normal sense of this word. He wrote:

> There are people who say that they are not such very bad weapons. Before the New Mexico test we sometimes said that too, writing down square miles and equivalent tonnages and looking at the picture of a ravaged Europe. After the test we did not say it any more. Some of you will have seen photographs of the Nagasaki strike, seen the great steel girders of factories twisted and wrecked; some of you may have noticed that these factories that were wrecked were miles apart. Some of you will have seen pictures of the people who were burned, or had a look at the wastes of Hiroshima. That bomb at Nagasaki would have taken out ten square miles, or a bit more, if there had been ten square miles to take out.[11]

This was a very compelling argument against using nuclear bombs, especially coming, as it did, from the man who was known as the father of the atomic bomb, but Kissinger's rejoinder to it was typical of modern prophets who are enchanted by a recent technical innovation into thinking it will in the future solve a host of problems, even non-technical problems of incredible magnitude. The gist of Kissinger's argument was that the age of absolute nuclear weapons was basically over because the bombs that had been dropped on Hiroshima and Nagasaki were now "obsolete." There had been a new innovation, small nuclear bombs, "nuclear weapons of low yield" as he called them, and they could be safely used in a "limited nuclear war." And, continuing in Blackett's vein, he proclaimed: "A distinction based on the difference between nuclear weapons and 'conventional armaments' is no more fruitful. Apart from the fact that the distinction becomes increasingly nebulous as we develop nuclear weapons of very low yield, *it will be impossible to reverse present trends. The very existence of nuclear armaments on both sides seems to insure that any future war will be nuclear.*" (emphasis added)[12] And then he concluded: "If we build our whole strategy around 'absolute' weapons of megaton size, professions of limited objectives will be meaningless and any use of nuclear weapons is likely to touch off an all-out war. The possibility of keeping a limited nuclear war limited depends on our ability to extend the range of low-yield weapons of a kiloton and below, and to devise tactics for their utilizations on the battlefield."[13]

It is impossible to tell whether or not Kissinger's emphasis on the importance of technological innovation in policy-making was disingenuous, because he vacillated in the statements he made about the importance of technology for determining theory and policy. In 1960 he evidently believed in technological determinism when he predicted: "Every war henceforth will be nuclear to a greater or lesser extent, whether or not nuclear weapons are used."[14] Kissinger's argument at that time was simply that all future wars will be nuclear just because the potential for using nuclear weapons will always exist. However, in later years, having already contributed through his writing to promoting technological dependency, he appears to have changed his mind and proceeded to deemphasize technology. For example, in 1965 he wrote: "Strategy henceforth cannot confine itself to expertise in designing weapons systems, but must involve a close understanding of the opponent's calculations."[15] So in the end, if he did not always wholeheartedly believe in technological determinism, he certainly seems to have had a great deal of

confidence in the ability of American leaders to understand
and calculate the behavior of their enemies, to control it with
threats of nuclear war and even to use nuclear war itself in
"limited" doses.

In any case, after their introduction by the United States
in 1954 and the Soviet Union in 1957, the small nuclear
warheads upon which Kissinger based his calculations have
naturally proliferated greatly on both sides. Today they represent perhaps the most unstable element in the constellation
of nuclear weapons systems: because of their number; because they are, in certain cases, interchangeable with conventional weapons; and because their use is in some cases
subject to the discretion of local commanders. And, as the
physicist Freeman Dyson has observed, whenever computer
simulations of battles are run using these weapons, the scenario always ends in chaos and utter destruction.[16]

Paul Nitze also shared Kissinger's view that the technical
problems of fighting nuclear wars would be manageable, if
not now, then at least at some point in the future. For example, with respect to one particularly touchy "technical
problem," the close proximity of civilian population centers
to nuclear installations, he wrote: "Is it possible to draw a
distinction between industrial and population centers and
air-atomic bases? Such a distinction presents real difficulties,
but the importance of overcoming them is so great that it
should be possible to do so."[17] It is extraordinary how
strongly Nitze believed that, given sufficient necessity, any
problem could be overcome. It is only because he was talking
abstractly about the future that he could maintain such conviction. Were he discussing a persistently intractable matter
of the present, it would have been much more difficult for
him to make a case for such boundless faith. How could he
argue, for example, that just because there is a compelling
necessity to discover a cure for AIDS that a cure will in fact
be discovered?

Given the enormous destructive capacity of nuclear
weapons, and the desirability of using them only on soldiers
and not civilians, Nitze's point of departure and emphasis
was somewhat different from Kissinger's at this time. Instead
of emphasizing the role that new technology would play in
controlling and limiting future nuclear wars, Nitze placed

great emphasis on technique. But the technique that he promoted in his *Foreign Affairs* article was not battlefield technique but psychological calculation, the use of words to limit wars. He noted, quite rightly, that words, especially the words of belligerents, are ambiguous. Accordingly, he advocated developing a great deal of precision in talking to the enemy so that they would have no doubt about our intentions to keep these wars limited, and would likewise behave in appropriate, self-limiting ways. His main point was very reasonable as far as it went: it was that our "declared" policy (that is, our propaganda), and our "action policy" (what we would actually try to do in the event that we started to fight), should be as near to one another as possible so that the enemy would always know exactly what we are up to and what to expect.

Actually, both Nitze's and Kissinger's articles are full of psychological techniques that were designed to ensure that nuclear wars would, in fact, be limited. But not all of these were to be directed at the enemy. The last two of three that Kissinger mentions later in summing up his first paper are self-directed psychological techniques. Echoing Herman Kahn he wrote that we, that is, *our leaders,* must develop "the ability to create a climate of opinion in which national survival is not thought to be at stake in every issue," and that our leaders should also develop "the ability to keep control of public opinion should a disagreement arise over whether national survival is at stake." In this vein he also declared: "We cannot afford even the implication that nuclear weapons are in a special category, apart from modern weapons in general, for this undermines the psychological basis of the most effective United States strategy." In short, in order to make these scenarios of future nuclear wars seem plausible, Kissinger argued that politicians must learn to control not only the behavior of their strategists and those of the enemy, but also the way the home front thinks about such wars so that leaders would not be hindered in their actions. And, in the end, this great exercise of control is made possible, made reasonable, because somehow or other it is exercised under the rubric of the then fashionable mental artifacts called "game rules." He concluded: "The fact remains that the most fruitful area for current strategic thought is the conduct and efficacy of limited nuclear war, the 'war gaming' of situations in which nuclear weapons are used by *both* sides, and a consideration of what would constitute victory in such a war.''[18]

Considering their enormous influence, what is most remarkable about both Kissinger's and Nitze's scenarios is how calculating they thought one could be given the subject matter with which they were dealing. They seem to have both set and reflected the tone of excessive abstraction, all in the name of rationality, which has come to characterize nuclear strategic thinking. Both of their articles are peppered with pronouncements of what would be the "rational" way to fight such wars. However, when they do get down to psychology, the realm where the irrational side of human nature might also come into play, we have only the most impoverished psychology imaginable: the psychology of the adman and the modern business manager who avails himself of "gamesmanship" to prognosticate the outcome of market strategies. There are any number of psychological elements that should have been included in their visions in order to properly take into account the irrational side of human nature, a natural part of all wars. But missing from this psychology most conspicuously are not only a theory of aggression, aside from what is implied by self-interest, but also any theory of relationships aside from the mechanical ones contained in gamesmanship. Missing, too, are two other bulwarks of modern psychology which reflect the irrational side of human nature—the love-wish and the death-wish.

To his credit, assuming he was being sincere and not just cheering on the latest trend, four years after his paper was published in *Foreign Affairs,* Kissinger published an article in which he largely repudiated what he had said earlier.[19] He did not however repudiate the idea of using force to gain political objectives, but simply declared that, in spite of all of the calculating with weapons and with words, things might get out of hand in a nuclear war anyway. There had already been war games to suggest the latter, but above all some logistical problems had come to his attention which he had not foreseen and factored into his own abstract war-fighting equations. These included military infighting among the various branches of the U.S. armed forces branches (for some reason each branch of the U.S. military had its own pet theory about how to use these new small atomic bombs), the growth of the Soviet stockpile, and the long-range impact of arms control negotiations, all of which posed perhaps insurmountable problems for calculating and controlling the next war.

It was, perhaps, commendable that Kissinger should back off, at least formally, from championing an idea that he had worked so hard to promote, and this entire policy-propagating episode would now have no more interest than a historical footnote if his repudiation had been the end of the matter. It was not. Ideas have a life of their own, even bad ideas which are occasionally more or less disowned by their author. In fact, these ideas often have the unfortunate habit of getting worse with age: unanticipated conditions develop; other, perhaps less subtle minds take the ideas up; they become institutionalized and thus develop substance and meaning even more flawed than the original wrong-headed idea. As Hannah Arendt has observed in her essay "On Lying," the danger is that one eventually begins to believe one's own propaganda—if indeed propaganda is what it was originally meant to be. In any event, the idea of fighting limited nuclear wars worked its way into strategic thinking over the years and, far from fading away, eventually became an official part of U.S. military policy when President Carter signed Presidential Directive 59 (PD-59) a few months before he left office at the end of 1980.† By then, however, the Kissinger-Nitze calculus had worked its way into thinking and planning not only for limited nuclear wars with battle-field weapons, but also general nuclear wars using strategic weapons. It became the basis of the so-called nuclear war-*fighting,* as opposed to *deterring,* mentality.

Some of the circumstances attending the signing of PD-59 are worth mentioning because they reveal a great deal about the persistence of overly abstract thinking on the high-est levels of policy formulation and future war prediction. When PD-59 percolated up to Carter's desk from the De-fense Department eighteen months before he finally signed

† This directive changed official policy so that weapons would be used for fighting as well as for deterrence.

it, he equivocated about whether or not to go ahead with endorsing it. Even though others, besides Nitze and Kissinger, had made attempts to undermine it ever since the invention of the bomb, simple deterrence based on mutually assured destruction had been the only official doctrine up until then, and PD-59 represented the enshrinement of these war-fighting elements in that doctrine. So, by way of postponing his decision, Carter asked the Defense Department to commission certain "studies" to flesh out and legitimate this policy directive. There were a number of different "studies" commissioned for this purpose. One consulting firm, called the Analytic Assessment Corporation (ANASMC) of Marina Del Rey, California, was commissioned to "determine the nuclear weapon employment strategy that would eliminate the USSR as a functioning national entity . . . bring about the collapse of the government that now exists." Another firm in Vienna, Virginia, was asked to calculate "the viability of employing strategic nuclear weapons to achieve regionalization of the Soviet Union," as well as "strategic targetting against Soviet leadership."[20] Eliminate their leadership, destroy their government, repackage their national identity—simple objectives for future wars. These were the "limited" political objectives which by 1980 were to be solved by the now not so "limited" nuclear wars that were then being planned.

Most of this thinking was summarized by two disciples of Nitze and Kissinger, Colin Gray and Keith Payne, in a much-quoted paper which appeared in *Foreign Policy* just before Carter signed PD-59.[21] Their language and thinking are so similar to that of their mentors that one wonders why they were never sued for plagiarism. They wrote: "If American power is to support U.S. foreign policy objectives, the United States must possess the ability to wage nuclear war rationally."[22] But they carried the Kissinger doctrine even further when they declared: "To advocate LNOS (Limited Nuclear Options) and targeting flexibility and selectivity is not the same as to advocate a war-fighting, war-survival strategy,"[23] and concluded, apparently drawing from the think-tank scenarios that were commissioned by President Carter: "The USSR, with its gross overcentralization of authority epitomized by its vast bureaucracy in Moscow, should be highly vulnerable to such an attack. The Soviet Union might cease to function if its security agency, the KGB, were severely crippled. Judicious U.S. targeting and weapon procurement policies might be able to deny the USSR the assurance of political survival."[24]

What is most striking about the Gray and Payne doctrine, and very much in keeping with the Nitze-Kissinger doctrine, is its simplistic view of Soviet nationhood and society. The notion that the United States might be welcomed as liberators if they annihilated about twenty million Soviet citizens (Gray and Payne's estimate of the size of the so-called ruling elite) and largely destroyed the Russian economy is simply too fatuous to be taken seriously as insightful prophecy, but it certainly does speak volumes about the American military establishment's willingness in its collective prophetic mind to trivialize the integrity of Soviet nationhood.

In fact, this thinking is reminiscent of the prophetic fantasies that were being printed during the post–*The Battle of Dorking* period. The irony of this is particularly striking if one considers that in a French play published around the same time as Chesney's article, *The Invasion of England: A Prophecy in Two Acts,* one of the invading Frenchmen is made to say to the appreciative natives that have gathered round, "Englishmen! Now is your time to destroy the British Government which has caused all your misfortunes, desolated your neighbors, and set Europe on fire. It is time that the fate of the people should no longer depend on the caprice of an individual."[25] Substitute Russia for England in this passage, and Payne and Gray might have used it in their own prophecy.

The tendency to underestimate and caricature the enemy is typical of the thinking of futurologists, and is just another way in which they often tend to trivialize problems of every sort by projecting them into the future. If one is going to assume that a massive attack on the Soviet Union, if successful, will result in the attackers being welcomed as liberators, then one may as well also assume that certain "technical difficulties," like the close proximity of residential and military developments which Nitze was concerned about in developing his nuclear war scenarios, will undoubtedly also be solved. But nothing is more simple-minded in all of this than the enchantment with the so-called rationality of this most irrational of all enterprises.

When speaking publicly of PD-59, Harold Brown, Carter's defense secretary, justified this major alteration in official policy as being a mere adjustment to developments in the weapons procurement process, a supposedly rational accounting endeavor. Apparently, the number of strategic warheads had reached such a high level that the strategists had run out of targets. Another way of understanding PD-59, maintained Brown, was to think of it as merely offering a sort of release valve for targeting congestion. With this new policy, the new warheads that were coming on board could be targeted to suit the newly created military purposes not only to deter but to fight and win a nuclear war. No matter that the old warheads could just as easily be retargeted for this purpose, if the frightful occasion should ever arise. No matter that the two systems taken together were even more redundant than the system of deterrence based on mutually assured destruction alone had been. By a stroke of the pen, military planners could now plan two different kinds of nuclear wars at once, all the while protesting that they would probably only fight when provoked. And weapons procurement in this most "rational" system turned out to have been possessed of less rationality than a simple bucket brigade, which at least knows how to stop passing water when the fire is out.†

Since the recent arms reduction agreements have reduced the massive arsenals on both sides and, more importantly, eased up the horrifying dance of death between the United States and the Soviet Union, in some ways it is hard to imagine what our prophet-cum-policy-makers of the 1950s were thinking when they started putting into place all of

---

† The peacetime process of weapons procurement is riddled by innumerable irrationalities of other sorts. Perhaps most notable of all are procurements which tend to produce instability. One must remember that due to either a breakdown of interdepartmental communication or someone's malign intent, in the late 1970s, contrary to official policy, new weapons systems were coming on board that undermined the stability that is necessary for deterrence to work. (See Deborah Shapley, "Congress Seeks New Approach to Arms Control," in *Science*, February 9, 1979.)

their abstract nuclear war-fighting systems to fight the future nuclear war. At first glance it appears as if they were simply acting very impressionably—as their nineteenth-century predecessors had done in the war predictions business—on the possibilities which they believed were opened up by technological innovation. They also seem to have been characteristically very impressed by extremely abstract assessments of the situations they were confronting, and by their own rather worshipful approach to the power of reason. Reason, they believed, in spite of all history and practical experience, would continue to operate not only to avoid fighting, but even to control the situation once battle was already engaged. But one must also appreciate other more concrete conditions which may have inspired them. The war in Korea had recently been concluded—on an unsatisfactory basis as far as the American Right was concerned—and there was a great deal of talk of America's position in the world being "nibbled away" by the Soviet Union. Stalin's memory also loomed large then, and served well past his death as a symbol and constant reference point with which ideologues could caricature the Soviet leadership and the Soviet system. An ever present, supposedly implacable enemy; discontentment with how things had gone in the past; the promise of technological innovation: all of the icons that war prophets like to worship were abundantly present.

Another way of trying to understand their thinking is to bear in mind the old saying that soldiers are always prepared to fight their last war, the one which, with hindsight, they understand so well. Certainly the nuclear part of World War II—the bombing of Hiroshima and Nagasaki—could, on a certain level, inspire admiration and a desire to copy among leaders on the victorious side. After all the misery that had preceded it, the final phase of the war with Japan presented the Allied soldiers, after the testing of the bomb at Los Alamos, with a rather attractive situation: one side, America and her Allies, was in a position of almost complete control, the prophets favorite fantasy. Perhaps all of the postwar reasoning—with weapons and with words—concerning the nature of possible future nuclear wars has been no more than an attempt to recapture that moment in the past.

But perhaps more important than this consideration is

8

2

FUTUREHYPE

the fact that American isolationism was particularly strong
right after the war. America had entered World War II re-
luctantly, and compared to the Russians had demobilized
very rapidly as soon as it was over. This isolationism naturally
fed the desire of some western leaders on both sides of the
Atlantic that America help defend Europe against the perceived threat from Russia, but without at the same time
acting as an army of occupation. One can almost see the
attraction that tactical nuclear weapons represented to these
naive and essentially technologically romantic but non-adept
admirers of new military technology. Small-scale nuclear
weapons appeared to them to be an elegant solution to all
of the problems just mentioned: they represented the ability
to fight a large standing army, like that of the Soviet Union,
with a much smaller one. From the American perspective,
this could be done almost by remote-control; by using these
weapons America could do battle without directly risking its
own people or nation. And finally, nuclear armaments were
relatively inexpensive by then, and much cheaper to procure
and maintain than huge standing armies—a consideration
that was bound to have a broad appeal in a fiscally conservative administration like Eisenhower's.

In Chapter Two on the psychology of futurology, I noted
that one can aptly apply to modern prophecy the Heisenberg
principle, which states that you cannot observe a phenomenon without altering it; when you observe it, you are in-
terfering with it whether you realize it or not, and therefore
cannot claim to be viewing it with perfect objectivity. This
principle should be magnified a thousand times for politics.
The self-delusion of the cold warriors on both sides can
hardly be exaggerated; whatever so-called objective facts the
cold warriors of the 1950s may have pointed to in order to
justify their policies, eventually they themselves became the
most important factor in the belligerent confrontation between East and West—and a condition about which, needless
to say, they could not even begin to become objective. But
worse than this, if the maintenance of peace was ever really
their aim—the epithet "cold warrior" is, after all, not one
of their own choosing—their methods were extraordinarily
self-defeating. The thickety jargon of these bedazzled prognosticators of future wars is really not that difficult to master,

but as has often been said, it does numb the senses by mystifying a horrifying situation. Furthermore, it lends an air of mystery, mastery, science and rationality—all of the futurologist's arsenal—to a business which all ordinary people who are destined to fight and die know to be basically irrational and unpredictable.

During the decade of the American chapter of the war in Vietnam there were innumerable instances when reason was made to wither in the face of unpredictability; but these lessons seem to have been to no avail.† One of the most dramatic of these instances was reported by William Shawcross who, in writing about an early incident in the bombing of Cambodia, quotes one of the officers as saying, "We had been told, as had everybody . . . that these carpet bombing attacks by B-52 [were] totally devastating, that nothing could survive, and if they had a troop concentration there it would be annihilated. . . . We were told . . . that if there was anybody still alive out there they would be so stunned that all [we would] have to do [was] walk over and lead him by the arm to the helicopter." The American army then proceeded to do their worst, blitzing the area with a virtual blanket of bombs. But in the end they vastly overestimated the effect that their bombing would have and the effect of all of this devastating bombing was only to rile up the enemy, "to serve as taking a beehive the size of a basketball and poking it with a stick. They [the Viet Cong] were mad."[26]

Military futurology both reflects our obsession with trying to perfect the calculability of the incalculable and epitomizes the destructive, destabilizing, and paralytic role that futurology generally plays in human affairs. Because so much of our effort has been going into perfecting increasingly destabilizing weapons systems for the battlefields of the future, we have been unable properly to attend to the needs of the present, both for peace and for warfare of the conventional type. A few years ago Senator Sam Nunn conducted congressional hearings about a widely recognized crisis in America's

---

† Much of the same can be said of both the Israeli war in Lebanon and the war between Iran and Iraq, both of which were ostensibly started for limited objective purposes: Israel was trying to clean up its northern border of terrorist activity, and Iran wanted to change the Iraqi leadership for one more sympathetic to her own religious fundamentalist ambitions.

conventional forces: the acute shortage of ammunition.[27] This issue was raised at a number of meetings of the Atlantic Council which I attended in 1986, and the accepted explanation from the well-informed and high-ranking military men present was that all of the money has been going into developing the weapons systems of the future, and therefore there has not been enough to supply the weapons of the present. The unspoken fact is, of course, that the armed forces naturally do not feel inclined to purchase ammunition for guns that will soon be obsolete.† To the extent that this explanation is true, it implies that we cannot fight with conventional weapons any battles that are imposed upon us in the present because we are preparing only to fight the wars of the future. In any present battle we will quickly run out of bullets and then be forced to resort to nuclear arms, whether we want to use them or not.‡ In any case, in the recent arms reduction negotiations the West's lack of conventional preparedness has persistently been cited as an important reason for not going along with Soviet proposals for arms reduction.

"No alternative to peace" may seem paralyzing to certain politicians—as it certainly did to Kissinger and his colleagues in 1956—but that is probably because at that time the West was still so close to World War II and the Korean War that we were no longer used to peace, in the sense that we still had not learned to maneuver effectively within its very broad "confines." Over thirty years after Kissinger wrote his influential paper, in the future he was trying to anticipate, the irony, of course, is that nothing has proven to be more paralyzing than the arms race which he helped

† Richard Gabriel, a prominent military critic, has also argued that the munitions shortage is due to logistical problems caused by an inefficient, infighting and top-heavy military bureaucracy. This explanation is not, of course, mutually exclusive with the one cited above, but actually complements the one I have most often heard. If the United States does indeed decide to switch to a conventional rather than nuclear deterrence, this inconsistency may continue to be a problem.

‡ Another theory holds that we are purposely keeping our stocks of conventional ammunition low to tyrannize the enemy with the threat of imminent nuclear war should they wish to fight one using conventional weapons, with which they will supposedly be superior. If this is true, it is an institutionalized form of Dulles's "brinkmanship" or Nixon's "mad dog theory of diplomacy," and in any case represents just another form of pretense with respect to being able to understand and to calculate the opponent's every move.

to promote. The freedom that he and other cold warriors were trying to preserve has been severely undermined by the very methods they promoted. In the world that their thinking helped create, or at least perpetuate, until recently the choices for the leaders of both East and West were increasingly limited, to the point that they could choose only between one weapons system and another. And these are choices which were, and still are made not in tranquil forums, but in the context of partisan politicians and in the intense hard-sell atmosphere of military expos organized by defense contractors.

Writing about the atmosphere of arms promotion, engineering historian Joseph J. Corn has observed: "Defense contractors, in fact, often seemed to have the largest crystal ball when it came to envisioning the future. They had good reasons to foster rapid technological change and weapons obsolescence: Just as automobile makers depended on consumer dissatisfaction with present vehicles—and avidly cultivated it with "cars of tomorrow"—defense firms sought to keep the military hungry for new and improved weapons. Military contractors even exploited the techniques developed by auto makers to sell their future weapons systems. Believing in the adage of a picture being worth a thousand words, they hired illustrators to visualize futuristic weapons in action. These images have been promoted in trade shows and in the pages of periodicals such as *Army Information Digest*."[28] This hype has been the background to the clever and subtle reasoning about future wars which has been used by military policy-makers from the end of World War II to the present time.

But the irrationalities of the hyped-up military marketplace have perhaps amounted to little compared to the overarching fear that has justified so much military decision-making during the cold war years. Orwell's dictum that prophecy panders to fear can be true of no other area more than this one. Our age, of course, is a very fearful one, but it is also extraordinary that it is perhaps the first age in which fear is actually being promoted as a virtue. Some political analysts today have actually written about fear as if it were a virtue, slandering those who are unwilling to espouse it. For example, Richard Pipes, the émigré American historian and military consultant, has written: "In the United States, the consensus of the educated and affluent holds all recourse to force to be the result of the inability or unwillingness to apply rational analysis and patient negotiation to disagreements: the use of force is *prima facie* evidence of failure. Some segments of this class not only refuse to acknowledge the existence of violence as a fact of life, they have even come to regard fear—the organism's biological reaction to the threat of violence—as inadmissible." (emphasis in original) He then quotes with approval a distinguished colleague's prejudices along the same lines: " 'The notion of being threatened has acquired an almost class connotation,' Daniel P. Moynihan notes in connection with the refusal of America's 'sophisticated' elite to accept the reality of a Soviet threat. 'If you're not very educated you're easily frightened. And not being ever frightened can be a formula for self-destruction.' "[29] It is hard to tell who Pipes and Moynihan are slurring more—the educated, affluent elite, for not being fearful enough, or the uneducated lower classes, for supposedly being easily scared. In any case, this type of argument is wholly lacking in the kind of moral intelligence that can distinguish between courage, fear and recklessness. One can recognize and face danger without being fearful—in fact, that is precisely what courage is all about. But it is difficult to see the virtue of all of the reckless over-arming for the war of the future that we have been doing since the end of World War II. It is no wonder that Aristotle classified recklessness and fear as two extremes, two failures of virtue, both opposite from courage.

We have not yet experienced the unthinkable disaster that could result from the nuclear arms race, but recklessness in the present is still recklessness, even if it does not lead to a future disaster. In the election campaign of 1988, part of the Republican party's rhetoric was to claim that the reckless confrontational style of the first three-quarters of the Reagan administrations—a style which the party has preferred to call "dealing from strength"—is what led to the recent arms reductions. This is both absurd and vain. To realize how absurd it is, one has only to imagine what state the world would now be in were Brezhnev still alive and were Reagan's confrontational foreign policy not cooled off, as some have contended, because of the Contra-gate scandal. No one predicted, or could predict, that Brezhnev would die before the end of Reagan's terms, or that Andropov and Chernenko, his immediate successors and every bit the hard-liners that he was, would also die within months of assuming leadership of the Soviet Union. No one predicted or, given the entire modern history of Soviet succession, could predict that a reformer of Gorbachev's character and effectiveness would assume the Soviet stewardship. Even the deteriorating economic situation in the Soviet Union did not guarantee that economic, and certainly not political, reforms would be forthcoming: that nation, which both during the Napoleonic Wars and World War II has endured far worse without changing its course, is known for its tenacity. If not for these unpredicted developments, Reagan's confrontational style and Brezhnev's obduracy might very well have proven how truly reckless such posturing and massive arming can be.

One does not have to make a case for the fact that military futurology is driven by fear and the worship of power, the motives that George Orwell contended were at the heart of all prophecy; this much, at least, should be self-evident. But military futurology, more than any other area of modern prophecy, also exemplifies all of the other psychological and ideological devices which are contained in the futurologist's repertoire.

For example, very prominent in military prediction is the forecaster's characteristic tendency to minimize, or even trivialize, all problems which detract from his vision. But also rather common are the mystification of future problems and situations through the use of pseudo-scientific jargon, ambiguity and secrecy; the pretense of future mastery and control of complex environments like battlefields, usually on the basis of no more than mere visionary words; the tendency to caricature national and human psychology, particularly that of the enemy, but also that of the population that must be controlled at home. All of these ploys are designed to give the military forecaster an air of mastering the unfathomable irrationalities and complexities of future battlefields, the privileged leadership position that often follows from this and the protection of his forecasts from public scrutiny. Nowhere more than when it engages in the business of prophecy does the military behave like a cult. In fact, with the mystification of fact, the communication to the public by innuendo and the pretense to mastery of mind-boggling situations, the prophets and visionaries of war are cult-prophets *par excellence.*

It is difficult to think of the nuclear arms race without again recalling the story of Iphigenia, Agamemnon's wretched daughter. Many of the great Greek dramatists wrote plays about her sacrifice and the ensuing incidents that finally destroyed Agamemnon himself and his royal family. When he returned from the Trojan War, Agamemnon was assassinated by his wife Clytemnestra and her consort, and one of the reasons the queen gave to justify her action was that he had earlier sacrificed Iphigenia, their daughter. The great Greek dramatist Euripides wrote a sequel to the sacrifice called *Iphigenia in Tauris* in which he has Orestes, Iphigenia's brother, make the following remark about prophecy:

> The wisest men follow their own direction
> And listen to no prophet guiding them
> None but the fools believe in oracles,
> Forsaking their own judgement. Those who know,
> Know that such men can only come to grief.[30]†

Iphigenia's story symbolizes the present grace that is sacrificed for future glory. Had Agamemnon preserved his daughter's life, he would have at the same time been preserving innumerable other lives, including his own, and given his people the present opportunity to practice the arts of peace rather than those of war. Given the incalculability of the nuclear wars, limited or otherwise, that are now being planned, any politician who is really concerned about the judgment of the future would be far safer to steer in the

---

† Incidentally, Calchas, the futurologist who caused all of Iphigenia's troubles and for whom she openly expresses great hatred in Euripides's play, *Iphigenia in Tauris,* finally got his comeuppance. He is said to have committed suicide when he was outprophesied by a rival soothsayer by the name of Mopsus.

direction of peace, with all of its so-called constraints, instead
of war.

NOTES

1. For this account, and for much of what follows about early war prediction, I
   am greatly indebted to I.F. Clarke's excellent book, *Voices Prophesying War
   1763-1984* (Oxford: Oxford University Press, 1966).
2. Clarke, *Voices*, p. 10.
3. I.F. Clarke, *History Today* (1965), vol. 15, p. 110. To their credit, the English
   also displayed a great deal of humor about Chesney's predictive fantasy. For
   example, it was common banter during this period to say, when referring to any
   accidental injury, that it was a wound received in the Battle of Dorking.
4. Clarke, *Voices*, pp. 10–13.
5. Interview with Robert Sheer in *With Enough Shovels: Reagan, Bush and Nuclear War* (New York: Random House, 1982), pp. 218–219.
6. Robert Aldridge, *First Strike! The Pentagon's Strategy for Nuclear War* (Boston:
   South End Press, 1983), p. 268. Aldridge reports on Fiscal Year 1977 Author-
   ization for Military Procurement Research and Development, hearing before
   the Senate Armed Forces Committee, March 11, 1976, Part 11.
7. Richard Pipes, "Why the Soviet Union Thinks It Could Fight and Win a Nuclear
   War," in *Commentary* (July 1977), p. 24. This argument is also made by one
   military critic as a primary explanation for the decline in effectiveness of the
   U.S. armed forces during the last quarter century. See Richard Gabriel, *Military
   Incompetence*, 1985.
8. Robert Oppenheimer, "Atomic Weapons and the Crisis in Science," in *Saturday Review* (November 24, 1945), p. 10.
9. Henry Kissinger, "Force and Diplomacy in the Nuclear Age," in *Foreign Affairs*
   (April 1956), vol. 34, no. 3, p. 349.
10. Kissinger, "Force and Diplomacy," p. 351.
11. Oppenheimer, "Atomic Weapons," p. 10.
12. Kissinger, p. 356.
13. Kissinger, pp. 360–361.
14. Henry Kissinger, "Limited War: Conventional or Nuclear?—A Reassess-
    ment," in *Daedalus* (Fall 1960), p. 800.
15. Henry Kissinger, "American Strategic Doctrine and Diplomacy," in Michael
    Howard (ed.), *The Theory and Practice of War* (London: Cassell, 1965), p. 275.
16. Freeman Dyson, *Weapons and Hope* (New York: Harper and Row, 1984).
17. Paul Nitze, "Atoms, Strategy and Policy," in *Foreign Affairs* (January 1956),
    p. 197.
18. Kissinger, "Force and Diplomacy," pp. 361–62.
19. Kissinger, "Limited War," pp. 800–817.
20. The following account was reported by Walter Pincus, "Thinking the Unthink-
    able: Studying New Approaches to a Nuclear War," in the *Washington Post*
    (February 11, 1979), p. A21.
21. Colin Gray and Keith Payne, "Victory Is Possible," in *Foreign Policy* (Summer
    1980). Gray served as a top military adviser to the Reagan administration.
22. Gray and Payne, p. 14.
23. Gray and Payne, p. 19.
24. Gray and Payne, p. 21.

25. *La Descente en Angleterre: Prophétie en deux actes.* Cited in I.F. Clarke, *Voices.*
26. William Shawcross, *Sideshow: Nixon, Kissinger and the Destruction of Cambodia* (New York: Touchstone Books, 1987), p. 25.
27. See, "Where Did It All Go?" in *New Republic* (April 20, 1987).
28. Joseph J. Corn, *Yesterday's Tomorrows* (New York: Summit Books, 1984), p. 120. See also, John Markoff, "Welcome to the War Fair: Where the Hawks Hawk," in *Mother Jones* (July 1979), pp. 41–44.
29. Pipes, p. 25.
30. Euripides, *Iphigenia in Tauris* (trans. Witter Bynner), in *Greek Tragedies* (Chicago: University of Chicago Press, 1972), Volume 2, p. 137.

Did she put on his knowledge with his power
Before the indifferent beak could let her drop?

—W.B. YEATS

5

FUTUREHYPE IN EDUCATION

During the summer of 1985 the IBM Corporation launched an ambitious promotion scheme aimed at the education marketplace. With the help of a consulting firm called National Computer Training Institute (NCTI) and the Extension School at the University of California at Berkeley, they recruited two hundred teachers who had already had some experience in using computers in the classroom; the teachers were recruited in teams of two from cities located in every U.S. state. The recruitment brochure said that they were looking for "successful classroom teachers with organizational ability and entrepreneurial spirit." Through NCTI, who acted as middlemen, these teachers were brought to Berkeley, provided with room and board, and given a two-week minicourse in what the brochure called "educationally oriented technical training" at Berkeley Extension—all with the compliments of IBM.

After completing this training session, each of these teachers was provided with the use of fifteen IBM personal computers, along with the appropriate IBM software and instructional materials; they were then hired by the corporation on a part-time basis to pass their newly acquired skills on to colleagues at regional training centers which were established for this purpose. Between training sessions, these teachers-cum-entrepreneurs were allowed to keep a couple of computers for their own personal use, but told to bring the other thirteen to their schools for use with their students. Some of these teachers were otherwise unemployed or working at non-teaching jobs but, on the basis of the recruitment protocol described in NCTI's brochure, at least half of them were required to pursue these part-time jobs as educational computer-entrepreneurs as a sideline, along with the regular teaching duties which they were to resume in the fall. No mention was made of conflict of interest.

IBM is not the only computer company that has been promoting its products in the education marketplace with giveaways and training, but this scheme was unusual because of its scope. Undoubtedly it cost them a great deal to finance, but since the educational computing market is already large and lucrative, it takes little imagination to understand IBM's thinking behind this promotion scheme. For more than a decade there has been a great deal of talk in education circles about an imminent micro-computer revolution in the classroom. Not only did this corporation want to capture a large part of the present market, but it wanted to ensure that this revolution would, in fact, occur; the seeding effect of such a strategy was an attempt to hasten it on its way. From the corporation's point of view, this whole scheme was business as usual. They were pursuing the education marketplace in the same way they had earlier pursued the military and business marketplace before it: by trying to cultivate the present market and capture a large part of it, and by trying to insure their stake in the market of the future.

This is not the first time a revolution in education has loomed on the horizon. When I was a boy attending public schools in Toronto, I was at one time very taken by an article in a popular magazine about a great new innovation in education that was one day going to make learning virtually effortless. However, on that occasion, the revolutionary educational innovation was related not to computers but to subliminal suggestion, which was at that time a hot topic in the field of advertising. The theory behind subliminal suggestion is that a consumer can be induced to buy a product if its name or symbol is quickly and secretly flashed before his eyes on a movie or television screen, or if some other object of desire, usually sexual, is embedded, like camouflage, in a picture of the product when it appears in an advertisement on a billboard or in a newspaper or magazine. The article I read claimed that, in a similar way, you could learn anything in your sleep, ostensibly by suggestion, simply by listening to a tape recording of the subject matter while you were unconscious. Eventually, so the article predicted, we would be learning all sorts of things this way. Since school was insufferably boring and tedious for me at that time, this technique struck me as a perfect solution, a way of giving my courses precisely the amount and type of attention they deserved. Unfortunately, however, I could not afford to buy the system, and therefore had to continue to take a little precious time away from other activities in order to master my subjects.

The theory about learning in one's sleep was undoubtedly inspired by Aldous Huxley's then still very fashionable novel *Brave New World*. In Huxley's novel, this educational technique of the future was known as "hypnopaedia." However, it was forcefully rejected, along with other similar techniques of Huxley's visionary society, by John the Savage, one of the novel's principal protagonists, on the grounds that it contributed to what he called "civilized infantility." John the Savage believed that life was better if it had real challenges, and so he could not see the virtue of making learning and everything else in life effortless.

Hypnopaedia, as a disproven instruction technique, may seem droll or even outlandish at this point in educational history, but one thing it has in common with a great many modern educational innovations which are taken quite seriously and are supposed to be making our educational future, is that it is based on the premise that learning would be much more effective if only it could somehow be made at least effortless, and hopefully even enjoyable.

Of course the hypnopaedia of my boyhood turned out to be a groundless little fad, but as a fad, groundless or otherwise, it certainly has not been lacking for company. In ensuing years there have been a great many innovations in education, some of which were modest enough, and others which were supposed to herald a wonderful new age of teaching and learning. Because of this onslaught of educational innovation, I think my generation, the baby-boom generation, has been subject to more educational experiments based on both new techniques and technology than any generation before us.

All of us have been subjected to the parade of educational innovation of this century, from tape recorders, phonographs, and projectors, through educational television, teaching machines and now, finally, computer assisted instruction (CAI). Most of the mechanical innovations were designed to make learning and teaching a little easier, more effective and perhaps even more enjoyable. And though they were by no means revolutionary, many of these technologies, in fairly simple and straightforward ways, did indeed prove to be useful and effective when employed appropriately in the classroom.

Other techniques—like open classrooms, self-directed learning and schools without walls—made grander, more dramatic claims on our attention, and yet ended up producing very mixed results. But a special case has been made for CAI which, in its most recent incarnation on microcomputers, is still going strong: it is said to be both technology and technique, a new machine as well as a new approach to teaching, wholly different from everything that has come before it; it is said to be truly revolutionary, to be heralding the education system of the future.

Though the computer revolution in the classroom has loomed in the public consciousness only a few years, by some standards this talk about a computer revolution in our classrooms is getting pretty old. More than twenty years ago there was another flurry, minuscule compared to the scale of present activity, which predicted the same outcome. In those days, however, computer technology for educational purposes was less elaborate than it is today. Relatively inexpensive microcomputers did not appear on the market until the mid- to late-1970s, so these early computer assisted instruction systems required that students sit at time-sharing video-display terminals (VDTs) which were connected to mainframe computers. Naturally, time-sharing had to be carefully coordinated and this prohibited most spontaneous usage; computing capacity was much more limited and expensive; the terminals had none of the optional accessories like joysticks, digitized drawing pads, game paddles and light pens that make input into today's micros so varied and, to some students, so appealing; and when the mainframe went down, all of the terminals naturally went down with it.

Also, during this first round, educational software was more scarce and much harder to produce. Programmers who were producing it at that time had to use the earlier generations of machine languages then available, which are rather restrictive by present-day standards. They did not have the benefit of modern utilities programs, like authoring languages, which make programming much easier, or graphics utilities which greatly facilitate creating visual representations on the screen, or standard subroutines which simplify the correction of errors.

With the development of the micro, its accessories and these aids for producing software, many of the mechanical difficulties of introducing these teaching machines into our classrooms were solved, or seem to be imminently soluble. We have certainly arrived at the point where, if the money could be found today, we could quite easily and rapidly inundate our classrooms with vast amounts of hardware and software and give those of our teachers who are not yet using computers at least a minimum amount of technical training: IBM's promotion scheme is a perfect model for this.

But talk of a computer revolution in the classroom has been premature. An education revolution of the sort I have described, that is, by inundation, would be successful only in IBM's narrow marketing sense. In fact, in spite of the enormous amount of effort that has already gone into developing computing products for the education marketplace, the problems that have thus far been solved, largely technical ones, are trivial compared to those that remain, especially if one takes our forecasters' scenarios seriously. Given how little we know about the human issues involved here—the real education issues—it is impossible at present to predict even what a computer revolution might mean, much less how it might turn out.

When one hears talk of imminent revolutions in our education system, it is important to bear in mind that, next to the military, perhaps no other part of our culture is as susceptible to becoming the subject of propaganda as is our education system. Although the two are obviously in many ways very different, the one thing that our military and education systems do have in common is that they are both major repositories of our individual and collective hopes and fears. Our education system, like the military, is therefore particularly susceptible to the propagandist work of our modern-day prophets. Perhaps even more so because of the pervasive and often pivotal role the education system plays in our society and culture. However, if we consider this role carefully, we begin to have some inkling of what an education revolution might mean, and what our education prophets are really about.

Just as the individual is reproduced in the family, the education system has long been the formal center for the reproduction and renewal of our society and culture: for the transmission of knowledge, customs, and values, as anthropologists usually put it. It certainly does not do this job alone. It is obvious that this business also happens in many other places—in the home, on the street, in the workplace, and in personal relations—but it is in the education system that it is most clearly, unequivocally and formally vested. Furthermore, as we continue to delegate more and more authority and responsibility for all sorts of formerly personal and private matters to professionals outside of the family, it is in the education system, where so many family-serving professionals tend to congregate, that the process of social and cultural reproduction is increasingly carried out. That is why we often say that, whatever else may happen to an individual during the course of a lifetime, his educational experience will have a great impact on shaping his destiny. Because the education system is universal and compulsory, it is a common path and a common place. Because it is a staging ground for their future roles, it plays a major role in renewing our society and has come to represent both our individual and common destiny. Hence its attraction to our prophets: anyone who can present a convincing picture of future society and show both that it will be significantly different from present society and that the education system is not producing the future citizens that will thrive in and foster that civilization can also make a strong and appealing case for radical educational innovation.

Because social and cultural reproduction are the main functions of our education system, it is naturally also a major center of transformation: what better time to change something than when you are making it anew? In the process of reproducing a civilization, there exists always the tantalizing possibility of renewing it, renovating it on the basis of a grander, finer design. This possibility may even present itself as an imperative when parts of the culture appear to be, or are said to be, rapidly becoming obsolete. You never want to reproduce something that is no longer useful, so you transform it while you are making it anew in the hopes that it will be better adapted to the future environment. Of course transformations may also occur unintentionally, like mutations, when the education system fails to carry forward a skill or some knowledge that society continues to value. An example of this in recent times has been the failure of our education system to maintain the rates and standards of literacy that were so painstakingly developed during the first two-thirds of this century. At other times, as I will presently show, the transformation may be intentional, as when the system is consciously used to try to create a new society and culture. At these times, changes may be of a most sweeping and radical nature, designed not only to improve the process of education, but to act as a major lever for changing a civilization. This is what happens during periods of revolution. In fact, no successful revolution or revolutionary plan can fail to give education anything less than a major place on its agenda, and no vision of a new society would be complete without an elaborate description of how the education system will be used for creating and maintaining it.

In this context it is worth bearing in mind that the oldest visionary description of a society, which was to be shaped and maintained by a revolutionary education system is Plato's utopia, the *Republic*. Plato envisioned a society that would be sorted and divided into different classes, and to achieve this goal he advocated incorporating into the education system a technique which was already well developed in his time and of which he must have had some knowledge: the technique of the "thoroughbreeder."[1]

Since he made use of allusions to some of the now more obscure parts of Greek mythology, the terms of Plato's vision may sound a little quaint and precious to modern ears, but his educational prescriptions for a utopian society are fairly clear. He imagined that the population of his new society would be divided into four different classes based on the four types of soul: *gold, silver, bronze* and *iron*. Merit in the *Republic* was to be based primarily on an aptitude for two sorts of skills: the ability to philosophize on the one hand, and, on the other, the ability to excel at the types of sports that were current at the time, that is, those geared towards the development of good war-fighting skills.

But here is where the thoroughbreeder comes in. In Plato's utopia, people with *gold* and *silver* souls would be encouraged by customs and rituals insinuated by their rulers (also selected from the class of *gold* souls) to breed prolificly, and thus have a disproportionate, and presumably beneficial impact on the population mix of their society. On the other hand, the *bronze* and *iron* classes would be encouraged to breed very little or not at all. The best souls would be separated from the rest and raised and educated communally by professional nurses and tutors.[2] This weeding process would continue at different stages of their lives until, at the age of fifty, those who had passed all hurdles would themselves be selected to join the circle of leaders.

Plato's description of an ideal future society also had some telling things to say about the role of women. Formally, women were to be selected on an equal footing with men and could rise just as high; equal opportunity, very narrowly conceived, was one of his basic precepts. In this limited sense, Plato's thinking was somewhat more egalitarian than that of most of his contemporaries. But social mobility for women depended strictly on their ability to prove themselves proficient at the conventional male skills of philosophical abstraction and warfare. No other skill or craft—be it law or business, weaving or pottery—no matter how highly developed, was esteemed in Plato's utopia to the extent that it could act as a vehicle for the kind of upward social mobility that would result in political leadership. And poetry and fine arts were to be banished altogether because, as "imitative" processes, they were removed from philosophical "reality"; they detracted from Plato's overriding philosophical project, which was to try to discover the "essences" of things. So obsessed was Plato with promoting the skills of war that in his utopia women who aspired to positions of leadership were required to exercise naked in the marketplace, as the men did, presumably even into late middle age while they held office,[3] while even little children were to be taken out into the battlefield, on suitably safe occasions, and figuratively given a taste of blood as part of their education.[4] In short, the education system in Plato's new society was to be used to create and sustain a community dominated by a culture which heavily emphasized conventional male skills.

In our time, perhaps the closest thing to Plato's model is the Israeli kibbutz. Of course the kibbutz strives to be a classless society, and the values that have been created and sustained in these communities are very different from the ones Plato promoted. While Plato demeaned tilling the soil, on the kibbutz this activity, especially at the outset, was elevated to the highest level. And another difference between the kibbutz and Plato's vision is that in time, with prosperity, it became possible to achieve distinction on the kibbutz on the basis of art and poetry as well as agriculture and industry. But what these modern utopian communities do have in common with Plato's vision is that children raised and educated in them are separated from their parents at a very early age and raised by communal care-givers and teachers. Moreover, one of the main purposes of this separation on the kibbutz, very much in keeping with Plato's idea, was to create a new society by making a revolutionary break with the past and to separate, or at least significantly decrease, the influence of the family. Aside from the very real economic considerations which were particularly relevant in the beginning, the founders of the kibbutzim wanted their chil-

dren to be freed from the debilitating neurosis of family and
small town culture which they had brought from their Eastern European backgrounds.[5]

In more recent times, we have seen many other examples of the education system being used to create a brave
new society. One is the ambitious scheme initiated by the
United States to upgrade its science education system following the dramatic Soviet launch of the first man-made
satellite in 1957; the aim was to produce scientists and technicians that would equal or surpass the Soviet achievements.[†] Another is the paroxysm of infighting between the
old and new guard in China, commonly known as the Cultural Revolution, which closed the universities for a decade
and sent intellectuals into the countryside to labor on the
land. And a third is the literacy campaign launched in Nic-
aragua following the Sandinista Revolution in order to upgrade the skills of the population and get them into the
mainstream of modern life.

But these movements, using only tools and techniques
already in existence, have produced nothing compared to
what some of our contemporary prophets have said will be
the outcome of the present period of computer-based innovation in the education systems of the industrialized world.
We have been told by its promoters that this revolution will
change not only the way we learn but even the way we think,
the very nature of how we work in science, and perhaps even
lead to the very disestablishment of our school systems themselves. For example, Seymour Papert, a prominent computer
scientist and psychologist at MIT and undoubtedly the foremost among these prophets, has written:

> I have described myself as an educational utopian—
> not because I have projected a future of education
> in which children are surrounded by high technol-

[†] The Soviet sputnik launch was really just another Texas Alamo. It did not signify
that the Soviet Union was technologically superior to the United States. On the
contrary, this innovation, in which the Soviet monopoly was very short-lived, was
the first and only significant military innovation the Soviet Union has achieved
during the entire post–World War II arms race. But the event had great symbolic
impact, and could therefore be used by the military and those who wanted educational change to promote it.

ogy, but because I believe that certain uses of very powerful computational technology and computational ideas can provide children with new possibilities for learning, thinking, and growing emotionally as well as cognitively . . . many of which depend on a computer-rich future, a future where a computer will be a significant part of every child's life.[6]

Depending on one's taste, this vision of the future may or may not be appealing. But given the role that the education system plays in society, this vision, if it is to be realized, immediately raises a simple but fundamental question: If computers are to be used in the reproduction and renewal of our culture and society, exactly how will they do this? What is the nature of human society and what is the nature of machines, and how can the latter be used by the former to reproduce itself?

Since the Industrial Revolution, machines have played a dramatic and significant role in the production of *things*. What generally characterizes the production of *things* by machines is that they are all supposed to come out the same—in fact, our engineers have coined the now rather familiar phrase, "production to specification," to describe this goal. This sameness is precisely what engineers have striven for during the course of the last two centuries and continue to strive for to this day. It is the basis not only for uniformity but also for standards of a sort because, as far as machines go, quality is basically uniformity on a high level: an engine block with no cracks in it, a piece of fabric with high uniform density of fiber and dye, pistons that are sealed and seated with the precision that leads to uniform compression, and so forth. Those who have sung the praises of machines have praised not only their power but also their precision, that is, their uniformity and the uniformity that they produce. Indeed if *things* that are produced by machines do not, for some reason or other, come out according to specification, then this is usually considered to be a failure of the production system.

What characterizes people, however, is that they are not produced to specifications. We are different from one

another because of the number and variety of traits in the
human gene pool and the incessantly stirring and churning
nature of genetic recombination which occurs when we reproduce ourselves. Though people have a great deal in common with one another (and in some ways this is just as
important as the fact that they are different), the fact of
diversity, of individual differences, is nevertheless one of the
hallmarks of humanity, and ultimately of all of nature. In
this light, perhaps the most fundamental question raised by
the idea of an education revolution based on computers is
this: How can machines both respond to natural human diversity and help produce a diverse future human society? Or
put another way, how can that which is basically geared
towards producing *sameness* assist in the production of those
who are by nature *different?*

　　Perhaps it is not fair to put the question in these terms.
Most computer scientists, especially those who belong to the
artificial intelligence movement, would make the claim that
computers are very special—Papert calls them the Proteus
of machines.† Theoretically, what distinguishes computers
from other machines is that they are very flexible, can perform different functions at different times, can simulate—
or "imitate" to use Alan Turing's term—any function that
anything or anyone else can do, providing it can be described
in formal terms. This, at least, is the theory of computers
and the battle-cry of the artificial intelligence movement.
Therefore, not surprisingly, one of the major premises
upon which the promotion of the computerized classroom
of the future has been based is that computers actually have
the capacity to optimize learning by tailoring instruction to
the individual learner's abilities and idiosyncrasies.[7] The
claim is made, in other words, that not only do students
learn *individually* with the assistance of the computer—quite
obviously this happens on other occasions too—but that their
very instruction is *individualized,* somehow made to suit their
particular natures as learners. In a sense, then, the CAI

† Poor Proteus! How easily this little god's name has been taken in vain. This
minor Greek deity, the son of Poseidon, was known primarily for his powers as a
seer who knew present, past and future, but was reluctant to talk. In order to make
him speak one had to catch him, and he evaded capture by assuming different
forms and shapes—hence Papert's allusion.

revolution has faced the question of human individual differences head-on, by claiming that much of its strength lies precisely in being ideally suited, perhaps even more so than human teachers, for dealing with this problem.

This is a very substantial claim, especially because a great deal of the appeal of computerized instruction and justification for the educational revolution rests on it. The educational philosophies of the western democracies place a high value on individual growth and development. But what does the CAI claim to individualized instruction actually mean? The best way to answer this question would be to look briefly at the development of this Proteus of teachers during the last quarter century in order to elucidate the meaning behind the myth of individualized CAI and thus put at least some of the hype about the coming revolution in education into perspective.

In spite of the fact that computers can supposedly simulate machines of any sort, in point of fact, most of the first computers used for teaching were simply designed to simulate B.F. Skinner's mechanical teaching machines. Masters often disown their disciples—even Marx, who loved to have a following, made a point of stating that he himself was not a Marxist—but it is nevertheless ironic when it happens. It was certainly ironic, for example, that Skinner himself expressed a rather dim view of educational computers when he first encountered them at the Seattle Exposition in 1961. He expressed this displeasure in an address to the French Psychological Association. In particular, he ridiculed the claim made by the boosters of these machines that the computer could be used effectively to individualize instruction:

> They told me with a great deal of pride that the machine [computer] was capable of addressing students by their given names. I have no doubt that in French they would address students by using the familiar form. In this way one adds the personal element to education! It is obvious that in all of these cases there is not one new idea, not one new conception of the processes of instruction. Such a machine serves only to perpetuate the most regrettable methods of education.[8]

However, the fact that Skinner, the father of programmed and machine-assisted instruction, chose to deprecate CAI did not prevent its proponents from using his learning theory and his model of programmed instruction for developing their own systems. So the first CAI programs, the linear programs, were based on the principles of conditioned learning, to the development of which Skinner himself had devoted most of his career.[9]

It is said that imitation is a form of flattery. To Skinner's credit—but obviously, from the above statement, against his best intentions—the majority of the first linear programs developed for CAI were no more than electrified and automated programmed learning books. In the simplest types of "tutorial" CAI, the subject matter is presented to the learner sequentially and systematically. All students are presented with exactly the same material, and whenever the student responds correctly to a question or problem, he gets a positive reinforcement, usually in the form of a message appearing on the video display screen saying that he is right. Because the learner is working on his own, and because, practically speaking, the computer is capable of presenting the material as fast as the student can handle it, the learning is self-paced.

In fact, given that every learner must go through all of the same material in exactly the same way, this self-pacing feature is the only sense in which the simplest linear educational software, or "courseware," can be characterized as being individualized. In other words, the learner who uses this type of linear program is treated as an individual by it, only in the sense that he is permitted to work at his own speed. But what does even this narrow form of individualization actually mean?

Consider two different hypothetical learners, both of whom would achieve the same credit for working through any given linear tutorial. The first learner is the kind who can anticipate very little or nothing at all of the material which is being presented by the machine, but nevertheless is able, in a reasonable amount of time, to comprehend and respond correctly to every question. The second is the learner who finds every question or problem immediately comprehensible and is able to anticipate some of these even before they are posed. This student is encumbered only by the speed at which he or she can physically transmit correct answers back to the machine.

Clearly, the learning experiences of these two very different kinds of students using the same "tutorial" will be very different, just as will be the experiences of two musicians, one of whom can sight-read only one note at a time, and the other of whom can sight-read a whole phrase, or a passage, or even an entire section at a time. Yet both students will get the same credit for completing the course, even though their experiences in doing so will have been considerably different. More important, insofar as these students do have different experiences—after all, scores certainly are not everything—it is because of what *they* bring to the computer, not what *the computer* brings to them. And as far as the product which results from this human-machine interaction is concerned, since all learners master the same material, then, for all intents and purposes, all come out the same. This is basically the kind of result that engineers hope for and expect from machine production. This is manufacturing to specification.

The obvious limitations of linear courseware were somewhat ameliorated by the development of a more sophisticated type called "branching tutorials." Branching programs are still based on Skinner's conditioning principles, but they do have some additional features which allow them to be flexible in their relationship to the learner's performance record. Corrective feedback, and thereby additional opportunities to learn the correct responses, are offered to students who fail to respond correctly at the beginning of each instructional sequence. (Conversely, this process is short-circuited or entirely eliminated for faster learners.) And, as another form of feedback, these programs are also capable of engaging the learner in highly structured tutorial dialogues—really only pre-recorded and pre-rehearsed sequences—and of posing questions in forms which are not explicitly multiple choice. However, *not explicitly multiple choice* is the key here, since these programs are capable of comparing a student's answer only with a set of pre-specified alternative responses which are invisible to the student but embedded in the program.

No one has more succinctly summarized the limitations of branching tutorials than Anthony Oettinger, an early critic of the movement towards computerization of education. Writing about them almost two decades ago, when the computer revolution in education was still in its first incarnation, he said: "Some claim that the advantage of a computer over simpler 'teaching machines' lies in its capability for practically infinite branching. But the real bottleneck is our inability to foresee more than a very few of the most common possible learner responses."[10]

Another variation of Skinner's basic linear tutorial which is worth a brief description is the so-called "generative courseware." These programs are capable of presenting wholly different problems to different students, generally at certain appropriate points in standardized routines. For example, in a drill-and-practice program in math, after a certain number of principles have been presented, each learner might be given problems that are different in the sense that the numbers in them are randomly generated. One learner might be asked to subtract 13 from 27, another 19 from 28, and so forth. But what is noteworthy and also ironic, about this type of computerized tutorial is that the *learner*'s individuality is generally defined, not with reference to the learner himself, but by the *computer*'s ability to generate random numbers. For example, if the object of the program is to present progressively more difficult problems, which is often the case, then "progressively more difficult" must be pre-defined, and it usually is, but on an average or random, rather than on an individual basis.

Yet another type of courseware is based on mathematically modeling learning behavior, and attempts to reduce learning based on the problem-solving model to mathematically describable situations, specifically to situations describable by game-theory.† Learning behavior is thus reduced to

† It is in the nature of game-theory to reduce complex behavior situations to a relatively small number of easily understandable variables based on simple human motives and simple probabilities of certain kinds of behavior. It is therefore not surprising that it has had a great deal of appeal to military strategists and has also been attractive to other kinds of strategists, including learning strategists. From the "gaming" of wars to the "gaming" of learning, this paltry theory certainly has got around for the purposes of trying to capture extremely complex situations in the simplest of terms. I shall have little to say about this type of courseware,

decision-making, based on a sort of game-playing, which is in turn based on a very mechanistic psychology and the rules of probability. The problem that game-theory encounters in education, however, is that aside from the fact that very few learning situations are well enough understood to be reduced to such terms, this type of courseware has been so strongly tied to its particular problem-solving theory that everything else has effectively been squeezed out. It turns out that, in practice, it has been forced to make a fatal trade-off: it has proven to be incapable of simultaneously both modeling the student's learning behavior and properly representing the subject matter at hand. The individual learner is defined by this type of program simply as a game-player, a "rational and normal" decision-maker, but *directly at the expense of the substance of the "game" he is playing,* that is, of the subject he is trying to learn. Because of this great shortcoming, one of the original theorists and authors of this type of courseware has commented on its well recognized failure that "the reason for stochastic learning models failing as models of instruction is *their lack of representing the content to be taught.*" (emphasis added)[11]

This brings us to the most progressive and probably the most famous type of CAI system, which also takes as its theoretical point of departure the notion of learner as problem-solver, but does not, however, burden itself by attempting to model the learning process on the basis of a mathematical formula. Essentially, what happens in this system is that the learner is taught, or teaches himself, a computer language, LOGO, and uses it in order both to set and solve problems, specifically *programming* problems. In other words, the student learns to program in a certain language and, since computer languages are mathematical constructs, he learns to pose and solve problems within the confines of these constructs.

It is interesting to observe that by the 1980s the rhetoric used to promote the LOGO system began to echo that used by the progressive education movement at the turn of the

---

however, beyond describing what it tries to do because it is generally regarded, even by its original proponents, as a failed system. It is therefore presently interesting only for what it tells us about another characteristic approach to individualizing instruction on the computer.

century. In 1982, Seymour Papert, the most prominent developer and promoter of LOGO, wrote: "My conjecture is that the computer can concretize (and *personalize*) the formal." (emphasis added)[12] This contention is part of the now familiar argument that computers are not merely a learning medium but an actual mathematical culture in which the learner acquires mathematical knowledge by programming in LOGO, by becoming, in other words, *acculturated* to what Papert calls "Mathland."

Papert's basic idea is really very old—older even than the progressive education movement—but has lost some of its familiarity since he embellishes it so much. It is therefore worth briefly unpacking here. He begins by asserting the theory that language is generally acquired rather effortlessly by most children, and attributes this phenomenon to the fact that children usually live in a language-rich environment. In this he is clearly a "nurturist" because he significantly does not likewise assert that the ability to acquire language has always been highly adaptive and, according to evolutionary theory, would therefore naturally be very widespread in the gene pool. Based on the questionable assumption that among humans the predisposition for learning math is just as strong as for learning language, his premise is that if we were to create an environment equally rich in mathematical as it is in verbal content, then mathematics would be acquired by our children with equal ease, and from this second conquest, somehow or other, the whole world of education would follow. A couple of years after publishing *Mindstorms,* his very influential prophecy, he described the future world that he envisioned in glowing terms.

> Then school, defined as a place where the three R's are imposed by force (or by the kind of subterfuge called "motivation" which is just as bad), will no longer be necessary. Society will be able to face the task of inventing environments in which children can develop as social, loving, honest human beings without distorting this goal by the crudely technical one of stuffing the multiplication tables into their heads.[13]

On the surface all of this may sound very romantic and appealing—perhaps that is why this school is often called the "techno-romantic" school of CAI—and there is no question that some children do indeed find it very appealing to learn certain mathematical concepts by programming with LOGO. But the theory does not stand up very well to close scrutiny, and, as scientists always insist, where theory is weak, predictions are bound to be wrong.

First of all, accepting Papert's claims at face value for the moment, it is revealing to probe some of their implications in order to see how this type of CAI relates to the individuality of the learner. If LOGO is indeed a *culture,* then one should ask the question: What is the process of becoming acculturated to it? One common way in which cultures are commonly characterized is as systems of shared values, symbols, customs and so forth. However, the process of sharing, almost by definition, entails some loss of individuality. In real cultures this is usually an acceptable trade-off. But consider what is lost in learning with LOGO.

Consider, for example, some of the earliest "lessons" in LOGO, in which the acculturation process is most manifest. Learning to "draw"—this is the term that Papert himself uses—with LOGO is tantamount to learning to program the computer to represent on its screen the figure one has in mind. To draw a circle the learner types on the keyboard: TO CIRCLE REPEAT FORWARD I RIGHT I, END; to draw a triangle: TO TRIANGLE, REPEAT 3 FORWARD 30, LEFT 120, END; to draw a square: TO SQUARE, REPEAT 4 FORWARD 30, LEFT 90, END. If one inspects these three programs, what is immediately striking about them is that they are all very much the same, that is, in form they are far more like one another than the figures in question. This observation is particularly true if one considers the great variety of ways in which individual learners might execute these drawings using other media or, sticking with Papert's terminology, I suppose one ought to say, in other "cultures."

Papert's ideas about drawing bring Plato to mind again. Plato dismissed art because it detracted from his great project: the pursuit of the immortal essences, which he called "the forms." He dismissed making art as a falling away from—worse, a negation of—his great project, which was to try to discover the essences of things. Plato felt that art removed ideas one step back from the essences rather than pushing them one step forward, as he hoped logic would do. The interpretive side of art would not have interested him because it is too ephemeral—precisely its virtue if one looks at art a certain way—while the creative side of art seems entirely to have escaped his notice. He would not have recognized it. To Plato, art was basically part of the false and deceiving world of flux, appearances and circumstances.

Papert's education program would probably have pleased Plato, his prophet predecessor, at least a little. By reducing art, as Papert's system does, to a kind of production which is based on a reductionist machine language, and by equating asymmetry, idiosyncrasy, deliberateness and all of the other marks of authentic, individualistic creation with the mere artifacts of duplication and randomization, two of the computer's most facile tricks, Papert trivialized art by emphasizing its merely imitative aspect and ignoring its creative, interpretive side, and reduced it to an essence, a symbolic machine language. In this way, he paid homage to Plato and at the same time tamed art by reducing it to production formulas. In this way, Papert also trivialized the problem of aesthetic creativity by obliterating not all, but a great deal of personality, context, individuality and judgment from the process. All this Papert—even given the most sophisticated of present developments—is logically willing to sacrifice in the future of education in pursuit of the power which the computer readily gives, and with which he is so obviously enchanted.

In the final analysis, individualization of instruction in the LOGO system consists, then, in the degree to which the individual learner can find ways of expressing himself within a formal, mathematical environment. After the preliminary stages there is indeed some freedom for individualized exploration in such a system, but the question arises: Where does all of this narrowly defined formal freedom ultimately lead? Consideration of this question points to a number of observations which throw light on how problematic the notion of individualized instruction really is.

Consider the following. LOGO, as its promoters claim,

is not a "tutor" but a "tool"; it is a system for exploring mathematico-logical ideas. However, practically speaking, this is not strictly true. In most LOGO teaching situations a human teacher will indeed be present to help formulate the next question or problem to be solved with LOGO, with the purpose of guiding the learner through what can rightly be regarded as a hidden curriculum of useful and perhaps systematic ideas. However, in the rare case when there is not a human teacher working as adjunct to the system and offering guidance as to its fruitful use, then there are two possible developments. Either the learner, in his own independent explorations, will be forced to reinvent the wheel; or, unless he can create an entirely new system which he can relate to old ones and/or share with others, he will lapse into solipsistic thinking. He may, for example, create a neat little geometric form, something like a butterfly, and use copies of these "butterflies" as building blocks to fashion more elaborate objects on the screen; if this works, he may well conclude that he has discovered one of nature's own building blocks. In the end, Papert's brave new world of learning turns out to be a precariously bare new world.

As it turns out, Papert has, in a sense, anticipated these troublesome outcomes, but decided to make a virtue of them. His vision is that you take whatever ideas you invent in your little computer environment to the marketplace and try to sell them. He writes:

> Increasingly, the computers of the very near future will be the private property of individuals, and this will gradually return to the individual the power to determine patterns of education. Education will become more of a private act, and people with good ideas, different ideas, exciting ideas will no longer be faced with a dilemma where they either have to "sell" their ideas to a conservative bureaucracy or shelve them. They will be able to offer them in an open marketplace directly to consumers. There will be new opportunities for imagination and originality. There might be a renaissance of thinking about education.[14]

But what can he possibly mean by an "open marketplace" when the product will be a computer program? What Papert neglects to mention in this clever formulation is that every marketplace must have a common coin. In Papert's marketplace the common coin would be a particular machine language, LOGO, the one he developed. This would, of course, be a logical perversion of individualization, and far from what any thoughtful proponent of progressive education might have in mind. So, in a somewhat different sense, for the LOGO learner, as for the learner who uses a program which models his learning behavior mathematically, the problem may arise that the system simply fails to represent the subject matter, the world of shareable knowledge.

The problem of adequately representing subject matter is persistent in all types of CAI programs, as is the problem of representing a model of the learner, or of learning, that can recognize the learner's individuality in more than one or two dimensions. Both of these problems are explicitly recognized in CAI that is informed with artificial intelligence (AI). This type of courseware, which is presently still in the developmental stages, is depending for its successful realization on the eventual solving of a number of formidable problems. They are worth listing because AI-informed CAI is the great hope of the CAI movement, and because they epitomize the problems which have always been faced by the entire field of CAI. First, in CAI knowledge must be representable as production rules and consist, therefore, of a reasonable number of related facts which can be logically extended. Furthermore, these facts must be comprehensible through natural and logical modes of reasoning. And finally, the computer must be able to engage the student in relatively open-ended dialogue and explain its thinking, that is, its decisions to him.

It is too early to judge how successful CAI informed by artificial intelligence will be. The task it has set for itself is clearly enormous. Simply representing all knowledge formally will itself present the greatest of difficulties, especially—it has become a commonplace by now—all of the humanities and most of the social sciences, where such knowledge is not "scientific," that is, does not come from a tradition which is already highly reductionist. As to the theory of learning that must be embedded in such programs, similar problems arise. All present theories of learning taken together present only a partial and sketchy picture of what learning may be. Even incorporating one of them in a CAI program presents great difficulties. After all, the work of Bruner, Piaget, Gagne, Atkinson and Skinner—to name only some of the major twentieth-century theorists that come to mind—are not parts of a puzzle, contributions to a general theory of instruction. No single learning theory, in and of itself, is nearly complete, but even taken together they are no more than distinct and loosely related approaches to a general theory of instruction. A general theory of instruction would be difficult if not impossible to devise, precisely because, among other things, learning is such an individualized process.

In the final analysis, then, it is characteristic of all educational software that the *learner*'s individuality is defined in terms of the *computer*'s capabilities. This is the hallmark of all people/machine interactions and a natural consequence of what Lewis Mumford long ago referred to as the "assimilation of the machine." In spite of appearances and claims to the contrary, even in computers the mark of the machine is very persistent. The malleability of this "Proteus of machines" is still largely a matter of theory; in practice it has been, and continues to be, greatly exaggerated.

It is impossible to say what the computerization of our education system will accomplish in the very long run, but, like the quest for a cure for cancer, there is no good reason, except for wishful thinking, to believe that in the foreseeable future it will accomplish even a small part of what it has set out to do. The reality of the present situation is that, after more than a quarter of a century of development, this ongoing project to revolutionize instruction with the use of computers continues to demonstrate persistent limitations based not only on the structural nature of machines and machine language, but also on the lack of imagination and skill among even the most talented programmers. But more important, it is also based on the individualistic nature of human beings and the indeterminate nature of a great deal of the knowledge contained in our culture, both of which are highly resistant to being captured in mechanical forms.

In the face of these enormous problems, and in spite of the predictions of the brave new world of education they will usher in, computers remain very machine-like in their instructional functions. They are indeed powerful in some ways, certainly as calculators, but the price of all of this much vaunted power is that they leave their mark on all knowledge and act as a sort of sieve through which, were the revolution ever completed, all knowledge would have to pass or run the risk of being discarded.

For elementary lessons Skinner's teaching machines and some computer programs have been very helpful and have made a real contribution. For these lessons the computer's sieve-like qualities do not matter very much because most of the knowledge at this level is simple enough to pass through the holes of the screen relatively unscathed. But beyond these elementary lessons the computer as an aid to instruction, be it in the form of tutor or tool, time and again keeps proving itself to be painfully literal, especially in instructional situations where this simply will not do, where ambiguity, context, and metaphor are not failures or aberrations of communication but simply the name of the game. At present, this includes the vast majority of learning situations, including those in all but the most elementary of sciences and mathematics.

This would be a merely cautionary observation if computers in education were usually used appropriately, as was largely true during the first phase of their introduction and development in the schools. However, because of the hype both from members of the "artificial intelligentsia" like Papert and corporations like IBM, there has been a rush to find uses for computers in the classroom, the vast majority of which are obviously inappropriate, in order to usher in the new era of education. The danger is that a great deal will be lost as the final consequence of all of this hectic activity. This is due to the fact that the computer's severe limitations in acting as bearer of culture are simply inadequate for the education system's enormously complex and critical role in reproducing our society and culture, even accepting the fact that that society and culture are changing.

Signs of this are already with us. Here are some typical examples. We now have an instructional program in geography that makes a logical game out of the founding of a city, based solely on simple geographical variables like access to water, transportation, resources. The city in the program in question happens to be my town, Toronto, a city which, in keeping with the severe constraints of this program, does in fact happen to lie logically on a sheltered harbor at the confluence of two rivers. But what if one were to consider the founding of cities that were established for ideological rather than rational reasons? How would one account in this program for the founding of Salt Lake City, which was established by religious refugees, or one of the large metropolises in Siberia which were built and populated by political prisoners? I know of another program which claims to teach something about poetry: the student is asked to input a list of words which are consequently made to appear on the screen in the form of a Christmas tree or some other designated object. Imagine how heartwarming such pyrotechnics of automated concretism would be to Apollinaire were he alive today! I also know of a project which is presently trying to develop software to teach the classics. With respect to the *Iliad,* one imagines such questions as: Why was the hero Achilles feeling sore? Did he miss his concubine Briseis? Did he want Agamemnon's job? Was he getting tired of Hector's hectoring? These examples should speak for themselves.

But even with respect to what computers are supposed to be best at doing, that is, teaching about themselves, there are other questionable practices going on, even in this "age of computers." In the cases that I now have in mind, however, these practices have to do with the all too human nature of people, and not machines.

The problem is that, in spite of the claims of future possibilities, the CAI system itself has already become somewhat stultified. Most software writers work within the confines of the instructional categories that were identified by Robert Taylor in 1980 in his well-known book, *The Computer in the School: Tutor, Tool, Tutee*—the title tells it all. But this stultification goes far beyond working in categories; it relates to the ongoing development of machine language itself. All machine languages have their strengths and weaknesses, but as this field is developed we are naturally working

out the flaws in some of the older ones in the new generations
that are coming on board. Nevertheless, one of the most
flawed of these older ones, the well-known pioneering language called BASIC, is still persistently being taught in our
schools in spite of all of its considerable shortcomings. John
Laski, a specialist in computer languages, has eloquently
spelled out the reasons, as well as the unfortunate, self-
defeating implications of this fact:

> How one thinks and what one thinks about are
> molded by the language one uses to express one's
> thoughts. Whorf originally proposed this for cul-
> tures and natural languages. It always surprises me
> that its analogue in programming languages and
> programs is not as widely recognized. For it ex-
> plains why people resist so passionately new
> programming language capabilities, and why pi-
> oneering languages like FORTRAN, BASIC and
> COBOL still flourish today.[15]

But Laski's argument can be taken even further. Why teach
the archaic machine-language called BASIC at all? What
stake is there in preserving this stepping-stone in the development of computer languages? Is it like Ancient Greek or
Latin, archaic languages in which great literature was written
and which served for hundreds of years as the communication
medium for entire civilizations? Little if anything has been
written in BASIC that could not be better written in a more
recently developed machine language, or in one of the others
that will be coming down the line in the future.

But beyond this, it is questionable whether we should
even be teaching programming universally. It is a skill which
for the purposes of most of the population is itself rapidly
becoming obsolete. Most people who are using computers
now are already using them more as clever appliances than
malleable machines. Clever appliances rather than sophisticated tools are precisely what most personal computers
have become over the last decade—after all, this is what
"user-friendliness" is all about. Why on earth, if they could
help it, which they now certainly can, would manufacturers
allow their potential sales to be constrained, as they were

even a decade ago, by the impediment of the consumer actually having to learn something even moderately difficult in order to be able to use their product? In the end, the rush to herald the new age of education by teaching languages like BASIC has been misguided and self-defeating, even if one takes the conservative view that most people will in the long run have to learn programming; it is simply wasteful and frivolous if one takes the more optimistic view that they will not.

Furthermore, whatever may be lost or constrained by allowing the computerization of education to turn our schools into a cultural sieve is exacerbated by the social losses that this process also entails. Creating an educationally rich environment out of a vacuum is far more complicated than what Papert in his facile talk about "computer-rich" environments and "Mathland" even vaguely begins to suggest. After all, we are not talking here about cultivating molds in a petri dish. The human population is extremely heterogeneous, and an environment that may be rich for one sector is bound to be adverse or poisonous for others. When Papert first introduced LOGO he was opposed to having it evaluated on the grounds that it was still in its developmental stages. However, now that it is finally being evaluated, there is evidence that suggests precisely the problem I have just described. We now have studies that suggest that female students, on the whole, seem to have less aptitude, less ability and, most important of all, less *interest* in learning with LOGO than do most male students.[16] These effects may be due to conditioning, or they may be due to innate differences—obviously this is an issue worth trying to sort out—but whatever the case may turn out to be, if such differences persist and this type of computer use becomes a significant sorting factor in our schools, it would have a very regressive influence on the academic fate of our female students—shades of Plato's *Republic*.

Furthermore, females are not the only part of the population being excluded by the cultural narrowing necessitated by the computerization of our education systems. A survey of 18,000 American students between the ages of nine and seventeen years indicated that a number of inequities exist in patterns of computer use among our school-age population.[17] Age, sex, region of the country and type of community are all factors which relate to the amount of exposure to the computer that students are getting. It is all too familiar by now, but those students from inner cities, from the American south and from rural areas are getting the least amount of exposure, while middle-class suburban white males from the northeast and southwest are getting the most—and since the first survey in 1978 this situation has worsened. Of course middle-class families are more likely to have a computer at home, thereby increasing accessibility. But beyond the accessibility issue, which is basically quantitative, is a much more important qualitative one: Arthur Luehrman of Computer Literacy Inc. has also reported that students in wealthier middle-class schools are given more independent access to their equipment and use it to develop new skills through exploration of its potential. In contrast, however, the passive and rather more limited use of computers for drill-and-practice is more prevalent in poorer schools.[18]

Finally, in addition to the software development problems and social issues, there are a number of health questions which an honest revolution should also be addressing. From our rapidly accumulating experience in using computers in commerce and industry have emerged a number of symptoms and syndromes associated with the use of or exposure to video-display terminals (VDTs). These include eyestrain, fatigue, headaches and anxiety. It is not clear what causes these and other symptoms. They may be brought on by radiation from the VDTs themselves or by other environmental factors associated with the use of micros, like room lighting, video brightness, air supply and proportion of negative ions. Unfortunately, our knowledge of the effects of low-level radiation is incomplete and controversial, but surely these effects, found in other places, cannot be dismissed with impunity when bringing computers into our classrooms. There is a great deal of conventional wisdom in the field of human development which holds that there are critical early ages in child development in which children are particularly susceptible to environmental effects. Since our children are being introduced to video-display terminals at ever earlier ages, we should be more circumspect than we are at present about exposing them to more low-level radiation.

Considering the pedagogical, social and health issues, it should be clear that there are no simple remedies for dealing with the difficulties and dangers inherent in the movement to computerize education—and the payoffs for doing so would seem to be rather questionable. So what does the future really hold in store for the computer revolution? It is surely impossible to say with any certainty. What is certain, however, is that in the rush to make this revolution happen, the future, rather than being broadened, has already been attenuated. Whatever has been gained by introducing computers into the classroom, a great deal has already been lost, all of it unnecessarily, and not just because of a further crowding of the curriculum. The machine's lust for uniformity is leaving its mark in many ways as our society and culture reproduce themselves and conform to the contours of this newly constructed educational mold.

The mechanical response to human individuality and knowledge, far from being liberating, has proven in all too many cases to be not only inadequate but actually stifling. This is the problem at the heart of the revolution, a problem that arises from the very nature of what it is trying to do: reduce humanity and knowledge to machine constructs. What is revolutionary about the CAI movement finally is not what it contributes but what it loses in the process of trying to simulate, to imitate people and knowledge. More than any other discipline or method, the computer's nature is not to coexist with but to transform every form of knowledge around it, to reduce to its own often paltry terms all of the diverse methods that have been developed to explore the diversity of knowledge that man has accumulated over the ages.

As far as prophets like Papert go, it is their lack of understanding of what the present is all about—particularly with respect to individuality and knowledge—that has made it so easy for them to recommend this impoverished future as if it were actually richer. Whatever the inadequacies of the present—and there is certainly no point in trying to minimize these—at least up until about twenty years ago the education system suffered from, among other things, an embarrassment of riches. Even as recently as two decades ago there was a greater variety of knowledge being pursued in

different ways with methodologies appropriate to each discipline than ever before in the history of the human race.
There have been serious problems, of course, with overspe-
cialization and the management of information, but the computer has merely trivialized them, not solved them.

This fact is masked, of course, by its power, power that
is often more apparent than real. Papert's writing is liberally
peppered with references to power. He speaks of computer
power, powerful ideas, empowering students by having them
learn to program, and so forth. Computers are indeed powerful, in a limited sort of way, but a great deal of freedom
and detail in life are lost by harnessing their power, just as
a great deal of freedom of another sort is lost in driving a
car rather than walking. If you break off the leg of an insect
and place it under a powerful microscope you can make that
leg appear many times larger than the original insect itself
and then claim to have gained a great deal, all the while
ignoring what you have really lost or discarded. Computer
power works in much the same way, and it is only an impressionable futurologist like Papert who thinks that computer
environments will inevitably be richer than the ones they
replace.

Knowledge is not the same as power. But if and when
we lose the ability to distinguish between power and knowledge, the computer revolution in the classrooms will be complete. (If Alan Turing's prophecy is correct, that will
probably happen around the same time as we lose the ability
to distinguish between simulated events and the reality they
are supposed to represent, between thinking and computing.) At that point our lives in the schools, as elsewhere,
will be simulated lives.

Earlier I observed that Papert's thinking about education,
with its abstract reductionist tendencies, can be traced back
to Plato. But Papert and Plato really both represent extremes. Plato's educational system, with its inbreeding and
selection, is elitist to an extreme, and Papert's, with its willingness to trivialize culture, is egalitarian to another extreme.
Plato wants education to be hard and unpleasant so it can
perform its selective function, whereas Papert wants it to be
easy and enjoyable so that no selection occurs, no one fails.

But Papert also shares common ground with a more modern futurist, Karl Marx. The common ground between Papert and Marx is that they both believe that the present state of affairs is somehow unnatural, somehow false, a degradation into which society has fallen. Both believe that the true potential of the individual has been greatly hindered by the growth and development of unnatural social arrangements based on social domination. That is why they both want a new start made possible by a revolution that will destroy these false and degrading relationships. Their analyses are compelling because they have a superficial humanistic flavor. But in the end their prescriptions, their cures, are at least as bad as the diseases they are attacking because each prophecy, a barely concealed call to arms, proposes to substitute one form of cultural domination for another.

This is not the first time an education revolution based on an ascendant form of cultural domination has reared its benevolent-seeming head. One does not have to go back as far as Plato to find an earlier example of this, although I have often referred to his vision because it is so distant and its prejudices are so obvious to our present-day eyes. This drama also played itself out in the nineteenth century in the growth of the high school and reform school movements. Writing about this period, the American education historian Michael Katz has remarked that "despite the intellectual's acceptance of cultural relativity, first apparent in the work of many of the intellectual reformers of the progressive era, the mentality of cultural absolutism has persisted."[19] The high school movement of the nineteenth century proved to be no more a panacea than the computerization of education will prove to be now. In the wake of its failure it did not, however, merely shrivel up and disappear. Katz later remarks that "as the ideology became ever more divorced from reality, as crime and poverty increased despite the extension of schooling, teachers turned inward, and within a couple of decades their growing network of bureaucracies became private worlds, sterile and rigid."[20] This has already begun to happen in the CAI movement, but it is not likely to do IBM any harm, aside from stabilizing its revenues from this field.

Beyond the fact that a great deal is being lost and squeezed out of the curriculum in the attempt to computerize it, and beyond the fact that the computer revolution in the classrooms is serving the purposes of one part of the culture which is trying to dominate the rest, what a tremendous distraction this revolution has turned out to be. In the meantime, what has now become a litany of educational problems still persists. Some of these, like declining literacy and increasing dropout rates, are getting worse. In the end the problem is not merely that the prophets like Papert are proving to be false, or that the movement they have promoted has proven to be a great distraction: this movement has also placed a great burden on educators who are having enough trouble mastering the system as it now stands.

As the U.S. Army learned in Vietnam, mastery does not simply follow from mechanization. This lesson is even more true for the more complex education system: if you get a person in your sights, given the best available technology in either field, it is much easier to kill him than to educate him. But one fortunate thing about the education system, compared to its military counterpart, is that in education field tests under real life circumstances usually occur very early on so that one does not have situations, like the present one in the military, where whole systems are developed and put in place without ever having had to face the test of reality. This means that the futurehype in education can be more easily refuted once it has bumped up against reality. This is already happening with the computer revolution in the classrooms, and indeed was already under way even when IBM launched its promotion campaign in the summer of 1985: damn the torpedos, full steam ahead! Meanwhile, Papert, ever the stalwart futurologist, has recently and characteristically not only claimed to be misunderstood, but has also attributed the criticism, which he calls journalistic backlash, to a conspiracy inspired by the media who are simply starved for another story.[21]

In spite of the hype about creating a master race of programmers by starting very early, computer programming can be learned at almost any stage of life, as many people who are now pursuing careers in this field have proven. And it should not be difficult, through the normal channels of graduate and professional training, to furnish our society with whatever number of higher-level computer scientists it may need without squeezing the whole education system in the process. But in the present, because learning is so much a mastery of the here and now, we would do well to devote our energies to taking responsibility by mastering rather than mechanizing the subtle arts of education.

NOTES

1. Winston Churchill was certainly no revolutionary but, in spite of its placid tones, his vision of the future, at least with respect to societal reproduction, certainly was. The reader will recall from the chapter on the ideology of futurology that in this vision the test-tube reproduction of babies, coupled with some sort of "expert suggestion," was to be geared towards radically influencing societal reproduction *at the source*, circumventing the usual social selection and sorting processes by producing two ready-made classes, one for "thought" and the other for "toil," Churchill said nothing of education in his prediction of the future, but the logic of his vision suggests that, in his new society, the genetic predispositions of these two classes would be so powerfully directed towards one or the other of these roles that education would then have the easy job of having only to reinforce and refine what was already set.
2. Plato, *Republic* (London: Oxford University Press, 1945), VII, 541a.
3. Plato, V, 457a,b.
4. Plato, V, 466e; VII, 537a.
5. See Melford Spiro, *Kibbutz: Venture in Utopia* (Cambridge, Mass.: Harvard University Press, 1975), p. 128.
6. Seymour Papert, *Mindstorms: Children, Computers and Powerful Ideas* (New York: Harper and Row, Basic Books, 1982), pp. 17–18.
7. For a distinguished educator's version of this claim see John I. Goodlad's article in *School, Curriculum and the Individual* (Waltham, Mass.: Blaisdell), 1966; for a more recent version emanating from the circles of "official" science see Stuart Smith, Chairman, Science Council of Canada, speech to Canadian Education Association on "Electronics in Education" (September 28, 1982).
8. (Author's translation) On m'a dit avec beaucoup de fierté que la machine peut s'adresser à l'étudiant par son prénom. Je ne doute pas qu'en français elle le tutoyerait. De cette façon on remet l'élément personnel dans l'éducation! Dans tous ces cas, bien entendu, il n'y a pas une nouvelle idée, pas une nouvelle conception des processus d'instruction. Une telle machine ne sert qu'à perpétuer les méthodes de l'éducation les plus regrettables. (B. F. Skinner, "L'avenir des machines à enseigner." *Psychologie Française*, vol. 8 (1963), p. 171.)
9. There is a certain logic behind the fact that Skinnerian learning theory forms the basis for this earliest type of CAI program. A quick glance at the historical context in which this courseware was born renders this logic very clearly. The earliest computers were used for military applications because this was the area which experienced the greatest amount of rationalization and also received the greatest amount of resources during both World War II and the Korean War. With the advent of a more or less real peacetime economy and the military market already having been captured, business and education, in that order, became the next logical areas to be captured by computer applications in the process of expansion of this field. As it turned out, programmed instruction by book experienced its heyday in the late 1950s and early 1960s concomitant with

Skinnerian psychology which, at least in America, was also at the peak of its esteem and prestige at this time. For a penetrating analysis of why the United States, above all, would have been hospitable to both Skinnerian teaching theory and CAI see Hannah Arendt's essay, "The Crisis in Education" (1968).

10. Anthony Oettinger, *Run, Computer, Run: The Mythology of Educational Innovation* (Cambridge, Mass.: Harvard University Press, 1969), p. 181.

11. J. H. Laubsch, "Some Thoughts about Representing Knowledge in Instructional Systems," Proceedings of the Fourth International Conference on Artificial Intelligence, Tbilisi, 1975.

12. Papert, *Mindstorms*, pp. 17–18.

13. Seymour Papert, "Tomorrow's Classroom?" in *The Times Educational Supplement* (May 5, 1982), p. 41.

14. Papert, *Mindstorms*, p. 37.

15. John Laski, "Basic Confusions," in *The Times Educational Supplement* (November 13, 1981), p. 30. This article spells out in laymen's terms exactly why BASIC should not be taught in our schools.

16. Studies executed by the Toronto Board of Education and Queen's University in 1985.

17. A. Anderson, reported at the American Micro Computer—Computer Literacy Conference, Baltimore, 1985.

18. Arthur Luehrman, reported at the American Micro Computer—Computer Literacy Conference, Baltimore, 1985.

19. Michael B. Katz, *The Irony of Early School Reform* (Boston: Beacon Press, 1970), p. 215.

20. Katz, p. 215.

21. See Seymour Papert, "Are Computers Bad for Children?" in Pat Campbell and Gieta Fine (eds.), *Young Children and Microcomputers* (Englewood Cliffs, N.J.: Prentice-Hall, 1986), pp. 172–179.

Parents are now able to choose personal characteristics for children, with very low incidence of selective abortion for defective (including wrong sex) children. . . . This has allowed expanded criteria for what is defective in children; what used to be considered merely unusual is now recognized as pathological. It also allows the design of special purpose humans. Some patriotic parents, for example, who wanted to maximize the United States' chance of winning Olympic gold medals were able to choose children with specific musculature potentials. (And there are even reports of the creation of rudimentary types of webbed feet for would-be swimmers).
—AMERICAN COUNCIL OF LIFE INSURANCE

FUTUREHYPE IN HEALTH

Of all of the realms of human existence in which our obsession with the future most clearly manifests itself, the one which seems persistently to retain the strongest hold on the popular imagination is health. Undoubtedly the popular concern about the "health future" stems largely from what is commonly regarded as a prominent characteristic of present-day western culture: the reluctance to accept sickness and death.[1] Almost every day there is a report in the news to the effect that scientists have made a major breakthrough in the treatment of one of the seemingly intractable diseases of our time, like cancer, cardiovascular disease, or mental illness, the cure for which is said to have appeared on the horizon and will be arriving in the not too distant future. These claims are often corroborated by testimony from a desperate patient seeking a cure. René Dubos, whose dis-

tinguished career as a microbiologist did not, however, include these kinds of press conferences, once observed:
"There are always men starved for hope or greedy for sen-
sation who will testify to the healing power of a spectacular
surgical feat or a new miracle drug. They provide the tes-
timonies of the new religions for which scientists with theories unproved or incomplete are always ready to provide
the mystic language."[2] Undoubtedly the way in which health
futurologists have come to play on our hopes and fears on
a day-to-day basis is more stark than in any other area.

In spite of the many remarkable discoveries and innovations in medicine which have occurred during this century,
and which might be used to justify the prophetic vision of
our time, the tradition of prophecy in medicine is not new.
In fact, it can be traced back to the famous Greek physician
Hippocrates. It was during his time that western civilization
witnessed for the first time a rapid and dramatic rise in medical science: a rise in which, it should be noted, he himself
played a very prominent role. The ability to predict events
on the basis of a deep understanding of the forces that shape
them has always been regarded as one of the hallmarks of
true science, and it appears as though this is the reason that
Hippocrates advised his students and disciples to use forecasting to inspire confidence in their patients. He wrote: "I
hold that it is an excellent thing for a physician to practice
forecasting. For if he discover and declare unaided by the
side of his patients the present, the past, and the future, and
fill in the gaps in the account given by the sick he will be
the more believed to understand the cases so that men will
confidently entrust themselves to him for treatment."[3]

Plato was greatly impressed by the developments in
medicine which had been brought about by Hippocrates and
his followers, and therefore made extensive use of the metaphor of health, along with allusions to the physician's art,
in writing about all sorts of philosophical questions. Like
education, health also figured in Plato's vision of utopia. In
fact, the health system which he prescribed for his visionary
society can best be viewed as basically being an elaboration
of the program of social selection which was to play a decisive
role in the education system of that state. In Plato's vision,
on the one hand, the state was to take it upon itself to

encourage all citizens to take good care of themselves by following sound nutrition and practicing gymnastics to develop sound bodies. But, on the other hand, Plato also maintained that those who had poor constitutions, or were unwilling or unable to take care of themselves, should be left to die. He wrote:

> Then you will establish in your state physicians and judges such as we have described. They will look after those citizens whose bodies and souls are constitutionally sound. The physically unsound they will leave to die; and they will actually put to death those who are incurably corrupt in mind.[4]

Though Plato was in some ways very subtle when it came to thinking about justice, he was rather reluctant to temper it with compassion or kindness, especially when the welfare of the state as a whole seemed to be at stake. Today, many people would probably describe Plato's health policy as a form of "blaming the victim," but no matter how you look at it, Plato's position was definitely both a moral judgment and an ideological statement. And Plato's thinking is characteristic of the ways in which health futurology is tainted by the prejudices of our modern-day prophets.

Although Plato's vision of the health future is shared by some modern prophets, the ideological roots of modern medical futurology, as with military futurology, can be traced more readily to the nineteenth century, and especially to England, than to the world of antiquity. Around the same time that Sir George Chesney published *The Battle of Dorking,* one of his fellow countrymen, Benjamin Ward Richardson, also published a future scenario which is generally regarded as the first piece of modern health futurology. It is a description of a future society that is based on the precepts of health, and Richardson got his title, and the name of the society he envisioned, from Hygeia, the minor Greek goddess who served as one of the assistants to Asklepius, the Greek god of health.

A comparison between *Hygeia* and *The Battle of Dorking* is interesting well beyond the coincidental closeness of their dates of publication. Like *The Battle of Dorking, Hy-*

geia struck a very deep chord in the heart of its Victorian audience, a chord which has continued to resonate with ever increasing strength to our time. In the literature of prediction *The Battle of Dorking* and *Hygeia* also make a pair because, in some ways, the intensity of our interest in the health future stems from the same source as our intense interest in the military future. It originates in that part of us that feels, not that the future will be very much the same, but, on the contrary, that it may hold great danger or great gain.

Unlike Chesney's *The Battle of Dorking* which was, in a sense, a new prophetic genre, Richardson's *Hygeia* was in some ways akin to earlier English utopian thinking, as well as being a logical extension of the philosophy of the British Public Health movement of the late nineteenth century. Earlier, however, images of the health future had appeared only incidentally, in bits and pieces in fiction, and in the context of more sweeping visions. In 1516 Sir Thomas More had published his famous *Utopia,* in which he described a society that placed the emphasis in health care on the prevention of illness rather than on its cure, and in which temperate living, first-class hospitals and enlightened sanitary measures brought a great measure of health and longevity to the people of the land. On the other hand, in *The New Atlantis,* published in 1626, Francis Bacon, who idolized the powers of science, placed the emphasis on the cure rather than the prevention of disease in the health system of his visionary society. He described a society in which scientists performed remarkable feats of curing disease by the use of drugs and medicines, prolonged life by means of "artificial waters of Paradise" or "air chambers" and prevented infectious disease by means of a certain fruit which, to our ears, sounds strikingly similar to the orange. Bacon also advocated the establishment of a research and development system similar to the ones which exist at present in all advanced industrial nations. Finally, in 1872 Samuel Butler published his celebrated visionary novel *Erewhon,* which foreshadowed the collapse of the Victorian illusion of eternal progress. Butler, unflatteringly but logically following in the footsteps of Plato, portrayed a dark vision of a society in which illness was punished as a crime, sometimes even subject to capital punishment, in order to promote the propagation of a beautiful race; physicians in this society, on the other hand, were satirized as members of the underworld. But unlike all of these utopias and dystopias, *Hygeia* was a vision of a city of the future that would be based on health to the extent that all of its governance would be dominated by precepts of health. Before any other needs or considerations, before politics, before economics, before religion, before art, would come health.

The impression that Richardson's *Hygeia* made on his contemporaries is quite extraordinary, much like that made by *The Battle of Dorking* a few years earlier. In describing it, the historian James Cassedy has observed that "both British and continental newspapers reported it at length. . . . Uncounted numbers of young British doctors and sanitarians read it and were permanently impressed. Rich old ladies began to build 'Hygeian residences'; tradesmen advertised Hygeian goods. Busy Fabian reformers incorporated elements of Hygeia into their plans for national health services."[5]

There are several reasons why *Hygeia* captured the public imagination. First, since it followed on the heels of the passage of the British Public Health Act of 1875, on one level the publication of *Hygeia* was a sort of celebration of the triumph of the advocacy movement which had promoted the newly enacted public health measures. It was also a simple projection of continued progress along these lines. On another level, there were parts of *Hygeia* that undoubtedly appealed to the ideals of large sectors of the educated public because these parts pointed towards relief from the messy world in which almost everyone lived. Most of these measures are commonplace by now: in this city of the future garbage would be collected daily, streets would be well paved, properly graded for drainage and regularly hosed down, transportation would be underground, industry that was noxious or noisy would be located outside of town and hospitals would be clean, efficient, commodious, flexible and up-to-date.

But although on one level Richardson's vision was simply the embodiment of best practice in public health, he was certainly not content to stop there. Richardson published *Hygeia* in 1875, eighteen years after Louis Pasteur had pub-

lished his first seminal paper on the germ theory of disease.
It is no exaggeration to say that Pasteur's work was nothing
less than revolutionary, but Richardson, far from being an
easy or early convert, belonged to a school of thought which
did not accept the germ theory as it was expounded by Pasteur and by Koch. In fact, Pasteur and Richardson are the
intellectual ancestors to two of the most prominent schools
of thought in health futurology. It would be worthwhile
therefore to examine briefly the apparent connection between Richardson's thinking and that of Pasteur.

Although Pasteur was in many ways a very subtle
thinker, the heart of his theory was decidedly mechanistic.
Up until Pasteur began to publish his brilliant papers on the
germ theory of disease, public health was based not on the
notion that germs were the enemy, but rather on philosophical notions that were not strictly based on scientific proof
or theory. These were notions to the effect that man must
live hygienically, moderately and in harmony with himself
and his environment. Many of the great triumphs of nineteenth-century public health, like Max von Pettenkofer's
cleaning up of the city of Munich, were based on these kinds
of principles, and not on mechanistic theories of cause and
effect, like the germ theory of disease.[6] And, as far as the
health of the individual was concerned, mid-nineteenth-
century medicine generally maintained that it is the distur-
bance of a person's inner and/or outer equilibrium—with
causes potentially emanating from any number of sources,
sometimes several at once—that initiates sickness. Because
they were so radical, Pasteur's ideas met very serious resistance in his time from both physicians and public health
advocates, and Richardson was a part of the resistance.

It should be noted that the germ theory of disease,
though based on good hard science, had effects other than
merely promoting a dispassionate search for simple causes
and simple effects. It also provided a basis for a philosophical
posture of a different sort, in part because of other Victorian
ideas with which it coincidentally became associated. René
Dubos describes this association very well:

> Pasteur's first paper on the germ theory, the *Mém-
> oire sur la fermentation appellée lactique,* appeared

in 1857 just one month before Charles Darwin sent to Asa Gray the famous letter stating for the first time in a precise form the theory of evolution. Through this historical accident the germ theory of disease developed during the gory phase of Darwinism, when the interplay between living things was regarded as a struggle for survival, when one had to be friend or foe, with no quarter given. This attitude molded from the beginning the pattern of all the attempts at the control of microbial diseases. It led to a kind of aggressive warfare against the microbes, aimed at their elimination from the sick individual and from the community.[7]

For followers of Pasteur and Koch, the enemy—microbes—was clear, and the weapons—drugs and vaccines that would destroy them—were either at hand or could be developed. But for Richardson, the first health futurologist, the battle for health was not simply a battle against germs. Like the battle between men, it was naturally to be a struggle which only the fittest would win. This battle, however, was to be fought not only against germs, but against some aspects of human nature as well.

Because of Richardson's zeal, his scenario went well beyond best public health practice, and in doing so proved that even such seemingly innocuous things as public health measures can be tyrannical when carried too far. His future health society simply did not respect any boundaries. It was extremely prejudiced and flawed—in that it appears to have neither known nor cared about human institutions, large parts of human nature and areas of human life that have little or nothing to do with health.

For example, he decreed that in this future city of health the walls of all dwellings were to be devoid of pictures or ornaments because these were deemed to collect unhealthy dust and mildew, and indeed even wallpaper was to be banned because of the supposedly toxic nature of the paste used to hang it. Instead, he predicted a sort of bathroom or laboratory architecture for the dwellings of Hygeia in which all walls were to be made of glazed brick so that they could be scrubbed down. And though at one point Richardson suggested that the brick might be done in a variety of colors to suit the individual taste, at a later point he recommended that a uniform gray would be most suitable for everyone's purposes. (He made an exception, however, for the rich who he expected would have the means to adorn their walls in what he called fancy "Pompeian" brickwork.)

But more than assaulting the aesthetic lives of the individuals of this city, *Hygeia* prescribed a certain form of social intolerance of all "unhealthy" habits, an intolerance, it should be added, which in Richardson's fanciful mind would be enforced by socially ostracizing those who would or could not shake them. Richardson wrote, "Practically, we are in a total abstainers' town, and a man seen intoxicated would be so avoided by the whole community, he would have no peace of mind to remain." Where this person would go, Richardson neglected to say but he did go on to predict:

> And, as smoking and drinking go largely together, as the two practices were, indeed, original exchanges of social degradations between the civilised man and the savage, the savage getting very much the worst of the bargain, so the practices largely disappear together. Pipe and glass, cigar and sherry-cobbler, like the Siamese twins, who could only live connected, have both died out in our model city. Tobacco, by far the most innocent partner of the firm, lived, as it perhaps deserved to do, a little the longest; but it passed away, and the tobacconist's counter, like the dram counter, has disappeared.[8]

From the above it should not surprise the reader to learn that, aside from being a prominent public health advocate, Richardson was also an active member of the temperance movement of his time. Whatever merits the temperance movement may have had in its earlier and less extreme phases, by Richardson's time large parts of it had already become extremely dogmatic and intolerant. Richardson must surely have belonged to one of the more extreme factions of this movement because in his scenario of the future city of health he displayed no tolerance for even moderate uses of alcohol; according to his beliefs and those of the more zealous activists of this movement, all uses were, by definition, abuse. His description of the way alcohol would be treated in this society suggests that he believed that the cause of alcohol abuse was basically to be found in the substance rather than in the person.† For Richardson, a simple, technical problem requires a simple, technical solution: eliminate alcohol from the pubs and people's homes and they will no longer be alcoholics. There was no room in Richardson's rigorously logical society of health for the moderate, pleasurable use of any drugs.

Furthermore, for Richardson, not only was alcohol in itself an unmitigated evil, it was also the source of many others. Later in his vision he went on to predict that "in a city from which that grand source of wild mirth, hopeless sorrow and confirmed madness, alcohol, has been expelled, it could hardly be expected that much insanity would be found. The few who are insane are placed in houses licensed as asylums, but not different in appearance to other houses in the city. Here the insane live, in small communities, under proper medical supervision, with their own gardens and pastimes."[9] Even for a Victorian, Richardson had a blissfully ignorant way of skirting or simplifying the variety of sources of mental illness which come both from within us and from without us. In his future scenario all mental illness that was not the direct consequence of alcohol abuse would be treated as a form of mental retardation. One had either raving alcoholics or village idiots—nothing else and nothing in between.

But as a temperance-activist-cum-futurologist, Richardson was playing the part not of a religious, but of a technocratic fundamentalist. It is clear from his approach to alcohol abuse that he believed ardently in the efficacy of

---

† The temperance movement had its origins in religious fundamentalism in New England in the early nineteenth century. In its more extreme forms, aside from categorically opposing the consumption of alcohol it was also, among other things, anti-immigrant and anti-Roman Catholic. The idea that alcohol abuse is inherent to the substance rather than the person uses the same logic that is presently driving the American war on drug abuse, a movement that is focusing on trying to stop the flow of drugs rather than on restoring drug abusers to health.

technique and technology in solving all problems, even those that were not solely technical problems. But more than this, he believed that institutions that were not grounded in his very narrow view of nature were superfluous, much as alcohol and music are superfluous to the religious fundamentalist. Therefore, in his vision of the future city of health, Richardson opposed even profound religious practices, like the erection of tombstones, if they in any way undermined his precepts of health. In Richardson's completely rational mind the burial of the dead was to be little more than an exercise in replenishment of the soil. He wrote:

> The burial ground is artificially made of a fine carboniferous earth. Vegetation of rapid growth is cultivated over it. The dead are placed in the earth from the bier, either in basket work or simply in the shroud; and the monumental slab, instead of being set over or at the head or foot of a raised grave, is placed in a spacious covered hall or temple, and records simply the fact that the person commemorated was recommitted to earth in these grounds. In a few months, indeed, no monument would indicate the remains of any dead. In that rapidly-resolving soil the transformation of dust into dust is too perfect to leave a trace of residuum. The natural circle of transmutation is harmlessly completed, and the economy of nature conserved.[10]

Richardson's health prophecy, with its plethora of sterile and paternalistic precepts, was in some ways a sort of hypochondriac's heaven. Following ideals, this city of the future was to be constantly sterilized, or, to use the more modern term which has developed political connotations, it is forever being *disinfected*. It is not too difficult to imagine why *Hygeia* appealed to the educated and well-to-do Victorian public, but though parts of it may have appealed to their idealism, other parts must surely have appealed to the vanity and hypocrisy, rather than the logic, of those who actually read all of this little book.

What is most striking about this prophetic vision, now

that we have attained some distance from it, is that in this elaborate picture of a future city of health there are no recognizable, flesh-and-blood, all-too-human people—in a word, no individuals—except for the occasional caricatures of individuals which are so typical of the futurologist's portraiture. Richardson portrays the crazed and raving alcoholic but not the sometimes dull and sometimes witty, sometimes celebratory and sometimes silly, seldom inspiring but usually basically innocuous social drinker. Obsessively tied to precepts of health, Richardson's future society was prepared to expunge everything else of value in the human fabric from its midst. It was to be a society devoid of aesthetics, insensitive to religious sensibilities and unwilling or perhaps unable to distinguish between harmless little pleasures and harmful overindulgences. And, perhaps more important, devoid of choice and challenge. In the final analysis, Richardson's Hygeia is an extremely mechanical place, a sterile city in which the strongest emotions that one can imagine, if these can be called emotions at all, are contentedness and a feeling of safety. In the end, this little book reads more like a manual for good husbandry than a portrait of a human society.

Both *Hygeia* and *The Battle of Dorking* represent a battle fought and won. In the case of *The Battle of Dorking,* the battle was won by the wrong side, of course, but even this is as it should be because as warning this makes the prophecy even more salutary. In the end, whatever else it may be, *Hygeia* is also the story of a battle, the story of a victorious future war against all of the causes of disease. If the enemies are germs, then it is necessary to defoliate and eliminate their hiding places—even if these happen to be pictures on the wall or wallpaper. If the enemies are toxins, in whatever form or whatever quantity, in alcohol, tobacco, noise and pollution, then they too must be eliminated—*completely.* All of the precepts in *Hygeia* are based on the premise that the enemy is clear and obvious, can always be identified and, when identified, can be eliminated. These are the precepts of war.

We have seen how flawed and dangerous this kind of thinking can be in the context of war, and with respect to health it is, in some ways, just as flawed but not so obviously dangerous.† Yet this simplistic thinking is very attractive to futurologists. From their perspective we need above all to have a clearly defined enemy—in war as in the battle against disease—and on both types of battlefield it is always easier when we can persuade ourselves that the enemy is outside of us rather than within, that the enemy is another person or a thing rather than, as is often the case, ourselves.

Since Richardson's time, the war against disease has moved to new fronts. In our time there are three major schools of thought competing in the field of health care and, because modern prophecy is generally a projection of the present and usually likes to associate itself with some sort of power base, most of the innumerable health scenarios in the literature of health futurology represent one of these three. Character-istically, however, these scenarios are mere caricatures of the present. Whatever cooperation and tolerance may exist in the present complex health scene is banished from the future one, which is often portrayed as being both exclusive and intolerant. Ironically, therefore, along with the external battle against disease, we also have in the future world of health which these scenarios collectively portray a three-way civil war among the schools of thought. The three combatants in this civil war are physicians, purveyors of the so-called alternative therapies and health bureaucrats. Of course the seeds of all three schools of thought, along with the battle-front mentality, were already contained in germinal form in Richardson's future city of health, but there, at least, they did not compete. It took the modern rationalization and institutionalization of health care, with the accompanying growth of professional rivalry on the one hand and heavy pressure on national resources on the other, to create the present state of competition among the three sectors of the health care field. To end this rivalry and competition—which

† In our time we have even seen extreme and oversimplistic metaphors of health used to promote racism and applied to the most horrifying practices of war. As has been commonly observed, we have heard the term extermination applied to humans instead of to pests, all in the name of promoting the health of the fittest, who were eventually to become a master race. No more extreme form of social Darwinism is imaginable, yet it is easily enough buried in the metaphor of health.

naturally goes against the grain of most futurologists, who cannot bear to contemplate a "messy" world—what each of the three types of scenarios portrays, among other things, is the establishment of the domination of one school of health thought over all of the others.[11]

The first characteristic scenario is a description of the triumph of medical technology—the weapons in the war against disease—but also the triumph of physicians, the heroes who wield them. This scenario also, incidentally, describes the triumph of a basically unregulated laissez-faire marketplace for the provision of health care; somehow or other, physician heroes and the laissez-faire provision of health care services are deemed to belong together and destined to triumph together in the future world portrayed by this vision. The second type of future health care scenario has the patient as hero. He either eliminates disease by an act of will, metaphorically referred to by some futurologists as the "hospital-in-the-mind," or exercises his consumer sovereignty in what turns out to be a wonderfully varied health marketplace where he picks and chooses, at reasonable cost, the therapies he needs to heal himself. Needless to say, in this scenario the health consumer's completely rational approach to the maintenance of his health easily and naturally triumphs over any other drives that might motivate or defeat him. And the third type portrays the public health administrator in the role of soldier-hero. His weapons, not surprisingly, are legislation, public health programs and, as we shall soon see, the power to enforce them.

Unfortunately, over the years since Richardson published *Hygeia,* the mechanistic tendencies of health futurology have only increased—and, interestingly enough, so have its paternalistic tendencies. A brief glance at a fairly recent set of future health scenarios which are very representative of the three basic types I have just described demonstrate what I mean. The scenarios are published by the American Council of Life Insurance (ACLI) which sponsors an ongoing project called the Trend Analysis Program (TAP) to monitor trends in health care. The ones I have in mind are contained in a report called *Health Care: Three Reports from 2030 A.D.,* which is divided into three sections, each representing one of the three schools of thought in health futurology as well as in the field of health care in general.†

The first section, entitled "A Fifty Year Report from the American Association for the Advancement of Medical Technology 1980–2030," represents the school that believes that physicians and technology will continue to be the center of the health care system of the future just as they are today. Assuming the voice of the future historian, this section boastfully begins: "The stunning triumphs of the last half-century prove that most of our problems had technological solutions. Technology has extended man's medical prowess beyond the once-finite limits of cradle to grave. In the process, Americans have come close to eradicating disease, have created primitive forms of artificial life and appear to be on the verge of conquering death itself."[12] Many of the predictions which are made in this section of the insurance council report are just the sort of thing one might expect from a world view that feels that technology can and will solve any and all human problems. Human individuality in this view is not overtly avoided but, as was the case with the mechanical individualization of instruction, it is finessed in what are by now all too familiar terms: it is treated as a *problem,* a rationally definable problem with a mechanical solution. The report from 2030 A.D. glibly observes: "Preventive medicine has come to recognize that each individual is genetically and biochemically unique. This has meant that it is now routine to determine what occupational and lifestyle choices are optimal for newborn infants. . . . The use of computerized, problem-oriented record systems led to the creation and wide availability of model treatment profiles and higher standards for medical data. (Problem-oriented medical records noted *all the physiological, emotional, social and economic problems associated with a patient's life.*)"[13] (emphasis added)

Having trivialized the question of human individuality, both as problem and solution, by assuming it to be both

† Their methodology is the same as that used by Naisbitt to produce his newsletter and his book *Megatrends.* The way this project works is that over one hundred life insurance executives around the United States routinely monitor and prepare abstracts of relevant articles which may appear in any of a large number of designated publications. From time to time, these abstracts are summarized in reports to the life insurance industry and are then ostensibly drawn upon for the purposes of thinking about and planning for the industry's future.

comprehensible enough to be defined by rational terms and then simply absorbed into medical routine, the report then goes on to dispose of the physical problems of the human condition, large and small, with similarly unhesitating dispatch and with the neatest solutions: "The original breakthroughs in technologies for the handicapped were soon converted to augment the 'normals' who wanted, for example, to see in the dark, speak and eat at the same time, or regenerate limbs. . . . The computer in their 'hospitals on the wrist' can diagnose and suggest treatment for a disease before individuals even notice symptoms. . . . The recognition that senile dementia was caused by a virus and the ability to cure senility with anti-viral drugs saved many Americans from fear of aging. Initial tests of an anti-aging vaccine led to significant breakthroughs in 1997 and broad application by 2020."[14]

The elaborate pacemaker known in the health futurology trade as the "hospital-on-the-wrist" makes many appearances in the technology-driven model of future health care delivery. In some predictions, less constrained than the one above in describing its uses, these little machines get to make *automated* decisions. For example, Peter Goldschmidt of the Health Futures Project at the Policy Research Institute in Baltimore writes: "The hospital-on-the-wrist is the apex of medical technology. This device not only monitors body functions but also adjust them to maintain homeostasis."[15] How will the hospital-on-the-wrist adjust bodily functions to maintain homeostasis? This is spelled out in another version of this scenario by health futurologist Clement Bezold, who predicts that "such communications advances as the 'hospital on the wrist,' . . . monitors bodily functions and *administers appropriate doses of drugs and electrical charges directly through the skin.* (Remember when Dick Tracy's two-way wristwatch radio was science fiction?)" (emphasis added)[16] What is most striking about these hospital-on-the-wrist visionaries is that, aside from likening them to Dick Tracy radios, they seem unable to imagine how these devices might work out in real life situations, where even bodily states require context in order to be properly interpreted, understood and treated. It takes very little imagination to realize that, should these devices ever be developed for popular use, they would probably also be accompanied by newspaper accounts telling how hundreds of young people who had forgotten to reprogram their wrist-hospitals were carried out of rock concerts on stretchers, not on account of having fainted, but on account of having been oversedated by their sophisticated wrist-equalizers in reaction to the states of extreme excitation which are naturally produced at these events.

However, the reader should not imagine the American Association for the Advancement of Medical Technology to be naive in thinking that there will be no problems in introducing so much technological innovation into an ill-prepared society. It laments, for example, that "because technology has displaced so many health care workers, it has created a labor pool for services like the franchised Lov'n-Care stores. Clients now rent an older person for an hour or more to tell stories, soothe injured feelings, or just cuddle an ailing child."[17] It also observes that "problems with health care technology in the past often arose because society couldn't keep up with the hardware. Life and death ethical questions tended to overwhelm many proposed advances. Once we could directly modify and design organisms, new social forms were required to protect the democratic process. Today, of course, technology is being used to explore ethical questions more rapidly. It is possible for citizens all over the world to actively debate weighty social questions in a matter of hours."[18] The only thing that is missing from this scenario is that, given communication technology and the very short time frame allowed for these debates, they will undoubtedly be done with all of the incisiveness, conclusiveness and dispatch of a call-in radio show! Later on, this report also whimsically envisions that "parents are now able to choose personal characteristics for children, with very low incidence of selective abortion for defective (including wrong sex) children. . . . This has allowed expanded criteria for what is defective in children; what used to be considered merely unusual is now recognized as pathological. It also allows the design of special purpose humans. Some patriotic parents, for example, who wanted to maximize the United States' chance of winning Olympic gold medals were able to choose children with specific musculature potentials. (And there are even reports of the creation of rudimentary types of webbed feet for would-be swimmers)."[19]

The second section of the ACLI report, called "Comprehensive Report of the Cooperative Commission on Wellness 2030," describes a future scenario that ostensibly represents the philosophy of the alternative healing movement. It is not nearly as systematic or monolithic as the section reflecting the philosophy of the technophiles but is more of a hodgepodge caricature of New Age truisms. The great good that it promotes is the sovereignty and self-possession of the individual patient. It begins: "A cultural transformation has touched every aspect of Western industrial civilization, and as we all know, a change in the conceptual model of the world has an all pervading influence on the forms of human life and its institutions."[20] What is the nature of this "all pervading influence"? Well, for one thing, the report tells us that "trends in health care indicate that androgyny, or the realization of both masculine and feminine attributes in every individual, has become a cultural goal." A concept for explaining the sometimes ambiguous boundaries of sex will become a cultural goal? In that case, any state of being can become a policy goal, and so they do. Therefore, among the more enlightened members of this society, "it seems that human beings may have an innate biological awareness of their physical state down to the level of the single cell and that the human mind can intervene in and direct any physiologic function."[21] Furthermore, according to the philosophy of this school of future health thought, all disease is in the mind. For example, it observes that "comprehensive National Health Insurance bills failed to pass since the public had grown to recognize the ineffectiveness of such programs and place such great emphasis on individual responsibility."† For some reason or other, in this future nation of health, individual and collective responsibility for health are viewed as being mutually exclusive. If the individual takes responsibility for his or her own health, it simply leaves no room for the state, the natural enemy, to get involved even to facilitate individual decisions.

Of course this scenario, like its counterparts, also en-

---

† This view, of course, is a milder version of that stated by Plato in the *Republic*.

visions problems, but they are as much caricatures as the so-called solutions. The report observes that "professionals, particularly MDs, had an especially difficult time adjusting to the decreased reliance on professionals and more egalitarian relationships between professionals and consumers," and also that "research efforts were redirected because of the feeling that biomedical research could no longer rest on reductionist assumptions (e.g. separation of body/mind/spirit) which directed 20th century medicine. Throughout the closing years of the 20th century, researchers devoted themselves to finding techniques for *motivating wellness-enhancing behavior in populations that were not so inclined.*" (emphasis added)[22] Conclusion: since the mind is so important in controlling an individual's health, it is important that we discover ways of controlling the minds of those who are not inclined to control their own health as they ought to.

Of the three scenarios in this set, the one which is both the most direct heir to Richardson's *Hygeia,* and to Plato's relentless pursuit of "health justice" in the *Republic,* is the vision of the future in which public health triumphs over the other two as the dominant philosophy. It also happens to describe the most tyrannical future of all. Called "The National Health Caucus 2030 A.D.," this scenario begins, tamely enough, with the retrospective observation that "over the last half century, developments in two areas combined to create the enviable health care system we have today. Technology and political wisdom were those two areas, and it is our purpose now to briefly outline their simultaneous contributions to progress." But what passes for "political wisdom" and "progress" in this scenario, were it ever to come into being, would undoubtedly make a great many people in the year 2030 hanker for the good old days of political stupidity.

From this harmless little prelude the insurance council proceeds to sketch, in progressively more shocking terms, what can only be described not as "The City of Health" but rather as "The Third Reich of Health": "Perhaps the greatest administrative successes resulted from one simple Congressional directive issued in 1998. Everyone involved was to do whatever was necessary to find out which health care procedures really worked. . . . Model treatment data bases were set up describing those treatments which had been found effective, and were automatically triggered when the appropriate set of symptoms was entered into the computer. To reinforce the new system, penalties were imposed if it was discovered that model treatment plans had been ignored."[23] Presumably these penalties would be imposed even if, in certain cases, it could be demonstrated that a treatment other than the model treatment was more appropriate and effective. "Personnel in particularly hazardous occupations were monitored by remote control. Readings were then fed into a central data base and analyzed by personnel skilled in the early identification of actual and potential stressors. The unexpected success in the workplace led officials to conduct similar experiments in the home. Since, by 1990, many consumers used their two-way television systems to order goods, it became feasible to keep track of purchasing patterns. Hyperactive children who upset their biochemical balance by ordering candy bars, adults at high risk of divorce who placed numerous orders for sedatives and grandparents who were abusing recreational drugs could all be identified."[24] The authoritarian implications of this school of thought are inescapable: never underestimate the importance of knowing the enemy, even if it happens to be the unenlightened children, spouses and grandparents of the nation.

The report then continues along other lines that are still authoritarian but overtly more benign: "Citizens with criminal or anti-social tendencies can be monitored and prevented from doing themselves or others any harm. And there are hopes that by coordinating information about the gene pool, the government can help insure that only those most fit for a stressful environment encounter the challenges of today's world. One way to see that this happens is through the use of routine screening of the population for genetic markers. Counselors routinely use this information to help clients make decisions about how they should live. In some instances, of course, decisions have to be made for them." A simple program in eugenics to usher in the superior race, much as Plato hoped to do. "Everyone understood by the beginning of this century that health care costs were determined by the way people lived. To hold down costs and to promote public health, the government was forced to intervene in individual life decisions . . . it makes sense to ration potentially harmful substances and to treat people who pursue unwarranted risks as social criminals."[25] Rock climbers and hang-gliders, watch out!

The above scenarios all describe the future triumph of one school of health thought over the other two. However, in keeping with the social Darwinist tradition that originally set the stage for Richardson's *Hygeia,* some of our modern prophets even relish the struggle itself, that is, the competitiveness that reengineering and rebuilding our bodies ultimately implies. According to American health futurologist Jerrold Maxmen, the health future will hold some very interesting twists in the struggle for survival of the fittest. He writes:

> Despite nature's ingenious artistry, artificial devices may improve upon the human product, and eventually people may replace their organs freely. If so, humanity would enter a new stage of history in which the semiartificial man becomes a reality. Man and machine could be intermeshed so completely that the two would become indistinguishable. This hybrid, known as a "cyborg" (an abbreviation for cybernetic organism), would be capable of two-way communication between its human and mechanical parts. Computers and other sophisticated devices could be implanted in man to amplify his intellectual or physical powers. The potential implications are mind boggling. Pessimists fear that conflicts between men and cyborgs could lead to nothing less than a total annihilation of human culture. Conversely, optimists proclaim that eventually natural selection will allow cyborgs to dominate and enrich civilization."[26]

What is noteworthy about these two alternative scenarios is that whether the pessimists or the optimists are right does not really seem to matter in the sense that, in both cases, the "cyborgs" are predicted to be destined to win the struggle with ordinary human beings. In keeping with the mind-set of many forecasters in other fields, in this scenario the machine-human hybrids are once again expected to evolve further and be more successful than ordinary humans.

Later in this book, anticipating his critics, this prophet continues: "My opposition to social, legal, and theologically imposed restrictions of the development and use of biomedical innovations does not rest solely upon pragmatic considerations. If we are forced to follow absolute ethical standards that are not adjusted to historical change or individual need, our capacity to cope effectively with the future will be undermined. . . . We cannot and will not increase man's sense of free will by depriving him of the freedom to make his own ethical decisions."[27] Apparently this futurologist is unable to distinguish between freedom and license in medical ethics.

It is interesting, moreover, that for this modern-day prophet "coping effectively with the future" will necessitate, among other things, the adoption of Hobbesian postures of each against all. The apparent assumption behind this premise seems to be that those who are willing to buy into the new technologies deserve to triumph over their fellows. But the struggle for health supremacy is not always expressed in the graphic and vulgar terms of a war between ordinary humans and cyborgs.† Sometimes it becomes a simple class struggle and is expressed in the utilitarian terms of the dispassionate economist. This came out in a debate which was carried out at the National Heart and Lung Institute of the United States in 1973 on the appropriateness of developing a nuclear-powered artificial heart.

The program to develop a totally implantable artificial heart (TIAH), of which the nuclear-powered heart was the centerpiece, was initiated as a very large research and developmemnt program by the Johnson administration in the early 1960s shortly after Dr. Christiaan Barnard performed the first human heart transplant. The first artificial heart, designed by Domingo Liotta, was implanted in an American by the name of Haskell Carp in 1969, and sustained him for three days, whereupon it was replaced by a human heart

† One wonders what it takes to be considered a cyborg? Would an ordinary hip replacement do? When the warring factions are finally mustered at some point in the future, do people get to decide whether they want to be considered humans or cyborgs?

which sustained him for another thirty-six hours, and then he died. Carp's wife accused Dr. Denton Cooley, the surgeon who performed the operation, of making her husband "the unfortunate victim of human experimentation," and the FDA banned further artificial heart transplants until these machines and techniques for using them could be properly developed. The artificial heart that Cooley used had been privately developed. The NIH program, of which this device was not a part, was officially launched in 1964 with the establishment of the Artificial Heart Program Office. During one period in the artificial heart development project, the NIH collaborated with the Atomic Energy Commission in developing the nuclear-powered artificial heart, but bureaucratic infighting broke up this collaboration. NIH's program nevertheless grew very large, at one point being as large as the navy's program to develop the Trident missile. In 1973 dollars, a nuclear-powered artificial heart was projected to cost $25,000 for the appliance itself (mainly on account of the high cost of Plutonium-238) and another $15,000 for the surgical procedure.

Had the program succeeded, it would undoubtedly have ranked with the first moonshot as a great technological accomplishment. Several models of this mechanical heart were developed simultaneously, but the one which was at once most attractive to the NIH and most controversial was the nuclear-powered artificial heart. It was attractive because it would not require follow-up procedures for recharging the battery since, being nuclear, it would never require recharging. However it was controversial for several reasons: its production and dissemination would require supervision by the Atomic Energy Commission since it was to employ Plutonium-238; it presented a health hazard both to its user and to other people, especially potential offspring who would be at particular risk from radiation exposure; and it would be very expensive. A prototype was completed by Westinghouse by 1975, but it was abandoned because of its controversial nature.

Dissenting from the majority position of the advisory panel that rejected the nuclear heart, Prof. Clark Havighurst of Duke Law School began by accusing the majority of the panel of "moralizing." Then, after lamenting the fact that they had not come up with a set of "neutral values" upon which to make their judgment, he offered what he considered to be the following elegant solution to this problem:

> Sometimes, because the social arrangements being made today for the future do not benefit specific individuals at the expense of identifiable others, it may be possible to justify a pure utilitarian approach by viewing the stakes of individuals probabilistically, making each a possible gainer as well as a possible loser. Thus viewed, if potential gains exceed potential losses, the action might be deemed appropriate without concern for compensation of the actual losers. Difficulties remain, of course, if the advantages (disadvantages) are likely to accrue only to the more (less) affluent or to some other group to which all do not have a roughly equal expectation of belonging. But, even if compensation is impossible in such circumstances and injustice therefore inevitable, it may still be unjust not to take the action, since that would be to impose uncompensated costs (in the form of benefits denied) on the would-be beneficiaries. Justice demands not that perfect justice be done, for that is impossible, but that every effort be made to design public programs and the legal environment of private activities—if they are justified because the benefits outweigh the costs—so that uncompensated harms are minimized. It is hard to conceive of circumstances when it would not be wrong to require that a large benefit be forgone in order to avoid imposing a small harm.[28]

There is nothing original about Havighurst's arguments for developing the nuclear-powered artificial heart. Similar arguments were used to promote the development of nuclear power plants long before we knew anything about the effects of small doses of radiation. But by 1973, when Havighurst was writing the above dissent, there was already evidence that even very small doses were enough to cause cancer. This is spelled out in the report: the report acknowledges the fact that future recipients of nuclear-powered artificial hearts, although prolonging their lives by preventing heart failure, would nevertheless almost certainly assure themselves of later dying of leukemia or some other form of cancer induced by their appliance. If you unpack Havighurst's argument from its econo-legalistic wrapper and consider it in terms of real human beings, it is obvious why he stood alone against the rest of the committee.

Since Havighurst's was the dissenting opinion, this is partially a cautionary tale. But it is more than a merely cautionary tale because, although the project was eventually abandoned, the implications of its having been almost completely developed at great public expense, given how obviously ridiculous it was from the very outset, are rather disturbing. And, Havighurst's arguments are worth examining because they are so typical of the kinds of spurious arguments that are so often presented by our false prophets. In fact, his arguments are strikingly similar to the arguments offered by those who promoted the build-up of huge nuclear arsenals. These arguments are all calculation and probability, without taking into account either the enemies of calculability—human fallibility and irrationality—or the specific, real and palpable harm that can and will be done to the vast majority of vulnerable and uninformed people were the program put into operation.

What does it mean, for example, when thinking of the future that we should consider only probabilities and speak of small harms versus large benefits? It means that humans are, in effect, entirely removed from the picture. When you get cancer from low-level radiation, the severity of the cancer is not determined by the amount of radiation that started it, or by the probability that you might have got it in the first place, any more than the severity of a fall from a high precipice is determined by the strength of the push that sends the body plunging. Suppose the person to get cancer from exposure to radiation from someone else's nuclear heart were a child; it would most likely be the recipient's own child or grandchild. How would one weigh the value of the life that might be lost because of this exposure against the value that might be gained by the person whose nuclear heart is emitting the radiation? It takes little imagination to see how this new medical phenomenon, no matter what efforts were expended to regulate it, might play itself out in the singles dating scene, or in the context of nuclear terrorists who might be inspired to kidnap recipients of these nuclear-powered artificial hearts in order to steal the nuclear fuel that kept them going. But instead of these obvious considerations and a host of others, all that we get from Havighurst is a vain and sterile calculus of potential small harms versus potential huge gains.

Although each of the three factions in health futurology supposedly represents a different philosophy of health, in the final analysis they all have a great deal in common with one another and are also an elaboration of the world view expressed in Richardson's *Hygeia*. All three characteristically view the human population as being basically homogeneous, or if they recognize human individuality they either trivialize or depreciate it. They usually view the processes of staying well and healing as being basically mechanical— even the "hospital-in-the-mind" sounds more like an organization or a machine than a state of being. They typically display an unawareness of or insensitivity to the irrational side of human nature. And, just as classical economists assume that greed is the prime motivating drive in all economic affairs, they likewise assume that risk-avoidance functions the same way in the realm of health: they forget the side of human nature that might consider some risk-taking to be worthwhile, even essential to human existence, and the side that might consider self-sacrifice rather than selfishness appropriate human behavior; they forget even the great health *benefits* that may accrue from risk-taking and self-sacrifice. In the end, instead of celebrating the plurality of possible approaches to healing, health preservation and disease prevention that can concurrently exist, these futurist health scenarios are images of a future in which all approaches have been subordinated to one—either to the high-tech model, the public health model, or the self-help model—and that one is exaggerated to such a degree that it becomes a caricature of its present self, as well as a monster that preys upon all of the other approaches.

    Yet some of our modern-day prophets seem to delight

in pushing the caricature which health futurology has become to ever greater extremes. For example, Stanley Lesse, a psychiatrist turned futurologist, seems actually to relish predicting the demise of individuality in his vision of the health future. In his book *The Future of the Health Sciences* he writes that "in some ways individualism may be antithetical to basic human nature," and predicts:

> Individuals, rather than being preoccupied with their personal selves, will find it necessary to change their orientation, to fit themselves as part of an integrated group, in order to be accepted by their society—indeed, to survive. It is likely that they will strive to become an integral and, paradoxically, an easily replaceable element of the group. They will be dependent members of the interdependent structure, for it is from this source that they will gain their main physical, psychological, economic and philosophic nourishment. In turn, they will probably, as a matter of course, perform specific functions and tasks. In this process, certain of their capacities, functions, and possibly eventually even some of their body structure will change, with some areas undergoing atrophy and others hypertrophy.[29]

For Lesse, a real neo-Malthusian in psychiatrist's clothing, the individuality of patients seems to get in the way of efficient and effective delivery of health services. His book is heavily spiced with carping on this theme; one gets the sense in reading it that in the war against germs the individuality of the patient is an unnecessary luxury with which we simply must dispense in order to fight effectively. In another attack on humans as individuals he predicts: "Since patients will be group rather than individually oriented, they will probably have far fewer individual expectations as to treatment. Most likely they will not object to a more impersonalized type of care. These trends are already poignantly evident in socialist countries. Emphasis will be focused upon the need for patients to integrate themselves into the group as quickly as possible. Indeed, they will be constantly reminded of their position as subordinate members of the group by the very fact that treatment will be group oriented."[30] For this health futurist, it appears that the war is between the hero physician with his high-tech weapons and the enemy germs; the individual patient is merely the battleground where all of this takes place.†

The other side of Lesse's anti-individualist coin is a sort of dark glamorization of the most exaggerated and caricatured types of professionalism. Here we have no Philistines of the ordinary variety—only Goliaths. But whereas Goliath had a superiority complex, the health experts in Lesse's future have far more interesting complexes of their own, complexes that Lesse considers to be indispensable to doing the job right. For example, writing about the future of health academicians, his own professional group, he declares:

> One of the main functions of the health academician will be to interrelate human values, both individual and social with technologic phenomena. As he or she scans information drawn from any computer-health technical expert terms, various factors will be given properly weighed values.
>
> This will require that health academicians have unique characteristics. Their positions [sic] should be one in which there would be guaranteed recognition and status. . . . They would ideally also have the capacity to "love" other beings and have a love of humanity, in general, coupled with appreciation and respect for themselves, requiring a capacity to be at one with the cosmos or allness.[31]

† This brings to mind E.O. Wilson's briefly famous dictum—borrowed from Samuel Butler—that the organism is merely DNA's way of making more DNA. The extent to which ordinary humans are regarded as mere battleground was starkly spelled out by the eminent biologist J.S.B. Haldane in response to the problem of evolving resistant microbes that are the consequence of the development of antibiotics, "I think there may be enough intelligent people to deal with the emergence of resistent bacteria and the like. I am very glad that it is going to keep us on our toes, but we shan't be able to do it all by means of computers; we shall have to start thinking. Even if it means that a few million people will die prematurely every year, it is worth it in order to keep biologists on their toes, in my humble opinion." (J.S.B. Haldane, "Health and Disease," in *Man and His Future*, G. Wolstonholme [ed.], Boston, Little, Brown, 1963, p. 234.)

Elsewhere, never losing touch with his self-professed humanism (although for some reason in the above passage he feels inclined to put the word love in quotation marks), Lesse calls the health academician a "humanistic cybernator," which is basically a master computer programmer or systems analyst. Another master in Lesse's health future is the health technical expert, who has a fascinating set of personal problems of his own. Lesse predicts: "The health technical experts, in common with today's super specialists, will be obsessive-compulsive personalities. The collecting of data is likely to satisfy their psychodynamic needs. In contrast to the health academician, the health technical expert is likely to react with anxiety, if bombarded with new information, particularly information reflecting a dramatic technical change. In a parallel fashion, he or she would likely be distressed by information coming from sources other than the health sciences.[32]

Jerrold Maxmen, on the other hand, sets his sights on eliminating even physicians in the battle against germs. In his book, *The Post-Physician Era: Medicine in the Twenty-first Century,* Maxmen predicts the demise of the physician sometime during the first half of the twenty-first century. He argues that physicians will disappear for a number of reasons but mainly because they will be too expensive to maintain. Furthermore, they will have outgrown their usefulness by then because technology will be able to perform most of their tasks better than they themselves can. But since, as we all know, technology cannot quite perform all of its tasks on its own, who then will replace physicians to perform, if nothing else, their mediating function between patients and machines? Well, for starters, technicians, of course, will help patients get into the space-suit type monitors that they will feel inclined to don from time to time to keep track of their health. But what about the other needs of patients, the human needs that are so often touted nowadays? Well, to satisfy these needs another kind of specialist will be introduced onto the scene. Asserting the futurologist's prerogative of renaming things in order to bestow novelty upon them, Maxmen calls this new professional a "medic," and has him specialize in two things. First, though his training will be suspiciously similar to the training of physicians today, the medic will make a point of not using the outmoded name "physician." And second, he will specialize in being human. What will this mean? According to Maxmen it will mean, among other things, that he will become a pro at cultivating what is commonly referred to as bedside manner—but not like an amateur, like a professional. He will be rather like a psychiatrist or clinical psychologist—like Maxmen himself—and he will master categorical formulas such as Kahana and Bibring's seven personality patient-types—presumably so that he can treat each patient like an individual human being![33]

Between the rampant anti-individualism of most health futurists and the worship of superspecialization of some, it is impossible to conclude that they are actually writing about a human society, one in which conscious individuals make decisions by the day, by the hour, and by the minute, and take actions, both rational and irrational, which ultimately affect their health. Instead they seem to be writing about a society of social bees, in which most members function merely as thoughtless drones while a few individuals, equally thoughtless but more exalted in stature, play the heroic roles like that of queen. Obviously, such a society would have little to commend itself to most people, but it has one advantage that must make it eminently attractive to the banal minds of these futurologists: it appears to be perfectible. That which is static, as all of these images to all intents and purposes are, can conceivably be perfected. That is the delusion, and that is the obvious appeal of these future health visions. René Dubos has observed:

> A perfect policy of public health could be conceived for colonies of social ants or bees, whose habits have become stabilized by instincts. Likewise, it would be possible to devise for a herd of cows an ideal system of husbandry with the proper combinations of stables and pastures. But unless men become robots, their behavior and environment fully controllable and predictable, no formula can ever give them permanently the health and happiness symbolized by the contented cow. Free men will develop new urges, and these will give rise to

new habits and new problems, which will require
ever new solutions. New environmental factors are
introduced by technological innovations, by the
constant flux of tastes, habits, and mores, and by
the profound disturbances that culture and ethics
exert on the normal play of biological processes. It
is because of this instability of the physical and
social environment that the pattern of disease
changes with each phase of civilization.[34]

One can immediately see how deadly these visions are by
simply considering what is happening in health developments
in the present. How is one to account, in these static visions,
for recent cultural developments that have already had, and
promise to continue to have, a profound effect on our health?
We are living during a period, for example, when exercise
has again become a craze; but it is also a period when sports
medicine has become a rapidly growing specialty. Speaking
more esoterically, we are also living during the beginning of
the age of space exploration, and during the beginning of
the development of a specialty in space medicine. These are
the sorts of changes that Dubos had in mind when he wrote,
"Free men will develop new urges, and these will give rise
to new habits and new problems, which will require ever
new solutions." All of these urges represent unanticipated
new experiences, and sometimes risks. They do not, however, represent utopia or paradise on earth. Yet in 1958,
following steadfastly in the steps of Richardson's childish
vision, Dr. Axel Hojer of the World Health Organization
(WHO) wrote that "man seems to have found out how to
make his dreams of a paradise on earth come true," and
around the same time Dr. M.G. Candau, Director-General
of WHO predicted that "if the great advances gained in
science and technology are put at the service of all the people
of the world, our children will live in an age from which
most of the diseases our grandparents and parents took for
granted will be banished. It may no longer be Utopian to
envisage a new chapter in the history of medicine."[35]
    Of course, notwithstanding all of this existential cheer-
leading, there are and always will be perils ahead. The sit-

uation remains much the same as Dubos described it in 1959 when he wrote: "Who could have dreamt a generation ago that hypervitaminosis would become a common form of nutritional disease in the Western world? That the cigaret industry and the use of x-rays would be held responsible for the increase in certain types of cancers? That the introduction of detergents and various synthetics would increase the incidence of allergies? That advances in chemotherapy and other therapeutic procedures would create a new staphylococcus pathology? That alcoholism would become widespread in the Western world? That patients with all forms of iatrogenic diseases would occupy such a large number of beds in modern hospitals?"[36]

Dubos is not a pessimist, but as a biologist, he has come to realize that medicine will never become a finished science like chemistry because, though the number of elements in the universe seems now to be finite, the number of things that can and will threaten our health is not, and as we evolve as a species, so do they. As we adapt to the microbes that threaten our health, new ones, like the AIDS virus, continue to emerge. As we eliminate some of the toxins we have created, we create, willy-nilly, others to replace them. As we eliminate or avoid some forms of stress, others emerge in our ever changing culture. And beyond this, we are constantly redefining what health is and how we should think of it. This is not a pessimistic view, but the human condition as it has ever been. Nor is it cause for despair, because the microbes are merely one type of thing that challenges us.

The alternative to the change and flux which is now, as always, largely of our own making, is a sterile, static culture. But a sterile, static culture is precisely what, in different ways, most of our health futurists are describing—when they are not too busy describing superman or superbureaucrat or some other sort of vain vision. Yet between their visions of doctors chasing germs, programs chasing people and people chasing therapies, all at an increasingly frenzied pace, there seems to be little room for the day-to-day individual decision-making which makes the greatest difference in all of our health futures. This is why Dubos wisely observed a quarter of a century ago:

While it may be comforting to imagine a life free
of stresses and strains in a carefree world, this will
remain an idle dream. Man cannot hope to find
another paradise on earth, because paradise is a
static concept while human life is a dynamic process. Man could escape danger only by renouncing
adventure, by abandoning that which has given to
the human condition its unique character and ge-
nius among the rest of living things. Since the days
of the cave man, the earth has never been a Garden
of Eden, but a Valley of Decision where resilience
is essential to survival. The earth is not a resting
place. Man has elected to fight, not necessarily for
himself, but for a process of emotional, intellectual,
and ethical growth that goes on forever. To grow
in the midst of dangers is the fate of the human
race, because it is the law of the spirit.[37]

Perhaps more than any other area of modern prophecy,
health futurology from Richardson on down likes to envision
what can only be described as the erasure of human decision-
making from day-to-day life, delegating most of it to machines or experts. Therefore, more than any other field of
modern prophecy, it envisions and promotes what Huxley
called "civilized infantility," the infantilization of the human
race. More than this, in the end these visions are all static
and contain a belief that change is the great enemy that must
incessantly be striven against. But that which is static is also
sterile, and all three of the major schools of thought of future
health are ultimately visions of sterility. They are decidedly
not visions, like Dubos's, of healthy adaptation to, and struggle with, change. In fact, they are visions in which change,
which must include some sickness, is regarded as being decidedly unhealthy. Therefore they are visions in which
change, if not entirely abolished, is at least completely controlled. In these visions, the powerful medical concept of
homeostasis (the way in which the body is constantly striving
to regain its equilibrium) is transmogrified from the fluid
concept which true scientists know it to be—recognizing that
after any change nothing returns again to being exactly what
it was before—to a caricature of itself, a static term, an icon

that wants to be worshipped in order to achieve . . . what? At bottom, one suspects that the sterile and static concepts that govern these visions of the health future, along with the characteristic obsession with control of the mechanically regarded human body, are as close as these futurologists can get to envisioning immortality.

NOTES

1. There are any number of books in the market today which cater to this mood, but probably the most popular recent one is *Life Extension* by Durk Pearson and Sandy Shaw. However, books like *Life Extension* are not uniquely twentieth-century phenomena that reflect the special nature of twentieth-century medical science. Rather, they are published whenever medical science seems to be gaining the upper hand. For example, at the end of the nineteenth century, when the most ravaging diseases were finally receding in Europe and medical science was once again beginning to feel confident in its powers, C.W. Hufeland published a similar book called *The Art of Prolonging Life*.
2. René Dubos, *Mirage of Health: Utopias, Progress and Biological Change* (Garden City, N.Y.: Doubleday & Company, 1959), p. 135. I am greatly indebted to this book, whose wisdom remains compelling even over a quarter of a century after it was written, for many of the perspectives I have gained about modern health futurology.
3. Hippocrates, "The Book of Prognostics," in *Hippocrates*, W.H.S. Jones and E.T. Whitington (ed. and trans.) (London: Heinemann, 1931), vol. 2, p. 7.
4. Plato, *Republic* (London: Oxford University Press, 1945), III, 410a.
5. James H. Cassedy, "Hygeia: A Mid-Victorian Dream of a City of Health," *Journal of the History of Medicine* (April 1962), p. 226.
6. Max von Pettenkofer was a pioneer public health practitioner in early nineteenth-century Germany. He persuaded the city fathers of Munich to institute simple sanitary measures like street cleaning, and sewage and garbage removal, and achieved dramatic results.
7. Dubos, *Mirage of Health*, pp. 68–69.
8. Benjamin Ward Richardson, *Hygeia: A City of Health*, address to the Social Science Association, Health Section (London: Social Science Association, 1876), pp. 29–30.
9. Richardson, p. 38.
10. Richardson, pp. 43–44.
11. Or sometimes the future is regarded as a *terra sancta* for the sake of which all fighting parties must lay down their arms. See, for example, Susan Jackson, "Health Planning in Turbulent Times," in *Man-Environment Systems* (September/November 1984).
12. American Council of Life Insurance (ACLI), *Health Care: Three Reports from 2030 A.D.* (Washington: American Council of Life Insurance, 1980), p. 3.
13. ACLI, pp. 3, 5.
14. ACLI, p. 4.
15. Peter G. Goldschmidt, "Health 2000" (Baltimore: Policy Research Institute, 1982), p. 12.
16. Clement Bezold, "Health Care in the U.S.: Four Alternative Futures," *Futurist* (August 1982), p. 17.

17. ACLI, p. 6.
18. ACLI, p. 5.
19. ACLI, pp. 5–6.
20. ACLI, p. 8.
21. ACLI, pp. 10, 11.
22. ACLI, pp. 10, 12.
23. ACLI, pp. 16–17.
24. ACLI, pp. 17–18.
25. ACLI, pp. 14–18.
26. Jerrold Maxmen, *The Post-Physician Era* (New York: Wiley, 1976), p. 181.
27. Maxmen, p. 214.
28. National Heart and Lung Institute, *The Totally Implantable Artificial Heart* (Washington: National Heart and Lung Institute, June 1973), pp. 235–236.
29. Stanley Lesse, *The Future of the Health Sciences* (New York: Irvington Publishers, 1981), p. 28.
30. Lesse, p. 28.
31. Lesse, p. 129.
32. Lesse, p. 131.
33. Maxmen, p. 223.
34. René Dubos, "Medical Utopias" in *Daedalus* (Summer 1959), p. 412.
35. Cited in Dubos, "Medical Utopias," pp. 413–414. Over a quarter of a century later, on the eve of the outbreak of the AIDS epidemic, and in light of the persistent intractability of certain diseases like cancer, cardiovascular disease, and mental illness, the WHO continued dauntlessly but somewhat more cautiously with this kind of forecasting, but by then the predictions were framed in a list of platitudes. Writing as true heirs to Richardson they predict: "Health for all does not mean that in the year 2000 doctors and nurses will provide medical care for everybody in the world for all existing ailments; nor does it mean that in the year 2000 nobody will be sick or disabled. It does mean that health begins at home, in schools and in factories. It is there, where people live and work, that health is made or broken. It does mean that people will use better approaches than they do now for preventing disease and alleviating unavoidable disease and disability, and have better ways of growing up, growing old and dying gracefully. It does mean that there will be an even distribution among the population of whatever resources for health are available. It does mean that essential health care will be accessible to all individuals and families in an acceptable and affordable way, and with their full involvement. And it does mean that people will realize that they themselves have the power to shape their lives and the lives of their families, free from the avoidable burden of disease, and aware that ill-health is not inevitable." (WHO, *Global Strategy for Health for All by the Year 2000*, pp. 31–32.)
36. Dubos, "Medical Utopias," p. 415.
37. Dubos, *Mirage of Health*, p. 230.

Our most serious problem, perhaps, is that we have become a nation of fantasists. We believe, apparently, in the infinite availability of finite resources.
—WENDELL BERRY

7

FUTUREHYPE ABOUT THE ENVIRONMENT

The most puzzling thing about the environmental movement, now that it has taken hold of the consciousness of vast numbers of the world's population, is that it was so long in coming. After all, predictions of environmental disaster have been around for centuries, and, in a way, their appeal would seem to be almost undeniable, having the logic and simplicity of the bathtub filling up. Yet it is probably fair to say that only since the dramatic discovery by scientists in 1986 of the development of a hole in the ozone layer has there been a large-scale popular awakening about environmental matters.

It is a commonplace to blame the late blooming of environmental consciousness on the all too common economic blinders of shortsightedness and greed, and there is undoubtedly a great deal of truth to this critique. But the world's earlier lack of consciousness about the environment is due to flaws in modern economic thinking that are much more profound than these two little demons suggest. Some of the incompetence of modern economic thinking is reflected in the telling fact, which a number of critics have observed, that pollution control is presently a greater priority in national and international policy than resource conservation "because pollution affects the present generation immediately, whereas the global endowment of energy and materials concerns future generations."[1] It is important to understand the reasons for our recent lack of consciousness about environmental issues, because if we do not understand them we will probably go back to being oblivious to the environment again after having made only a few cosmetic changes in the way we live. As it is, environmental consciousness is already being anesthetized by political babble and commercial cooptation. But, more important, it is systematically being undermined by modern economic thought, which is inept at understanding the world of nature except in the most superficial ways and therefore constitutionally incompetent at planning for the future of the earth.

There is a memorable little episode in Tolstoy's *Anna Karenina* that nicely illustrates one aspect of this ineptitude. It begins when a Moscow aristocrat, Prince Stepan Oblonsky, goes to visit his friend, Konstantin Levin, who owns and works a large estate in the country. Although the two friends go hunting together, it turns out that the real purpose of Oblonsky's visit is to sell a wood in the neighborhood of Levin's property to a dealer called Ryabinin. But when the Prince reveals the terms of the upcoming deal to his friend, Levin immediately realizes that Oblonsky is going to be underpaid by the shrewd dealer and bluntly tells him so. All to no avail. It is obvious from their conversation that Levin's good advice is going to be lost on Oblonsky because the Prince is sure he knows what he is doing and is determined to carry on. By the way Tolstoy describes their bantering about this matter you can tell that the author is himself a farmer. He writes:

"Oh, these farmers!" Oblonsky said jokingly. "Your tone of contempt for us poor city dwellers!

But when it comes to business, we do it better than anyone. Believe me, I've taken everything into account," he went on, "and the wood has been sold for a good price. Indeed, I am afraid he may change his mind. You see, it's not standing trees," said Oblonsky, hoping by the term 'standing trees' to convince Levin of the unfairness of his doubts, "but mostly only good for fuel. And it won't yield more than about forty cubic yards of wood per acre, and he's paying me at the rate of seventy rubles the acre."[2]

In the end, Oblonsky does indeed go ahead with the deal and, from the way he portrays the transaction, Tolstoy makes it clear that the Prince really does get taken. But Levin, acutely aware of the relationship between wealth and natural resources, is tenacious—and perhaps also a little ungracious—in his attitude about all of this, so afterwards he will not let his friend live this foolishness down and continues to needle him. Finally, in utter exasperation, Oblonsky asks, "Well, what would you have me do? Count every tree?" To which the farmer tersely replies, "Certainly count them. You have not counted them, but Ryabinin has. Ryabinin's children will have the means to live and to get an education, while yours may not!"[3]

This little episode is, of course, the opposite of the usual tale of the country bumpkin being taken by the city slicker, but there is a lot more to it than a lesson in the difference between real and pseudo-sophistication. At one point in their conversation Levin calls Oblonsky "innocent," and, in a sense, he really is. Oblonsky's wood, as Levin wisely observes, is no more to him than a monetary asset whose value he calculates from clever, but in this case ultimately empty, economic abstractions—"standing trees," "yield," "cubic yards per acre." Now, one might like to think that Oblonsky's "innocence" reflects no more than his impractical nature or the inadequacy of his own economic training, but that would be taking too narrow a view.

Oblonsky, like most city dwellers, is not only out of

touch with the natural world, but alienated from it. But, more to the point, not only is *he* alienated from the natural world but *economics,* the discipline which he uses to try to understand the material world, is also alienated from it. Even though the world of nature makes up the largest part of our material world and is the ultimate source of wealth, economics, the social discipline which is supposed to improve our happiness by giving us insight into our relationship with the material world, has, at best, a very tenuous grounding in the natural world—and this is true of both streams of modern economic thought, neoclassical as well as the now beleaguered Marxist school.

Probably the most important reason the environment is such a late bloomer in modern consciousness is that it has for centuries been systematically excluded from our thinking about the world by modern economic theory. It is worth remembering that Tolstoy was roughly contemporary not only with Karl Marx but also, on the other side of the spectrum of economic theory, with Vilfredo Pareto, Stanley Jevons, Leon Walras and the other major originators of modern economic thinking. Tolstoy wrote *Anna Karenina* in 1870 when he was in late middle age, but by that time most of the elements of modern economic thought were already in place. However, although Tolstoy's fictional character, Oblonsky, was merely a silly snob about his citified, pseudo-sophisticated economic thinking, Marx went so far as to hold rural culture in contempt, assigning to it the famous epithet "rural idiocy"—in spite of the fact that it was only due to the high level of productivity of those who worry and toil in the country that city dwellers like himself were able to live free of the burden of having to raise their own food.

Because of the obtuseness of the architects of modern economic thinking about environmental matters, Nicholas Georgescu-Roegen, the famous economist and philosopher of science, has written that they "succeeded so well with their grand plan that the conception of the economic process as a mechanical analogue has ever since dominated economic thought completely. In this representation, the economic process neither induces any qualitative change nor is affected by the qualitative change of the environment into which it is anchored. It is an isolated, self-contained and ahistorical process—a circular flow between production and consumption with no outlets and no inlets, as the elementary textbooks depict it." And, to emphasize the almost complete alienation of the quantitative overview of economics from the qualitative world we live in, this economist then goes on to note, "Economists do speak occasionally of natural resources. Yet the fact remains that, search as one may, in none of the numerous economic models in existence is there a variable standing for nature's perennial contribution. The contact some of these models have with the natural environment is confined to Ricardian land,† which is expressly defined as a factor immune to any qualitative change. We could very well refer to it simply as 'space.' "[4]

It is an indication of the deeply flawed nature of modern economics that it does not even provide us with adequate terms and concepts with which to think about the environment. On the contrary, when economic theory is confronted with certain kinds of environmental problems it tries to deal with them by systematic avoidance. The extent of this pathology is reflected in a formal economic concept that epitomizes this avoidance, the notion of external economies or externalities.

Simply speaking, an externality is an unintended consequence of an economic process or transaction, and it may be negative or positive. To cite a classic example, a negative externality occurs when a train transporting goods across a farmer's field sets fire to the crops adjacent to the track with sparks from its engine. When this happens, the problem in classical economics is that then the railway, or an insurance company in the railway's behalf, is required to compensate the farmer, and the cost of this compensation, which was not anticipated by the original economic calculations, becomes an "added" expense of doing business. Now the compensation can be sorted out in different ways: the railway can either pay the farmer the value of crops that are actually

† After David Ricardo (1772–1823), an English economist who developed a theory of rent.

destroyed or pay him a lesser value, equal to his potential profit from these crops, to discourage him from growing them near the tracks in the first place. Obviously, however it does get sorted out, this additional expense would naturally make transportation more expensive—but the point is that it is *dealing with the added expense* that is considered the real problem in the theory of externalities, not that the transportation does damage to the environment and/or may result in removing food from the market.

Clearly there are countless negative externalities which are more general than crop burning and therefore more difficult to assess. In fact, in principle, every incidence of pollution can properly be considered an externality of our economic processes because someone must pay for it one way or another somewhere down the line. Not surprisingly, it is in terms of this kind of economic thinking, which is, quite obviously, heavily based on the precepts of private property rights, that many classical economists, especially of conservative tendencies, are presently trying to deal with the problem of pollution and solve it for the future.

For example, in a recent article in the *National Review,* Fred Smith and Kathy Kushner write, "The most common cause of environmental degradation is a lack of clearly defined and transferrable property rights in the resource in question. If a thing has no owner then no one has an incentive to care for it. Few will act to safeguard or enhance the property of others."[5] From this premise Smith and Kushner make an elaborate argument for privatizing everything from wildlife preserves to air spaces. They assume that everything will be cared for and protected once it is simply owned by private individuals. It is difficult to imagine on what they base this assumption unless it is the common orderliness of middle-class *domestic* life. However, outside the domestic sphere, and sometimes even within it, there is only very limited reason to assume that proprietors will always protect and preserve what they own—especially if protection runs into conflict with exploitation. One of the things that Smith and Kushner blatantly ignore in their vision are the effects of absentee ownership: why not clear-cut your tract of timber wood if you do not live in or beside it and do not have to look at it afterwards?

In the end, the theory of externalities, far from being a promising solution to the problem of pollution, is really no more than a striking indication of the ineptness of economics in dealing with the environment. The real point of a negative externality, from the point of view of the environment and not of economic theory, is that unless the economic actors can force each other to pay for an external damage, for all intents and purposes the damage simply does not exist. Smith and Kushner's view is that there is nothing wrong with the economic engine that expanding it cannot cure. They imagine that through increased appropriation and litigation the economic engine will eventually include all of nature and thus automatically cure all of our environmental ills. Their vision of privatizing the whole world and then settling all infringements through negotiation and litigation is mind-boggling. It begins with the impossible task of causally tracing and assessing all incidents of trespass and ends with the equally impossible task of knowing when, where, and what to privatize at any given point in history. (As far as the second problem is concerned we should not forget that when oil was first discovered gurgling spontaneously up from the ground it was considered a contaminant and a nuisance.) Clearly externalities is a paltry precept for dealing with the enormous and pervasive problem of pollution, but the inability of classic economics to deal with environmental issues goes much deeper than the theory of externalities can even begin to suggest.

The fundamental flaw in economic thought is its mechanistic nature.[6] Now, the basic characteristic of mechanics is that it cannot account for *qualitative* change, that is, for a change that not only has never occurred before but may be irreversible, like the development of the hole in the ozone layer. According to the precepts of classical mechanics, all of nature is an enormous machine in which everything that goes forward can also always go backward like a pendulum or water turning to steam and back to water again. Since the mechanistic nature of economics makes it incapable of properly understanding qualitative change, it also alienates it from the environment, because most changes in the environment, like the pollution of a body of water or the erosion and exhaustion of soil, are manifestly qualitative. But until the appearance of the hole in the ozone layer these changes have, because of the narrowness of the economic perspective, been assumed to be susceptible to quantitative calculation. Higher interest rates, lower interest rates—the environment gets a little dirtier and then a little cleaner—the "economic engine" understands all operations only in terms of thinking that holds that all processes are, at least in principle, reversible. The development of the hole in the ozone layer was the first qualitative change to demonstrate dramatically and irrefutably that economic activity can have irreversible results that are detrimental to human welfare. Needless to say, precisely because it is a qualitative change and out of the perspective of mechanistic thinking, no one predicted it would happen.

Because no one predicted it would happen, the appearance of the hole in the ozone layer has lent the prognosticators of ecological doom, who have of course long been with us, a great deal of credibility. This is not because it vindicates their method, which is also decidedly mechanistic, but because it vindicates their outlook, which is bleak. When you look at them closely, the prophets of environmental doom are little more insightful and no more spiritually attractive than their counterparts who predict that endless rounds of technological innovation will solve all environmental problems that develop while the material standard of living of the world increases without abatement. In the end both kinds of environmental extremists, the doomsayers and the optimists, like their counterparts in politics, have a mechanistic view of the world and a childish view of human culture because they believe either too much or too little in the efficacy of human adaptation.

All of this was first brought home to me when I was a tutor in graduate school and the faculty associated with my residence convened a special colloquium to discuss Robert Heilbroner's book *An Inquiry into the Human Prospect,* which had just been serialized in *The New York Review of Books.*[7] Heilbroner's book is a vision of doom and gloom in the old tradition of Thomas Malthus and Stanley Jevons and in the more current genre of the Club of Rome's *Limits to Growth.*[8][†] At this colloquium two of the three speakers stood up and advised the audience not to worry about Heilbroner's thesis. One of them, Daniel Bell, observed that although the prophets of doom have always been with us, they have never been right. On the other hand, Roger Revell gave us a talk about the earth's seemingly endless resources and the seemingly infinite ways we may potentially be able to tap them. At that seminar the so-called optimists outnumbered the so-called pessimists—and, in any case, if you did not probe into the matter any more deeply than our speakers did, the optimistic and pessimistic prophecies seemed to cancel each other out so we were still able to enjoy our after-dinner drinks.

But if you did probe into the matter more deeply this was hardly the case. Take, for example, the Club of Rome's report, *The Limits of Growth,* and look at its fate. Looking back at that set of predictions now most people who are not sympathetic with it will say that the model was all wrong; those who are sympathetic will say the model was right but the variables were wrong. This is the short of it—the longer critique of the report had a much more elaborate form and its fallacies are worth recounting because they reflect much of what is pathological in current thought about the future of the environment.

For example, in the March 1975 issue of *Science* Glenn Hueckel published a critical analysis of the limits-to-growth thesis called "A Historical Approach to Future Economic Growth," which illustrates two of three great myths that contemporary prophets have promoted to sully our thinking about the environmental future.[9] One of these myths is that the marketplace will solve our environmental problems as they develop, the other is that technological innovation will always have the power to do the same thing.

† Thomas Malthus (see page 83) was the eighteenth-century English economist who predicted that England would starve at some point in the future because the growth of population was outstripping the growth of food production. He was proven wrong first through the import of surplus food from the New World and later by technological innovation. Stanley Jevons was a nineteenth-century English economist who, in a book called *The Coal Question,* predicted the demise of English industry because of the depletion of coal. He was proven wrong in the short run by the discovery of vast new reserves in America and in the long by the switch to petroleum—although English industry did eventually decline for other reasons.

These two myths are, of course, related, and Hueckel cites a typical example to illustrate how this works. In 1920 the chief geologist of the U.S. Geological Survey reported that only seven billion more barrels of oil could be recovered using existing techniques. He then predicted that at the contemporary rate of consumption the U.S. would run out of domestic supplies by 1934. But by the time that fateful year arrived, due to increasing demand twelve, not seven, billion barrels had been pumped out of the ground and there remained another twelve billion barrels of proved reserves. How did this miracle occur? Quite simply. As consumption proceeded and diminished supply, prices naturally rose, making it economically feasible to initiate hitherto uneconomical technological innovation and to make possible further, more costly, exploration and recovery.[10]

It would be nice to think that all of this is as it should be, and indeed many people seem to think just that, but this is an insupportably narrow view. Rising prices may make all sorts of development feasible, but they do not have a neutral effect on the economy or the environment. As prices for any given commodity rise that commodity consumes an ever greater part of a nation's resources, often with diminishing returns. This is precisely what is happening now in the United States as rising health care costs each year consume a larger part of the GNP. But this problem is exacerbated in the case of the rising price of a commodity like oil because it figures in the manufacture of a vast number of other commodities whose prices also rise.

Now all of this may be all right or even a good thing in the short run in an economy like that of the United States which is heavily capitalized and can therefore handle some of this dislocation and reallocation of resources. Rising prices may also even entail the benefit of reducing pollution by reducing consumption. But consider the effect of rising prices on poorer, less developed economies.

It is easy enough for an economist like Hueckel to be complacent about escalating prices of non-renewable resources. The United States, where Hueckel does his thinking, effectively had the privilege of a subsidized development because it occurred at a time before there existed international market pressure on non-renewable resources which would later drive the price up. He can therefore ignore the fact that presently developing countries, which are, in some respects, living in the U.S. past, have to develop in the context of severe market pressure. But price rises—whether they result from increased production expenses due to the capitalization of technology or can simply be attributed to economic cartel—affect the poorer countries more than the rich ones, as has consistently been demonstrated ever since OPEC hiked its prices in the early 1970s. This fact is seldom properly appreciated in the developed nations. In some ways, the most difficult thing for a developing nation to do is accumulate the reserve of capital that will make it resourceful enough to be responsive to changing economic conditions. An advanced economy's solution to rising prices is based on vast capital reserves which make stockpiling and technological innovation possible, but the lack of these reserves is precisely the problem of developing nations in a world market.

In a sense the relationship between poorer countries and richer ones is the same as the relationship between present and future generations. The point is that the price of a commodity does not necessarily represent its true value, because only those living at present can bid for it. If the commodity is based on a non-renewable resource, like oil, whose price has risen and will continue to rise in the future, then the market would only work equitably if future as well as present generations could bid on the commodity. Similarly, the market for oil could only work equitably if poorer, less developed nations could buy it as cheaply now as the developed nations did when they were starting out.

As to the ability of technology to keep providing the world with new sources of power, the picture is also not nearly as rosy as the market/innovation school would lead one to believe. For one thing, we need to get out of our minds the notion that the necessary technology for retrieving and generating energy will, like calculators and computers, always decrease in price and to bear in mind the common fact that most nuclear power plants have come on line at prices far above those predicted—which is to say nothing of the long-term cost of nuclear waste disposal, which will be dearer to future generations than to our own. On the other

hand, the idea that the development of nuclear fusion technology will solve all the world's energy problem from the
point it is commercially feasible until the end of time is one
of the most misleading notions of our time. As long as it is
credible, it is bound to hinder the kinds of changes that entail
a more sane and sensible approach to energy use. Ever since
we left the period when wood and coal were our main sources
of energy, there has always been a fantastic notion that there
exists an infinite supply of energy somewhere. This futuristic
fantasy is the modern counterpart in an age of disenchant-
ment—or enchantment only with scientific things—to the
genie in the bottle who can create infinite wealth out of thin
air. In the nineteenth century electricity, which is itself,
strictly speaking, not a form of energy but a method for
transforming and transporting other forms of energy, was
considered to be such a source—perhaps because one could
not see it being used up as one can see coal or wood used
up while one is burning it. In our time ordinary fission reactors were given the same attribute when they were first
introduced in the 1950s, and then the so-called breeder reactors were endowed with it in the 1970s. Now it is the turn
of nuclear fusion—but this time it is even before a single
viable fusion reactor has even been built.

If it should ever come, the price of infinite energy promises to be very dear for any foreseeable future. Jeremy Rifkin
has pointed out a few of the astounding difficulties entailed
in nuclear fusion technology: (1) The deuterium-tritium
model of the reactor, which is now the focus of development,
is based on lithium, niobium and vanadium, all elements
which are found in limited supply in the earth, and the first
of which is dangerous to mine. (2) The hydrogen reactor, if
it is ever developed, will have to operate at three billion
degrees centigrade, and no known substance is able to contain such temperatures. (3) Fusion plants will still produce
enormous amounts of nuclear waste every year. (4) The costs
of building these plants will be enormous and capital inten-
sive, which means not only that the energy will be expensive
but its production will not happen on a really competitive
basis because there will be very few players who can enter
at such stakes.[11] This is what technological genies cost, and

yet fusion is still being thoughtlessly billed as the latest panacea.

The third myth with which we have been anesthetized by thoughtless modern prophets is the notion that we are entering the age of post-industrial society. Supposedly we are about to enter or have already entered an age where information is the basis of economy, and in some versions of this vision because we are all, or will all be, trading in services rather than goods we will no longer draw on the earth's resources.[12] The notion of post-industrial society is based on certain trends in the industrialized nations and a very narrow view of what industrialization really is. The trends are very simple, but misleading, unless one looks at them in context. They entail, first, a shift of the labor force from agricultural work to industrial work, starting with the Industrial Revolution of the late eighteenth and early nineteenth centuries, and then, in the twentieth century, a further shift from industrial work to so-called service work, which ostensibly is low in resource and energy use. Second, information itself becomes the most common commodity and a component of all others.†

There is so much more to industrialization than this view implies. While it is true that industrialization, by definition, entailed a shift of labor into the industrial sector, it also entailed two other things which, far from abating, are actually increasing as time goes on. First, in light of mechanization, industrialization necessitated a substitution of non-renewable sources of power, like coal and oil, for renewable ones like human and animal energy, with the concomitant exploitation of other non-renewable resources that was driven by this shift. Second, it entailed a routinization and standardization of work processes in order to make them more efficient. Today the factory model has invaded all kinds of work, including a great deal of what is called information work, and has encroached on hitherto seemingly unen-

---

† It is interesting that just as modern economic theory was born in countries where resources were abundant and therefore could ignore the notion of "limits," the theory of post-industrial or information society was born in countries where automation was so advanced (and energy and resource use so profligate) that vast sectors of the population could be freed from industrial work.

croachable fields like the provision of health and education services. Most food production is now industrialized in factory farms, in processing plants, in "fast-food" eating places, and even in many specialized restaurants. Furthermore, in spite of modern efficiency and resource substitution, the per capita use of resources is extravagant and still growing to the point where it is more accurate to say that we are living in a hyperindustrial rather than a postindustrial age.† Though they may use very little energy while on the job, white-collar workers who drive automobiles in long commutes use more energy getting to and from work than their nineteenth-century counterparts used in order to get the job done. One need only add to this the enormous resources that are used for endless conferences and conventions attended by great numbers of privileged bureaucrats, consultants and academics, so many of which serve only as paid mini-vacations for those attending and produce, for all the energy entailed, far less intellectual payoff than a good correspondence or reading a good book, and the picture of the resource profligacy of the so-called post-industrial world is complete.

The information society would indeed be desirable if it meant that intellectual and spiritual goods were *substituted* for material ones. The telltale sign of what the information society really means is that it is symptomized by widespread rising illiteracy—which is just the opposite of what one would expect if it is ever going to really live up to its billing. As it is presently constituted, with its huge component of propaganda, advertising and bureaucratic blather, information exchange serves the purpose of intellectual and spiritual diminution, as well as serving as a catalyst and facilitator for material exchange.

As products of modern economic thinking—and especially the thinking of the developed nations—what all of the above myths have in common is their alienation from the world of nature: they all assume, in one way or another, that the laws of nature can be finessed. In the end, these future-minded myths about markets and innovation—and some ver-

† It is all too common to mistake high productivity for efficiency when labor and/ or resources are cheap because efficiency is defined by economics only as the *cost* of producing each unit.

sions of the myth of post-industrialism—are all consumerist oriented. Therefore they all ignore the simple yet irrefutable law of nature that gives the lie to consumerism and demonstrates that if one takes a long view it can only hasten environmental degradation. This law is the second law of thermodynamics, commonly called the law of entropy.

When it was first formalized by the German physicist Rudolf Clausius in the nineteenth century, the law of entropy revolutionized the thinking of physicists as much as quantum mechanics did in the twentieth century because it severely undermined the hitherto universally accepted world view of a mechanical universe. On the contrary the entropy law entails that the universe continually and irreversibly evolves only in one direction, toward total degradation. In all of its technicalities the law of entropy is very complex, but in informal terms it is easily graspable by laymen, and indeed was intuitively understood for millennia before being formalized in the nineteenth century. We see it in action around us all the time, from the accumulation of dust in our homes to the more dramatic process that occurs when we burn wood in the fireplace. When we burn some logs in the fireplace we see them transformed to heat and to ashes and we recognize intuitively that this process cannot be reversed. In slightly more formal terms we convert the logs from a state of low entropy to a state of high entropy. The law of entropy states that all matter in the universe is constantly undergoing this irreversible degradation and, in the end, trillions of years hence, will result in a formless and lifeless universe. This ultimate end, being trillions of years away and preceded by the explosion of our sun, is almost unimaginable and would seem to be irrelevant to everyday life, but it is not, because the rate at which this degradation occurs in any given corner of the universe, like our earth, is crucial to our long-term survival and is to a significant degree in our control.

The famous physicist Erwin Shrodinger has observed that living organisms sustain themselves by hastening the entropic process in the environment around them, that is, by consumption, by converting parts of their environment from a state of low entropy to one of high entropy.[13] This is the ultimate existential meaning of consumption, and all

economic activity, particularly that which encourages consumption of non-renewable resources, hastens the entropic
process. As Georgescu-Roegen has written, "A living being
can evade the entropic degradation of its own structure only.
It cannot prevent the increase of the entropy of the whole
system, consisting of its structure and its environment. On
the contrary, from all we can tell now, the presence of life
causes the entropy of a system to increase faster than it
otherwise would."[14] What the law of entropy tells us about
non-renewable resources is that their ultimate destruction
cannot be avoided but only postponed; they exist on earth
in finite supply and can only be used and/or reused a finite
number of times. The sun, on the other hand, though not
infinite, is a source of resources that is practically infinite for
us to draw upon because, as has often been said, every week
it beams towards the earth energy equivalent to all of the
earth's non-renewable resources. The sun represents a flow
of resources towards the earth that may, for all intents and
purposes, be regarded as infinite and is the only effective
check that we presently have or may ever have on drawing
from the earth's finite stock of resources to sustain our lives.

In this context the ultimate question is whether we will
draw our sustenance from an enduring flow, the sun, or from
a decidedly finite stock, the earth. Before we switched to
coal and oil and uranium for our power needs we were
forced, by default, to live from this flow. Now, through technological and conservation techniques, we have the choice
of adhering to it in other ways. Unless or until we transform
our individual lives and the world economy in this way we
will be consuming more than our fair share of stock resources
and depriving future generations of their use. There is no
getting around the law of entropy. However sophisticated
we become at information transfer and transformation we
will continue to live in an industrial or even a hyperindustrial
age as long as material consumption remains the basis of our
existence.

The law of entropy is what gives the universe direction
and stimulates our thinking about the future and about time
in general. If resources truly were infinite and if biological
life did not entail irreversible processes like growth, aging
and death—all manifestations of the entropic process—what

would make us think about the future? Without the entropic process the universe would indeed be the perpetual motion machine that physicists once thought it was. What one must remember is that the perpetual motion machine not only goes on forever, but it goes on forever doing *exactly the same thing*. Because of entropy, life and even the lifeless universe are not like that but, on the contrary, are always changing and evolving in unpredictable ways.

Given the law of entropy and what it tells us of the limits of the natural world the only way that we can live in a way that is responsible to future generations is by reducing consumption. Future generations will not rightly be able to blame us for using resources to sustain our lives and to allow ourselves reasonable material comfort, but they will be able to blame us if we squander resources as we are now doing by living materially profligate lives. With respect to the environment, as in all areas of life, living responsibly for the future is a matter of living responsibly now. On the level of the individual, this is a matter of character, and on the level of society, a matter of culture. For at least the last half-century, the cultural development of the advanced industrial nations has largely consisted of trading the intellectual and spiritual bases of existence for material ones, and it follows that one of the logical environmental disciplines for our present time would be to reverse that process as much as possible.

It is interesting that historically there is a precedent for doing this, and, since the environmental movement is often enamored of seeking alternate cultural precedents outside the mainstream of western tradition, there is some virtue in the fact that the precedent I have in mind is found in the Judeo-Christian tradition. It is described in the Bible near the end of the Book of Leviticus and has to do with the convention of the sabbath of the land.[15] The law of the sabbath of the land is very complicated and is also described in slightly different terms in different parts of the Bible, but its basic precepts are simple. According to Jewish law, the people were allowed to work the land for only six years in a row; the seventh year was considered a "sabbath of the land" and during that year all the land had to be left untouched. During that year the people were to live off only what grew spontaneously from the land, sharing it equally among themselves and the animals. It was traditional that during the year of the sabbath of the land the people were to occupy their time in study rather than work, trading a material existence for a spiritual one. In the Book of Deuteronomy (15:1–10) the sabbath of the land was also a time when all debts were to be forgiven, and in Hebrew the root of the word for letting the land rest and for forgiving debts is the same and means "to drop."

It is not clear how strictly ancient Jews adhered to this law, but it is clear from historical records that for centuries the sabbath of the land was in force to a great extent. It is recorded in the First Book of Maccabees and also by the historian Josephus that during a sabbatical year the city of Beth-zur was forced to surrender to the Syrians because it could not withstand a siege due to lack of provisions. Josephus also reports that Alexander the Great and Julius Caesar were both sufficiently appreciative of these laws and practices to exempt the Palestinian Jews from tributary taxes during these sabbatical years.[16]†

The law of entropy is as fundamental as the law of gravity. It may appear at times as if it can be beaten or finessed, just as we appear to beat gravity by taking off in rocket ships. But as far as everything we know or seem to know about the natural world is concerned, it cannot be disabled. What person who cares for humankind would stake the well-being of future generations on the undoing of the law of gravity? If, through our collective ingenuity, we should ever learn to reverse the entropic process, then scarcity will be abolished forever and humankind may, if it so wishes, adopt a course of uncontrolled and unabated consumerism. Until such a time, those who wantonly consume from the earth's stock now deprive those who must make a living on the earth tomorrow.

Whatever may be the virtues of stopping and controlling pollution, if the environmental movement does no more than

† It is interesting to note that Jewish tradition also holds that if the sabbatical year were not observed the earth would eventually make up the lost sabbaths by being laid waste (Leviticus 26:34, 43), and that much of the hardship and suffering the Jewish people endured in exile was considered punishment for not having faithfully kept the sabbath of the land.

achieve this goal it will have failed in its obligation to future generations. Ultimately, the abatement of pollution through any method other than the reduction of consumption is largely a victory for consumerism because the consumer will no longer have to consume anything involuntarily but will not have to consume any less. In the long run the law of entropy is a no-win game, and for humans the only advantage lies in playing it as little as possible.

What seems to militate most against our accepting this fact and minimizing the material basis of our existence is our selfishness, our shortsightedness, and our lack of responsibility to future generations, all of which are enforced by fantastic tales of futurists. In 1965, at a conference on the prospects of genetic engineering, the biologist Kimball Atwood envisioned that "we could, for example produce an organism that combines the happy qualities of animals and plants, such as one with a large brain so that it can indulge in philosophy and also a photosynthetic area on its back so that it would not have to eat."[17] Similarly, in 1990, writing in *The New Republic,* Gregg Easterbrook fantasized that we will eventually be able to alleviate the strain of unecological human activity and at the same time bestow the blessing of human life in other parts of the universe by kindling other planets with life-supporting properties. "The prospect of expanding life into the heavens may sound too remote to be relevant to today's environmental debates. Hardly. It's far more meaningful than such details as unburned hydrocarbon gram level or delayed Subtitle D regulations."[18] Atwood's vision may be a little more down-to-earth than Easterbrook's, and it certainly contains the virtue of relying on the enduring resources of the sun, but their visions have two things in common: both reflect alienation, and neither is able to accept limits. It is no wonder that Wendell Berry has written, "Our most serious problem, perhaps, is that we have become a nation of fantasists. We believe, apparently, in the infinite availability of finite resources."[19]

The debate about the environment—present, past and future—begins and ends with questions about the extent of our alienation from the world of nature. What are we to think of the earth? Are we to regard it, ultimately, as a disposable launching pad, to be left in the custody of those who lack the means or will to leave it? And with all its joys and riches, what do we expect we will ever learn to love and cherish if, by the time we are able to leave the earth, we have not learned to love and cherish it? Though it will not happen until the very distant future, our destiny may eventually be to explore and inhabit other parts of the universe, but unless we can first learn to care for and cherish this earth and live within its limits, it will be only a wanton destiny to which we cannot be spiritually entitled.

NOTES

1. Joseph C. Dragan and M.C. Demetrescu, *Entropy and Bioeconomics* (Rome: Nagard, 1986), p. 167.
2. Leo Tolstoy, *Anna Karenina* (trans. David Magarshack) (New York: New American Library, 1961), p. 178.
3. Tolstoy, p. 182.
4. Nicholas Georgescu-Roegen, *The Entropy Law and the Economic Process* (Cambridge, Mass.: Harvard University Press, 1971), p. 2.
5. Fred L. Smith and Kathy H. Kushner, "Good Fences Make Good Neighborhoods," in *National Review* (April 1, 1990), p. 31.
6. This mechanistic perspective may partly be a consequence of the scientism inherent in modern economics, but, as Georgescu-Roegen has pointed out, it is surely also partly the result of the fact that modern economics was originally formulated in lands of abundant resources. Since both streams of thought have this origin in common, with respect to the environment Marxist economics is no different from neoclassical in its mechanistic thinking. Perhaps the Marxist position is even more attenuated because it places so much emphasis on class struggle and the labor theory of value. In this scheme the natural world does not fit in either as a legitimate source of wealth or as an appropriate antagonist.
7. Robert L. Heilbroner, *An Inquiry into the Human Prospect* (New York: Norton, 1974).
8. D.H. Meadows, D.L. Meadows, J. Rangers, W.W. Behrens III, *The Limits to Growth: A Report for the Club of Rome's Project on the Predicament of Mankind* (New York: Potomac Associates-Universe Books, 1972).
9. Glenn Hueckel, "A Historical Approach to Future Economic Growth," in *Science* (March 14, 1975), pp. 925–931.
10. This example is taken from Hueckel, pp. 927–928.
11. See Jeremy Rifkin, *Entropy: A New World View* (New York: Viking, 1980), pp. 112–113.
12. See for example Yoneji Masuda, *Computopia: Information Society as Post-Industrial Society* (Bethesda, Md.: World Future Society, 1981).
13. Cited in Georgescu-Roegen, p. 10.
14. Georgescu-Roegen, p. 11.
15. Leviticus 25.
16. See Gunther Plaut, *The Torah* (New York: Union of American Hebrew Congregations, 1981), p. 941. See also T.H. Hertz, *The Pentateuch and Haftorahs*, 2nd ed. (London: Soncino Press, 1981), p. 531.
17. Kimball Atwood, "The Revolutionary New Biology: Discussion," in

T.M. Sonneborn (ed.), *The Control of Human Heredity and Evolution* (New York: Macmillan, 1965), p. 37.

18. Gregg Easterbrook, "Everything You Know about the Environment Is Wrong," in *The New Republic* (April 30, 1990), p. 27.

19. Wendell Berry, "Word and Flesh," in *Whole Earth Review* (Spring 1990), p. 71.

TRUTH AND POLITICS IN DEBATES ABOUT THE FUTURE

Even in the best of circumstances debates about the future are never straightforward because they are always pulled in two directions at once. All debates about the future are likely to deal with two things: what *will* be, which is a matter of truth, and therefore should fall under the authority of science, and what *should* be, which is a moral matter, and in our time falls under the authority of politics. But since, outside of some aspects of the world of nature, science usually cannot say what *will* be, it often finds itself at a disadvantage vis-à-vis politics in such debates. Today, in any case, science and politics have become hopelessly muddled: not only do scientific debates have wide political ramifications, but what would otherwise be hopelessly shoddy political debates often manage to achieve a certain degree of legitimacy and respectability by assuming scientific airs. As a consequence of all of this, both scientific and political debates about the future tend at best to be obscure and confusing and at worst to be mistaken and misleading.

All of these problems were very apparent in a recent debate about artificial intelligence (AI). In January of 1990 *Scientific American* published a debate between some prominent members of the artificial intelligence community about whether machines will ever be able to think. As it happened, in this particular contest neither side made any really new points—but the argument was still very interesting, not so much because of its content as because of its style.

In scientific circles, where cold-blooded objectivity is supposed to be the name of the game, one should be wary whenever the style of a debate is more interesting than its content. Of course, there is a place for flair even in the somber halls of science, but it is also a commonplace that if you cannot win an argument with facts you may still be able to "win" it with rhetoric. It has always been true that a wilful debater, using nothing more than fanciful language, jokes, personal attacks and similar devices, can win over an unwary audience and deflect its attention away from the question at hand. And, if the rhetorician is skillful enough, while he is at it he may even manage to quietly introduce a different agenda.

In the *Scientific American* debate the differences in style were apparent from the very first sentence of each paper. John Searle, on the side of the doubters, began by simply restating the question in its classic and most familiar terms. "Can a machine think?" he asked.[1] Then, in the typical style of the philosopher, he proceeded to define the terms "machine" and "think" and went on to present a case against the possibility that computing machines, as we know them, will ever be able to think in the conscious way that humans do.[2] Until the very end of his paper Searle did not once deviate from sober analysis and simple logical statements. And when, in concluding, he did depart from this style, it was only to speculate as to why, in spite of the mounting evidence against it, some people still believe that computers will someday be able to think. Searle blamed the persistence of this belief on the lingering influence of behaviorism, and concluded that adherents to this school of thought were being unscientific and fighting a retrograde battle to protect theories that have already been discredited.

Now, whereas Searle began his paper by restating the question, Paul and Patricia Churchland, who took the affirmative side in this debate, began theirs by bragging. This tone was also apparent in their very first sentence, where they made the archetypal hyperbolic proclamation: "Artificial-intelligence research is undergoing a revolution."[3] From here they proceeded to recount the accomplishments of the artificial intelligence movement in the most glowing terms. They called it "a well-defined research program" based on "deep theoretical underpinnings" which has come up with "deepest reasons" for having confidence in its enterprise. Furthermore, not only did the Churchlands praise their movement, they also found it appropriate to slander their detractors, calling them, on different occasions, "ill-motivated," "ill-informed," "short-sighted," "unsympathetic" and, with apparent reference to Searle himself, "logic-chopping."

A little academic name-calling—fine. But what is particularly interesting about the Churchland paper is that when the authors finally did get down to addressing the question of whether the artificial intelligence movement will ever produce a consciously thinking machine they were almost as doubtful as their adversary. "We believe that the prospects are poor," they concluded, "but we rest this opinion on reasons very different from Searle's. Our reasons derive from the specific performance failures of the classical research program in AI."[4] Having made this concession, however, the Churchlands then went right on to describe some recent—though, if you look at them closely, by no means *revolutionary*—research developments in AI and to make a plea for more time to carry them forward.[5] So in the end, far from being a concession of defeat, the Churchlands' admission of serious doubt was only the prelude to a plea for more time in the hope that somehow it will all work out in the future.

On one level the Churchlands' plea for more time is perfectly reasonable and, naturally, it is constantly being echoed by researchers in every field of science, even in the face of the most frustrating results. Since frustration in the sciences is very common but is often enough followed by success, a plea for more time is perfectly understandable— and, in any case, one would instinctively want to give sincere and honest researchers the benefit of the doubt. In this spirit Stevan Harnad, an AI theoretician at Princeton, has observed: "Whereas Searle's thought-experiment and scepticism lead nowhere, there is every reason to believe that AI's toys will grow and grow, until some day they will begin to look like the real thing, and some of them may even begin giving the Turing Test a run for its money."[6]† Harnad's point certainly makes the suspension of judgment about future outcomes very appealing: what, after all, is the use of Searle's skepticism—except that it may give him the intellectual self-satisfaction of thinking that he really can foresee the results of the long and complicated quest for artificial intelligence?

A number of years ago Arthur C. Clarke, the famous British futurist and science fiction writer, wrote an essay called *Profiles of the Future: An Inquiry into the Limits of the Possible* in which, among other things, he tried to make a case for completely open-minded thinking about what science and technology will be capable of accomplishing in the future. At the same time, Clarke also attempted to put skeptics like Searle in their place. Yet, in spite of the fact that his book is written as a sort of tribute to science, what is interesting about Clarke's method in this essay is that it is patently unscientific.

He begins by giving a brief historical account of a number of technological feats which some skeptics believed to be impossible before they were accomplished. One could list any number of feats of this sort, but I will mention only a couple that Clarke himself cites to give the reader a feeling for what he was trying to do and how he was trying to do it. In the nineteenth century, after the invention of the locomotive, skeptics maintained that a person could not travel at the speed of thirty miles per hour without suffocating; in

---

† AI researchers commonly refer to their present, ostensibly provisional achievements as "toys"—partly as a matter of self-effacement, but also partly in self-assured expectation of achieving far greater results in the future. But the self-flattering nature of this terminology is evident if one compares AI to any other more vital field. For example, whatever their expectations may be for future results, cancer researchers would never refer to their present, provisional achievements as "toy" cures.

the early twentieth century, before airplanes were invented, many people believed that heavier-than-air-machines could not fly; and, after the airplane had become a reality, some skeptics continued to believe that these machines would never be able to carry many people or go very far or very fast and therefore would be impractical for commercial purposes. Of course, as history has shown, the skeptics in these particular cases proved to be wrong, but the conclusion that Clarke draws about skepticism in general, that it is useless in the short run and foolish in the long, is also wrong.

Good scientists are very reluctant to make generalizations about oddly assorted and/or carefully selected cases like the ones that Clarke cites. If a scientist feels inclined to draw conclusions about a number of cases he has studied he will tend to generalize to those cases alone and to no others—sometimes to the point where a layman, not understanding the spirit of this attitude, might even find it precious and laughable. The only conclusion that a sober scientist would draw from Clarke's cases is that in those *particular* instances—which he gives us no reason to believe are representative—the skeptics turned out to be wrong. But Clarke goes much further than this. He concludes, "Anything that is theoretically possible will be achieved in practice, no matter what the technical difficulties, if it is desired greatly enough."[7] From a scientific perspective such a sweeping generalization is almost meaningless, but it is worth looking at more closely because, in spite of its meaninglessness, it exemplifies the kind of thinking that forms a significant part of the background for all sorts of debates about what is possible.

The question of what is possible is an ancient one in philosophy and goes back as far as Aristotle, but the position Clarke has taken on it is closer to that taken by Descartes. Descartes believed that anything is possible provided that it can be clearly imagined and does not violate God's goodness. This is not the place to discuss Descartes' second condition, but an illustration of the first is that it might be possible to construct a round rectangle if only one could first get a clear picture of it in one's head. This is how Clarke thinks—he uses the term "theoretically possible" so loosely that it appears to be synonymous with "conceived" or "imagined."

Of course imagining something is certainly useful, and may even be necessary, to bringing it about, but Clarke would lead one to believe that it is also sufficient. Yet although he makes it sound simple and straightforward, the idea of theoretical possibility is actually fraught with problems. What, after all, does it really mean to say that something is "theoretically possible"? A couple of illustrations that countervail Clarke's argument will show how contrived his thinking really is.

Before they performed the first test of the atom bomb, Robert Oppenheimer and some of his colleagues on the Manhattan Project theorized that it was possible that when the bomb exploded it would set the earth's atmosphere on fire—perhaps even causing a worldwide conflagration. Presumably, the scientists who speculated about this astounding possibility were not idly conjecturing, but, as everyone knows, they went ahead with their test anyhow, and, in the event, the global conflagration did not actually occur. Since the bomb did not set the world on fire, what became of the theoretical possibility, which existed before the detonation, that this might actually happen? The simple answer is that presumably this possibility was obliterated, along with lots of other things, with the explosion of the bomb.

Of course, the conjectures of the atomic scientists about atmospheric conflagration was a bit of a sideshow: these speculations were not central to their main plan and purpose, nor did disproving the conflagration theory destroy the elaborate theoretical edifice which made the explosion of the bomb itself a possibility. Therefore my second example has to do with speculative theory that arose from the very heart of a long-standing scientific objective—this time in the field of biology—namely, cloning.

The idea of cloning, or exactly reproducing an individual, has been part of human fantasy for some time, but in the past it was generally regarded as a joke.[8] About a century ago, however, a German embryologist named Hans Driesch performed some famous experiments that showed that an organism may develop not only from a fertilized egg, but from an ordinary body-cell when that cell is taken from an embryo at the earliest stages of development. Half a century later a couple of experimental biologists called R. Briggs and

T.J. King pushed our practical and theoretical knowledge of cloning a big step further. They were able to pluck the nucleus from a single body-cell and use it to replace the nucleus of a fertilized egg, thus giving the egg the genetic material of the individual from whose body-cell the nucleus had been transplanted. Using this technique, in the early 1950s Briggs and King were able to clone reptiles from the body-cells of reptiles. Naturally, at that point in history, it seemed "theoretically possible" that one day we would also be able to clone humans, including everyone's favorite examples, Einsteins from Einsteins and Mozarts from Mozarts—if only some Einsteins or Mozarts managed to appear on the scene again.

However, one aspect of the Briggs-King experiments which did not appear to be particularly significant at the time of their early research but later proved to be crucial was that the nuclei they used for transplants had been consistently taken only from reptiles at the first stages of development. As it turned out, subsequent attempts to make clones using the body-cells of more mature organisms failed. For some reason—neither explained by nor anticipated by the theory as it then stood—the older the organism happened to be the less likely that the transplanted nucleus of one of its body-cells would make an egg develop into a similar organism.[9] With nuclei from mature organisms the process will not work at all. But until this was proven experimentally in the later investigations of Briggs and King and others there was no reason not to believe that it was "theoretically possible" that we would one day be able to clone humans from mature humans.†

The experiences of the Manhattan Project scientists and Briggs and King illustrate a little of what "theoretical possibility" actually means in science, and this meaning is obviously, to a greater or lesser extent, very contingent on new developments, on what is not yet known, unlike what Clarke's argument would lead one to believe. It should be clear from the preceding examples that Clarke confuses ap-

---

† Obviously, there would be little point in cloning humans from human embryos if this turned out to be feasible because, setting aside the problems of nurture, Einsteins and Mozarts are not identifiable at the embryo stage. One might as well use fertility drugs to induce identical multiple births.

parent but blind potentiality with real possibility. When we observe something in its earliest stages, be it an organism, an institution or a science, its potential seems unlimited, but this is largely due to our ignorance. The eggs of many species look superficially alike, and many species are superficially alike even at the stage of the embryo. It is not until development and differentiation have proceeded some way that it becomes obvious that one egg will develop only into a reptile and another into a human. What is left out of Clarke's equation is that development, be it of an organism, an institution, and even a science, along with being an expansive process is also a self-limiting one. The theoretical edifice in any science may lead to dead ends and blind alleys, some temporary, some permanent; it is more like a maze than like a long dark tunnel which will always and ever have a light at the end of it. The English philosopher R.G. Collingwood therefore once said of the development of science: "Natural science . . . consists of facts and theories. A scientific fact is an event in the world of nature. A scientific theory is an hypothesis about that event, which further events verify or disprove."[10] Because the hypothetical nature of theory, so central to science, is absent from Clarke's formula, it is certainly unscientific and almost meaningless. It does not describe real science, in which hypotheses are forever being proven or disproven, but an idealized, childish vision of science, as if it were a mechanical enterprise, a huge jigsaw puzzle in which all the missing pieces are somewhere to be found and their shapes will forever be discernible, a puzzle which we will always be able to complete simply by "desiring it greatly enough."

In debates about the future, misconceptions like Clarke's about the nature of scientific theory make for a lot of loose talk and wild speculation. Much of this could be avoided by simply bearing in mind what every scientist knows, that at bottom theory is only a shorthand way of representing and thinking about phenomena, both those that occur naturally in the world and those that result because of man's intervention but are still, of course, a part of nature. In a symbolic and economical way theory organizes and summarizes the world as we understand it at any given point in history, and, because we are curious, it does more than that:

it also provides a framework for speculating about what may be possible. This framework points to gaps in our knowledge and in our experience, and to the possibilities for filling them. But though theory allows us to speculate honestly about future developments, there is no scientific ground for assuming that all gaps can be filled and that all imaginable occurences will actually occur—and experimental developments, like the ones I have just described, demonstrate to the contrary.

Because of this, any statement about what is possible, especially about something that has never yet happened, cannot, strictly speaking, be taken as fact, but only as opinion. In particular the statement "anything is possible" is only an opinion—and a rather silly one at that, unless it is merely a way of stating the commonsense existential notion that all sorts of things may be possible that have not yet happened nor been imagined. But there is a world of difference between saying that "all sorts of things may be possible" when this is an existential position, and saying that "anything is possible" when this is meant to be a scientific statement reflecting the omnipotence of science when it is driven by imagination, human will and intelligence.

Whereas opinion is a necessary part of scientific speculation, it is a part of the scientific edifice about which scientists will always have mixed feelings. As long as science is driven by the quest for truth, its desire will always be to abolish opinions and get on to facts by proving or disproving a hypothesis one way or the other. Science thrives on facts and considers the opinion that is inherent in hypotheses to be no more than a necessary evil that will, it is hoped, ultimately lead to useful facts. But this places science, which thrives on "finding" truth, whatever it may turn out to be, directly opposite to politics, which thrives on "making" opinion—and often actually abhors facts either because they are dull or because their implications are threatening.

Yet, in spite of their uneasy relationship with facts, politicians will often seize on a fact in the form of an event if it will serve to shape opinion. Thus the fact of the recent arms reductions in Europe has been used by propagandists during the last year or so to vindicate the build-ups that preceded it, as if arms reduction were the only possible out-

come of the arms race. Because a nuclear war has not happened as a result of the arms race, propagandists who wish
to justify the build-up retrospectively would have us believe
that nuclear war was never a real possibility. In this sense
political rhetoric often tries to mimic scientific reasoning by
claiming that a development either proves or disproves a
given hypothesis. But in politics such a claim is always rhetorical because in human affairs nothing is "in the nature of
things" and one can therefore always rightly say that "it
could have been different in any number of possible ways."
Yet this kind of pseudo-scientific rhetoric is very powerful
because it is as true of human as of natural history that each
development does, in fact, partially or wholly negate the
possibility of others occurring—not because it reveals the
true nature of things, as in science, but because each event
in history exclusively occupies the moment in which it occurs.
Once the Allied powers had won World War II it was then
impossible for the Axis powers to do so. As Hannah Arendt
has observed: "It is true that in retrospect—that is, in historical perspective—every sequence of events looks as
though it could not have happened otherwise, but this is an
optical, or, rather, an existential illusion: nothing could ever
happen if reality did not kill, by definition, all the other
potentialities originally inherent in any given situation."[11]

However, although present events may erode, or even
kill, past potentialities, they do not kill future potentialities.
The present does, of course, have a great deal of bearing on
the future, but it is ridiculous to try to push historical logic
forward in the way one can, with a great deal of wilful con-
struction, more or less push it backwards, along a single path.
From any given present innumerable futures are always possible, but this fact does not sit well with politicians who like
to give the appearance of having completely mastered events
by having chosen the right path, the path that leads to the
best of all possible futures. In particular, when an event takes
the form of an intervention like a program or policy, the
instigating politicians will always attempt to prove that they
have privileged insight into its logic and know its future
outcome.

This kind of posturing was abundantly evident in Canada during the general election of 1988. The Canadian elec-

tion of 1988 was fought on the basis of only one policy issue: should Canada sign a free trade agreement with the United States. However, by the time they called the election, the incumbent party, the Conservatives, had already begun negotiating the deal, so there was no question what their policy was or where their commitment lay. Naturally, during the course of the campaign, they predicted that great good would come from this treaty but economic hardship would be inevitable without it. The opposition parties, in turn, devoted their campaign energies to making opposite predictions based on the "studies" of their own hired forecasters. Needless to say, during these elaborate exercises in prophecy, no party cared to mention the commonsense fact that although trade treaties may prove to be important, as the EEC has demonstrated over the last two decades, they are not decisive to economic well-being. Even in the EEC there are winners and losers, countries that are better off or worse off with respect to certain aspects of trade. Trade treaties offer no more than opportunities and potential benefits that must be realized—or not—through innumerable individual decisions which reflect a nation's overall level of industriousness, intelligence, natural advantage and so forth.†

The prophetic propaganda which dominated the 1988 general election campaign in Canada illustrates how compelling debates about the future can be even when they are patently used as forums for making political hay. In politics, which is highly dependent on image-management and opinion-making, such debates are all too common, and the legitimating function of supposedly scientific forecasters is all too transparent within them. Increasingly, however, we live in a world in which it is difficult to separate science from politics because governments routinely initiate huge scientific projects as the embodiment of national policies. In these cases the transparency of pseudo-science working in the ser-

† Since the Canadian electorate were treated, on this occasion, to a one-issue campaign based entirely on "scientifically" legitimated fantasies about the future, it was not surprising that the polls swayed dramatically during the contest as politicians of all parties persisted in making melodramatic predictions. In the end the Conservatives were returned because their propaganda was better managed, but this was certainly one of those elections, all too common during the last two decades, where the electorate went to the polls holding their noses.

vice of political will is usually lost and instead we have debates about the future in which science, some real and some sham, is obscurely interwoven with political rhetoric.

Probably the best example in recent years of how this works is to be found in the American debate about the Strategic Defense Initiative (SDI), or Star Wars as it was commonly known. The most telling thing about the SDI debate was how rapidly and broadly its grounds and terms of reference kept shifting and becoming more vague at each step. When President Reagan first announced his plans to develop and deploy the SDI system he was unequivocal about its purpose: it would be an impenetrable defense shield that would make the nuclear weapons of the enemy impotent and therefore obsolete. Whatever their judgment as to its feasibility may have been, there is no question that for a long time the public as well as the media took this goal at face value. No sooner had Reagan finished proclaiming this incredibly ambitious goal, however, than the U.S. Defense Department began to "explain" to the public that in reality the purpose of SDI would be far more modest, that the system would be deployed only as an added component of the existing system of deterrence. Then, by the late 1980s, after the credibility of SDI had been seriously eroded by its critics, its proponents and defenders trotted out the old standby justifications that the goal of SDI was to be neither invincible defense nor even deterrence but to act as a vehicle for funding worthwhile research. Finally, some defenders of SDI even went so far as to argue that one purpose of deploying the system was to bankrupt the Soviet Union by forcing it to increase its military spending in order to respond to it.

Much as a reluctant striptease dancer, who remains forever alluring but never revealing, casts a spell on her audience, the shedding of a more ambitious—but clearer—purpose for more conventional and vaguer ones managed to keep the public in thrall for a long time. Of course political initiatives can legitimately have multiple goals, but when this is so each should be valid in it own right in case the others fail. What is most telling about the stated aims of SDI was that none of them alone could have stood up to scrutiny for very long. Only the shadow game of all four goals taken together could possibly have allowed SDI to persist as long as it did under public analysis.

Ironically, however, in spite of its incredibly ambitious nature, of the four justifications for developing the system, the scientists who wished to argue objectively about it could take only Reagan's original goal, to construct a completely invulnerable shield, as a proper point of reference—otherwise there would have been nothing to argue about. None of the other goals were scientifically testable. This is why when David L. Parnas resigned in protest from the advisory panel that was supposed to explore the feasibility of SDI he insisted: "I've taken my requirements from the very highest and most reliable source, Ronald Reagan."[12]† Sophisticates of realpolitik probably consider Parnas's statement to be hopelessly naive, but however "naive" it may have been, from the point of view of such cynics his position was anything but posturing because, from the perspective of a hard scientist, as lofty and ambitious as Reagan's goal may have been compared to the others that followed it, it was the only one that was susceptible to scientific analysis. Like schoolyard morality in which children of a certain age will insist on constantly changing the rules whenever it is to their advantage, all of this ground-shifting may serve some fairly obvious political purposes but in the long run it can only be self-defeating, since it will prove to be extremely annoying to that part of the public that can see through it and confusing to the rest.

Unfortunately ground-shifting and rule-changing have become common traits of scientific as well as political debate.

---

† It should be noted that in making his assessment of whether it would be possible to write the software for such a system Parnas did not use perfection as his standard, but rather believable dependability. In his original papers justifying his resignation Parnas wrote, "The system has numerous technical characteristics that will make it more difficult than previous systems, independent of size. Because of the extreme demands on the system and our inability to test it, we will never be able to believe, with any confidence, that we have succeeded. Nuclear weapons will remain a potent threat" (in *Communications of the ACM*, vol. 28, no. 12, December 1985, p. 1329). And elsewhere he has written, "I have consistently used the work [*sic*] "trustworthy," explaining that what is required is a system with known, that is, predictable, effectiveness—one which we know, with great confidence is free of *catastrophic flaws*. That is far from perfection" (emphasis in original) (letter, in *Science* [July 25, 1986], p. 403).

Last year when the chemists Stanley Pons and Martin Fleischmann claimed to have created nuclear fusion at room temperature in a test-tube, they used the ground-shifting tactic to evade the ultimately devastating critiques of their colleagues. In commenting on the Pons-Fleischmann cold-fusion affair, Robert Crease and N.P. Samios, a philosopher and a scientist, compared the chemists to the French scientist René Blondlot, another famous ground-shifter, who imagined he had discovered n-rays, in the wake of the remarkable discovery of X rays by the German scientist Wilhelm Roentgen. Crease and Samios observed, "When someone claimed that it was not possible to produce cold fusion, the two Utah scientists would add more instructions—that the palladium cathode had to be prepared in a certain way, or the electrolyte had to be of a certain concentration."[13] (At least one can say of Pons and Fleischmann that they kept their shifting on scientific turf—some of Blondlot's followers eventually claimed that "only individuals of Latin descent had good enough eyesight to see evidence of the rays.")[14] Crease and Samios concluded that Pons and Fleischmann were self-deluded victims of "pathological science." Crease and Samios maintain that healthy science, far from trying to glorify new findings without first subjecting them to the rigor of peer replication and evaluation, will try to "kill the results" as did Roentgen, in case they should turn out to be only the consequence of experimental error.

Contrary to the schoolyard tactic of constantly shifting ground, those who are debating in good faith, be it in politics or in science, will always seek for common ground and common terms—in fact that quest alone is sometimes the substance of a debate. This makes for dullness at times, but it also makes for honesty. Ground-shifting is a sure sign that a debate about the future is political as opposed to scientific. Any side that uses the tactic is either deluding itself or not debating in good faith.

Unfortunately, in any debate, if one side is trying to argue from truth while the other is arguing from opinion the latter side will tend to have the upper hand, because factual truth is seldom self-evident. In fact, Hannah Arendt has gone so far as to claim that "factual truth is no more self-evident than opinion, and this may be among the reasons that opinion-holders find it relatively easy to discredit factual truth as just another opinion."[15] In this case the uses of skepticism, like John Searle's in the AI debate, should be obvious. Aside from the scientific use of trying to keep the debate as close to truth as possible, which honest skepticism always does, it brings to light the purely political aspects of such debates. If what might otherwise be scientific debates then become almost strictly political, at least we are in the position to insist that the other contingencies of political debate come into play, for example, that interests be spelled out and that any given interest be directly compared with competing interests. Getting back to the point of departure for this chapter, if the Churchlands insist on making the artificial intelligence debate a political one, then the claims of the artificial intelligence movement on the public purse should be weighed against the claims of other causes, like the educating of people, the cultivation of real intelligence. It would not do, after all, for any country to be a nation of smart machines and stupid people.

If politics were like science in every way one could say it was inherently "pathological." But part of the game of politics is forging consensus, and this may rightly necessitate shifting ground. We cannot expect politicians to have the integrity to try to "kill the results" the way honest scientists do before they publish them, because "results" in politics are always contingent, always created by forging consensus. But in the forging of consensus through the fostering of beliefs and opinion we can at least insist, as scientists will insist, that all the players stick to the facts as we know them and state their intentions honestly—otherwise, in our political culture, we will remain forever in the schoolyard.

NOTES

1. John R. Searle, "Is the Brain's Mind a Computer Program?," in *Scientific American* (January 1990), p. 26.
2. See John R. Searle, "Minds, Brains, and Programs," in *The Behavioral and Brain Sciences* (Cambridge University Press, 1980), vol. 3, pp. 417–457. Searle's refutation was, for the most part, a restatement of the famous rebuttal in the form of a thought-experiment that he had formulated for this purpose a decade earlier. In Searle's thought-experiment a person who does not understand a word of Chinese is sequestered in a room where he manipulates Chinese symbols

on the basis of a rule-book written in a language, like English, that he does understand. It follows in principle that if his rule-book is comprehensive and well written, he will give the appearance of understanding Chinese when in reality he does not understand a word. This thought-experiment was designed to show that a machine can display the appearance of thought by blindly manipulating symbols without actually thinking, that is, that computers have only syntax, the ability to follow rules, but not semantics, the ability to understand the meaning of the symbols which they manipulate. Searle's paper created quite a stir in the AI community when it was first published because it logically and directly countered Turing's thought-experiment, which had launched the AI movement. Searle's experiment demonstrated, among other things, what intentionality might mean even in the context of behaviorist psychology, and showed that, in spite of what behaviorists might claim, the "state" behind "appearances" can be very important. It was published along with comments from twenty-seven theoreticians and practitioners in the field. All but three of these comments were negative, but Searle refuted all of them with written responses. In any case the evidence that his paper has certainly struck a very raw nerve in the AI community is that it is still controversial and being debated over a decade later.

3. Paul M. Churchland and Patricia Smith Churchland, "Could a Machine Think?," in *Scientific American* (January 1990), p. 32.
4. Churchland and Churchland, p. 35.
5. At this point the reader finally gets to find out what the Churchlands mean by *revolutionary*. Apparently it is parallel architecture, a type of computer engineering which, although by no means new, is presently gaining a great deal of attention because it is superficially similar to the gross anatomic structure of the human brain. However, as Searle points out in his rebuttal, aside from decreasing computing time, there is nothing that can be done using this type of engineering that cannot likewise be done on the more common serial architecture. (See Searle, "Computer Program?," p. 28.)
6. Stevan Harnad, "Minds, Machines and Searle," in *Journal of Experimental and Theoretical Artificial Intelligence*, (1989) vol. 1, no. 1.
7. Arthur C. Clarke, *Profiles of the Future: An Inquiry into the Limits of the Possible*, 2nd rev. ed. (London: Victor Gollancz, 1982), p. 25.
8. In 1769 the French encyclopedist Denis Diderot published a satire which deals with this fantasy called *The Dream of d'Alembert*. Diderot imagined a room, like a large hothouse, which would contain potted people, pots of kings, of bishops, of stableboys, of courtesans and so forth. (See Denis Diderot, *La rêve de d'Alembert*, Paris: Librairie Marcel Didier, 1951, p. 54.)
9. See James D. Watson, *Molecular Biology of the Gene* (New York: W.A. Benjamin, 1965), pp. 416 ff.
10. R.G. Collingwood, *The Idea of Nature* (London: Oxford University Press, 1964), p. 176.
11. Hannah Arendt, "Truth and Politics," in *Between Past and Future* (New York, Viking, 1968), p. 243.
12. Quoted in M. Mitchell Waldrop, "Resolving the Star Wars Software Dilemma," in *Science* (May 9, 1986), p. 710.
13. Robert P. Crease and N.P. Samios, "Cold Fusion," in *The New York Times*, September 24, 1989.
14. Crease and Samios, p. 38.
15. Arendt, p. 243.

Actual life is full of false clues and sign-posts that lead nowhere. With infinite effort we nerve ourselves for a crisis that never comes. The most successful career must show a waste of strength that might have removed mountains, and the most unsuccessful is not that of the man who is taken unpreparedly, but of him who has prepared and is never taken. On a tragedy of that kind our national morality is duly silent. It assumes that preparation against danger is in itself good, and that men, like nations, are the better for staggering through life fully armed.

—E.M. FORSTER

EPILOGUE: EROS AND PLANNING: THE ANT AND THE GRASSHOPPER RETOLD

It is often said that we are living in the age of information, but insofar as this is true, it follows that we must also be living in the midst of a great deal of bad information, that is, misinformation, propaganda, nonsense and hype. In our time prophecy, in its various forms of prediction, forecasting, futurology and scenario writing, has become a major source of bad information—bad in the sense that it misleads us by distorting our regard for both the present and the future. It thereby brings out the worst in us, encouraging us to behave in narrow, selfish and self-defeating ways.

Because it so often works this way, notwithstanding the good that may sometimes come from trying to be mindful of the future, the role of prophecy today has become rather malign. Although our prophets like to tout themselves as being escorts along the avenues of salvation and exploration, all too often they act as legitimators of questionable schemes and programs that unleash the forces of abandonment, neglect, irresponsibility, destabilization and exploitation. But this is not surprising when you consider how simple-minded, self-serving and childishly impressionable most of our prophets are.

Yet the problem with modern prophecy cannot entirely be attributed to the fecklessness of our prophets; they are, after all, a product of our times and, as I have tried to demonstrate throughout this book, reflect the pathologies of their willing audiences. They exploit only that which is eminently exploitable. The problem with prophecy today and the source of our sometimes pathological obsession with the future is much the same as what Ivan Illich has said is the problem with medicine, that is, prophecy and medicine both represent major interventions in our lives that often cause harm.[1] They do not, of course, always cause harm, and if we wish to give them the benefit of the doubt we should say that they usually intend to do good. But they cause harm often enough and decisively enough so that we should be seriously concerned about the role they play in our lives, both unbidden and at our behest. And we should be particularly concerned because their malign side is not aberrant or accidental but part of their very nature, characteristic of the role these enterprises play today.

Illich's book *Limits to Medicine* is subtitled *Medical Nemesis: The Expropriation of Health*, and a large part of his argument is that, aside from any other harms the modern practice of medicine may entail, it also expropriates from individuals, with their consent, responsibility for their own health. Therefore, on the positive side, he argues that we should reappropriate the responsibility for our health, which we have both relinquished and had taken away from us, by learning to take better care of ourselves and relying less on health professionals. Modern prophecy, again with our consent, has also developed in such a way that it has come to rob us of an essentially human right and responsibility: the right to dream our own dreams and set our own goals; the right, ultimately, to exercise the freedom, individually and collectively, to make the decisions that will shape our destinies.

It is no accident that prophecy and medicine have both come to work this way; the same could be said of a great deal of present human endeavor. There are many areas in which we abdicate responsibility for our growth and development and for our regular duties and pass it on to professionals, to experts, thereby empowering them and at the same time rendering ourselves ever more irresponsible and helpless. On this level, prophecy today can be regarded as being no more than an attempt by self-appointed experts to rationalize the future. Rationalization today has become little more than an attempt to order and control just about everything by pressing it into the mold of formal logic, and into the paltry calculus of formal means geared towards the achievement of what usually turn out to be extremely narrow ends. In the process of trying to fit everything into this mold, we are constantly deluding ourselves about what can or cannot be done. We are ignoring a great deal of substance in life that cannot easily be fit into this mold, that cannot easily be defined as a problem to which an expert can apply a formal bag of tricks. In this way, we often avoid or ignore vast areas of human endeavor which rationalization cannot easily capture. Our tendency to ignore in the present that which cannot be easily defined and managed as a problem is the intellectual and spiritual precursor to the all-too-common habit of our prophets of trivializing the problems of the future.

The persistent themes of modern prophecy—including its penchant to trivialize and depersonalize all problems, its concomitant obsession with automated decision-making, its "gaming" of life situations, its anti-individualism and its view of the human population as being basically anonymous and homogeneous—are all extremely mechanistic ideas. They necessarily follow from our obsession with the mechanized world view represented by rationalization and the type of control that is supposed to come from it. However, individuality, diversity and heterogeneity are too difficult to capture and predict and therefore defy control. Notwithstanding their power and utility, all machines are a caricature of nature, and the mechanistic future is no more than a caricature of the present, that is, of life.

Yet the way we live is not in the nature of things. Our culture is of our own making, and the beginning of trying to ameliorate its faults is to try to become conscious of them. There are certainly alternative ways to look at the world and think about it than those suggested by our futurologists who, in addition to adopting a mechanistic view of the universe, often lack the imagination to envision a future world that is other than a mere extrapolation of the present, no matter how questionable some parts of that present may be, and who, as George Orwell rightly observed, so often appeal to our fears and our craving for power.

As a point of departure for exploring these alternative views, I will begin by trying to deal with a little unfinished business relating to the panic that so many people feel about the future, and which makes them turn to futurologists for guidance. Early in this book I made the observation that futurologists frequently justify their enterprise by making the claim that, because things are changing so rapidly, we need to be able to predict the future in order to be able, by anticipatory action, to adapt to it. To support this claim they usually refer to familiar slogans such as, "There are far more scientists and technologists alive and working to change the world today than in all the previous history of civilization," and, "The amount of information in the world is doubling every few years and increasing at a far more rapid rate than was previously imaginable." These commonplaces are said to be indisputable facts, and are supposed to portend revolutionary futures for everyone on earth.

However, if you scrutinize them closely, all such statements are questionable, if not simply false. For one thing, we should not mistake the hectic pace of modern life, which includes a great deal of wasted and duplicated effort, for rapid change, or even for forward motion. But even assuming, for the sake of argument, that all change is for the better, what does it mean, after all, to say that the rate of change is accelerating, and why should we assume that an accelerating—or even merely rapid—rate of change can and will be sustained indefinitely? There have been other bursts of scientific and technological activity followed by long or short lulls; is there any basis for assuming that our age will be different? Any number of developments can slow down or even halt the rate of technological innovation and the social and economic transformations that are said to follow it. These include: war; declining prosperity; a turning away of the human spirit from outer, materialistic matters towards inner, spiritual ones; and even a failure of intelligence and/ or imagination. Given the importance of mathematics, it is worth bearing in mind that in every age there are unsolved mathematical problems around. That most or even all of these will eventually be solved is highly probable; but exactly when any particular problem will be solved—no matter how important it may be to do so—is unpredictable. The serious decline during the Reagan administration in patent applications in the United States, a nation which prides itself on its innovative ability, is in and of itself evidence enough that these changes can happen to any nation, even during our age, which often likes to think of itself as being above the greater forces of history.

Furthermore, although social change is related to technological development, far less personal change is actually necessitated by such development than our prophets, who are typically so enamored with it, would like us to assume. This means, quite simply, that if we are only willing to exercise it, we can have much more control over our lives than is commonly supposed. To cite a crude example, just because televisions exist, and most of us are likely to bring them into our homes, does not mean that they have to be used as the centerpiece for social life in the family. Just because jet planes make traveling fast and relatively easy does not mean that any given married couple must keep houses in two cities at once in order to develop their individual careers, simply because it is possible to do so. There are perhaps difficult choices involved when a technological development makes a decision in personal life-style possible—many opportunities present precisely these kinds of difficult choices—but they are real choices nevertheless, choices which we can make to shape our own futures.

Now let me return again to the original question: How

fast are things really changing? The only way to answer this question is to compare our time with previous eras. Because we take electricity and mechanical power for granted, we have lost perspective on how dramatic was the introduction of these things in the world of the nineteenth century— dramatic not simply because the world at that time was technically naive, as our prophetic hucksters flatter us into assuming, but because these innovations were truly astounding. Perhaps what one considers to be earth-shaking is a matter of personal judgment, values and taste, but I know of no development in the twentieth century, including the computer and biotechnology, which has had and continues to have as dramatic and far-reaching an effect on our lives as the invention and development in the eighteenth and nineteenth centuries of the different kinds of mechanical engine and the electric generator.

In fact, it can be argued that, from the perspective of the power of its impact on our lives, technical innovation has been steadily slowing down during the entire course of this century. To understand what I mean by this statement, ask yourself which of the following innovations have had the greatest impact on your life: the refrigerator, which started making its appearance in the homes of the industrialized nations in the 1940s, or the microwave oven, which started becoming common in the 1970s? The automobile, which became common starting in the 1920s, or the home computer, which started to make its presence felt only in the 1980s? To assess the importance of these appliances, ask yourself the following questions: in each set, which would you sooner give up, the earlier or the later innovation? Which has made the greatest difference in your life?

As we press towards the end of this century, most innovations are no more than refinements of existing technologies: they enable us to do things faster or more neatly, in a glitzier fashion, or more precisely, but not *differently*. Furthermore, the existing technologies, upon whose development so much innovation depends, may themselves find their limits or be exhausted before they perform the miracles that our prophets tell us they will perform in the future. This has often happened in the past. For example, in the Middle Ages many communities in Europe competed with one another to see who could build the biggest and highest cathedral. Many of their accomplishments stand to this day as monuments to their ingenuity. Who has not heard of the cathedrals of Notre Dame, at Chartres, at Amiens and Rheims? But the biggest cathedral that was ever planned and erected was the cathedral at Beauvais. Sound familiar? It shouldn't, because this greatest of all cathedrals is no longer standing. Begun in 1247 and completed by 1557, this marvelous structure collapsed on Ascension Day of 1573. Its ambitious builders had pushed the technology of gothic architecture to the breaking point—and then beyond. This and similar lessons from history should teach us that we should not make predictions simply on the basis of extending present technologies; there is no basis for assuming that any technology is infinitely extensible.

Of course today, using the technologies of reinforced concrete and structural steel, we can build structures even higher and grander than the Beauvais cathedral. But when one technology reaches its limits, it is impossible to predict when a new one will be developed to replace it and push its logic forward. For example, the digital computer of today is based on the "analytic engine" which was invented by the Englishman Charles Babbit in the early nineteenth century. (The "analytic engine" was itself based on the Jacquard loom, the complete development of which, it should be noted, had to be delayed because of the advent of the French Revolution.) The theory of the modern digital computing machine is exactly the same as that of this early predecessor, so why wasn't the nineteenth century the computer age? The answer to this question is very simple: Babbit's "analytic engine" was completely mechanical and the mechanics, that is, the *practice* of the machine, simply could not do justice to its *theory*. There were no alloys in those days that were both light enough and strong enough to sustain the extremely rapid mechanical activity that computing with these machines required. The earliest computers used vacuum tubes and did present some problems with overheating, but the modern computer is basically electronic and therefore has very few mechanical parts so the problem of wear and tear caused by the extremely rapid movement of parts is no longer an issue, although other maintenance problems do remain.

Yet even the development of the modern computer has been limited by the development of software. In Chapter Five, I illustrated some of the software development problems that have now for a quarter of a century seriously limited the scope and effectiveness of the computerization of our education system. Admittedly, education is one of the most complex fields in existence for which one might try to develop software, but it is by no means unique. Similar problems are being experienced, for example, in the fields of meteorology and weapons systems.

These apparent limitations on innovation are not a pessimist's list of past and recent failures. Undoubtedly, with persistence, we will eventually be able to solve some, if not all, of the technical problems that now seem intractable. However problem solving, especially the way we practice it today, is not everything: not all of life's difficulties are reducible to these neat little things we call problems, and wishful thinking, intellectual dishonesty and half-baked answers solve nothing. Therefore we should not be basing human existence, including, especially, the existence of future generations, on premises and promises based on false predictions which stem from untried theories and claims of future mastery which may never exist.

It is much more effective, healthy and honest to recognize the complex nature of development as it occurs in this world and, as far as this pertains to definable problems, not to assume that anything can be solved until it has been solved—especially when there is an element of danger involved in failing to do so. It is, of course, morally questionable to create and bequeath any problems for future generations to solve when this is avoidable. But if we do convince ourselves that our development does indeed depend on this type of decision-making, we should ensure that problems that are created in the present will be solvable at some time in the future, and that we know how far in the future this will be likely to happen. The legacy of present problems that stem from the decisions of past actors who either did not care about the future—that is, *our present*—or assumed, conveniently, that we would be clever enough to deal with what, by disdain or neglect, they were preparing for us, is evidence of the importance of this care for the future. From crushing debt burdens—not only in the Third World but now also in the West—to exhausted and eroded soil, to unmanageable nuclear waste: there is ample evidence of this around us. The irony is that it was our prophets, who make the greatest claim to be mindful of the future, who encouraged us to get into these predicaments with their foolish, self-serving, dishonest and irresponsible predictions, and their assurance that if we pursued these paths to the future everything would turn out all right. It is all very well for a futurologist like Jerrold Maxmen to praise the virtue of making bold, optimistic predictions, but it is precisely these kinds of predictions that are likely to put us in greatest jeopardy if proven false.

Now let us look again at the premise that it is necessary to try to predict the future in order to adapt to it by anticipatory action. I said in the first chapter, and have illustrated throughout this book, that this kind of adaptation often has a bandwagon effect which can lead to making the prophecies in question self-fulfilling. On the other hand, why does one have to arrive in the future with, as it were, ready-made answers? Why does one have to predict to adapt? Do you have to know there will be a road in your future to be able to cross it? After all, it is not the prediction of the road but your eyes and legs, your intelligence and ability, that get you across. Likewise it is mastery of the present, which "living in the future" often makes us neglect, that will get us through the real future when it finally arrives.

Henry Kissinger has been the prophet of our time who, more than any other, has been enamored of the ready-made answer which can be persistently carried forward to the future. Characteristically, he likes to call this ready-made answer *doctrine*. Not surprisingly, therefore, he has had a strong aversion to, and very little patience with, real, that is, open-ended discussion. So he has written: "If there is no doctrine at all and a society operates pragmatically, solving problems 'on their merits' as the saying goes, every event becomes a special case. More energy is spent deciding where one is than where one is going."[2] And so obsessed has he been with where we are going that he has expressed great impatience with the sticky business of taking stock of where we presently are and where we are coming from. It is surprising that this kind of statement has been so appealing for so long in a country like America which prides itself on its pragmatism, which of course always entails dealing with issues "on their merits" and in context. Probably its sway and the closed-minded abstraction it entails have been major factors in America's decline, because in nations, as in individuals, there are few things that retard growth more than ready-made answers.

One cannot help but contrast Kissinger's penchant for ready-made answers with the views of Edmund Burke, the great English conservative statesman of the late eighteenth century. Burke once wrote: "In my course I have known and, according to my measure, have cooperated with great men; and I have never yet seen any plan which has not been mended by the observations of those who were much inferior in understanding to the person who took the lead in the business."[3] It is worth noting that, because of his willingness to consider all cases on their merits, and because he did not believe in approaching developments with ready-made answers, Burke was able in his time both to oppose the French Revolution on the one hand and to support the American Revolution on the other. Kissinger's statement may be appealing to foreign policy makers, but it would never appeal to airline pilots: they know the importance of knowing exactly where one is coming from and all of the other conditions of one's departure in order to be able to both depart and arrive safely. During the post-war years we have all been witness to how doctrine, precisely because of this aversion to open-ended discussion and the pragmatism that can flow from it, has degenerated to dogma; and we have all seen how this degeneration on both ideological fronts has prolonged and exacerbated the arms race.

The greatest development successes of this century have been based not on abstract goals or grand schemes, but on mastery of the concrete details relating to the situation at hand. This has often meant mastery of received technology, not of innovation. This was as true of the United States in the first half of this century as it has been of Japan in the second. No part of the automobile, except for the electric ignition system, was invented in the United States. But Ford and other pioneers in this industry were foremost at mastering quality control and efficiently producing mechanical systems that were invented in Europe, and thus they created the auto-industrial age. Similarly, Japan is not known to be an innovative country, but a masterful one. It is the high-level mastery of manufacturing technique and not innovation that has earned Japan her reputation for quality. By now it is a well-known fact that many of the things that Japan manufactures, from silicon chips to printed circuit boards, were invented in the United States and other countries; in fact even the much touted Japanese management techniques were invented in the United States.

For years after World War II, Japanese industry kept churning out the same dull and unimaginative models of everything from cars to transistor radios while they were mastering their production and quality-control techniques. In a sense, innovation would simply have been a distraction and an unnecessary luxury at that point. The Japanese were not concentrating on the model of the future, but on the one in front of their noses. Once they had complete control of the production process and were able to manufacture things exactly the way they wanted to, they began to introduce variety and to innovate on their own. By then their innovation was grounded in what they had already really mastered and could therefore do exceedingly well.

Likewise, the Soviet Union's remarkable accomplishments in space in recent years have been based on the mastery of received technology. It matters little whether they have stuck to the old technology out of necessity, that is, because of their relative technological backwardness, or out of choice. In 1969, when the United States won the race to the moon, all of the pundits predicted that the Soviet Union would never catch up in the race in space. And in the 1970s it appeared as if these prophets would be right. America surged forward with dazzling innovations and new programs to both broaden and deepen her lead, developing first the Skylab and then the Shuttle. Meanwhile the Soviets plodded on, using the same tried-and-true rocket systems over and over again, manufacturing them in large quantities and, with experience, with a high level of reliability. Needless to say, what has happened since then should embarrass the prophets of 1969. The Skylab came crashing down to earth and so too, tragically, did the American Shuttle. In the meantime, as they plodded on, the Soviets became very good at what they were doing. They logged an impressive number of man-hours, days, months and finally years in space so that now they are experts at dealing with the health consequences of prolonged stays outside of the earth's gravitational pull. This is acknowledged by observers in both the West and the East to be the type of experience that will be indispensable if a journey to Mars is to be undertaken, as it may be, towards the end of this century. The Soviets are also now close to the point where they will be able to build a space station, which could act as a stepping-stone for this proposed journey and would give them a permanent presence in space. Of course, any number of unanticipated things could happen to thwart the Soviet ambitions in space, but the point is that they are now universally acknowledged to be ahead in many of the most basic capabilities needed for getting to Mars, a development which no one could or would have predicted in 1969.

There are many races to the future going on now, cheered on by our prophets, and we are already beginning to see some of the consequences of the whole world chasing after the same goals. With more and more people and nations setting their sights on the same targets, the future is becoming like the small end of a funnel. One consequence of so many nations choosing the same developmental goals is that, with everyone heading for the same place, the way is very crowded and it is hard to find any standing room when one arrives. That is why it is said that we are living in such a competitive world. It is not because we are so masterful—too many of our goods, in spite of their glitz, are actually rather uninteresting and shoddy—but because there are too few goals being pursued by too many comers. Another consequence of the whole world chasing the same goals is that the globe is actually becoming increasingly homogeneous and losing some of its rich diversity. This has resulted, of course, in the boredom of finding the same sorts of goods and services all over the world; but it has also led to the loss of some invaluable cultural forms, from literacy to railways, that have been or are being abandoned in the process.

However, in the short run, just as bad as the sometimes harmful homogeneity that chasing after a narrow number of goals is imposing upon the world is the fact that the constant innovation upon which a great deal of futurology is based— and which it encourages—undermines our ability to act effectively in the present. Thinking about the past in moderation is a good thing and can enhance the present. That is why Goethe said that he who knows no history lives in darkness. But thinking about the past excessively, which is commonly referred to as "living in the past," is harmful because it undermines the present by halting human growth and development. The same can be said about thinking about the future: in moderation, it should enhance the present. But the modern obsession with the future is the same as "living in the future," and is simply the other side of the coin to "living in the past." It does not inhibit growth by fixing it at some stage in the past, as living in the past does; it inhibits it by limiting choice and paralyzing the capacity of individuals, communities and nations to maximize the discovery and creation which belong to the present. And it encourages us to live dishonestly and irresponsibly in the present in expectation of future redemption. Finally, living in the future undermines our ability to act effectively in the present because it forces us to constantly learn the "up-and-coming thing" regardless of its merits—sometimes even before the old one has been mastered.

Because of our obsession with the future, many of us have become innovation junkies, but this lust for innovation, often for its own sake, needlessly puts everyone, especially adults, who are often slow learners, into situations where they are periodically, sometimes permanently, being put off balance and rendered incompetent. And it puts children, who are fast learners, in the position of having to invest great amounts of energy in mastering ephemeral things, like rapidly obsolescing computer languages, while neglecting the proven and still necessary skills that would serve them in better stead in the long run. And the institutionalized lust for innovation often leads to institutionalized incompetence in all sorts of public and private organizations. When presented with proposals that are said to be our future salvation, we should always bear these problems in mind, and also bear in mind that today innovation is often no more than a racket. One student of this phenomenon, the educator Michael Fullan, has observed that, although few of the innovations in the education system have made any positive difference in the lives of students or teachers, they have made a great deal of difference in the lives of the innovators themselves; they help them develop their own careers. Just to get an idea of the magnitude of intervention which is here in question, one should bear in mind that in New York City alone there were no fewer than 781 innovative programs introduced into the education system between 1979 and 1981.[4]

Perhaps the best way to understand our obsession with the future and the lust for innovation which it engenders is to think of it as a trap in our culture into which our prophets have been able to lure us because of our fear. But there are other ways of understanding our susceptibility to being lured into this trap. In an illuminating study called *The Myth of the Eternal Return*, Mircea Eliade, the distinguished professor of comparative religion, discusses a phenomenon which he calls "the terror of history." The terror of history is an existential critique of the linear progress of modern history, and a way of comprehending why so many of its steps have been so horrifying. Eliade credits Hegel with formulating the existential position that accepts all historical developments, no matter how terrifying they may be, as being *necessary*. He writes:

> From Hegel on, every effort is directed toward saving and conferring value on the historical event as such, the event in itself and for itself. In his study of the German Constitution, Hegel wrote that if we recognize that things are necessarily as they are, that is, that they are not arbitrary and not the result of chance, we shall at the same time recognize that they *must* be as they are. A century later, the concept of historical necessity will enjoy a more and more triumphant practical application: in fact, all the cruelties, aberrations, and tragedies of history

have been, and still are, justified by the necessities of the "historical moment." (emphasis in original)[5]

Hegel's sense of historical necessity should sound familiar because the "necessary past" is basically just the other side of the coin of the "inevitable future" with which so many of our prophets are smitten. Both of these views are born of a linear view of the passage of time; they both act as a rationale for narrowing choice, for narrowing the scope of human endeavor; and ultimately they both act also as an apology for the loss of human freedom this entails. Therefore, Eliade concludes this part of his argument with the following painfully ironic observation: "How could Hegel know what was *necessary* in history, what, consequently, must occur exactly as it had occurred? Hegel believed that he knew what the Universal Spirit wanted. We shall not insist on the audacity of this thesis, which, after all, abolishes precisely what Hegel wanted to save in history—human freedom." (emphasis in original)[6]

The attack on human freedom by modern prophecy is perhaps the most disturbing aspect of futurology. Squeezed between the "terror of history" and the "tyranny of prophecy" people today—in spite of the freedom that is much vaunted, especially in the West—find that they have little room to maneuver. No wonder our prophets appeal, as Orwell observed, to our fear and our craving for power: these are precisely the drives that dominate those who feel trapped.

The futurologists' arguments about inevitability and necessity are absurd. After all, what does the future represent except a mental construct which contains possibilities? The future seems ominous, not because it is rushing in on us and forcing us to make decisions about an unknown time, but because we are crowded by the failures of the present and immediate past, many of which are based on the irresponsible programs of our contemporary prophets: over forty years of failure to disarm, to properly end World War II; over twenty years of decline in the education system; a health system which in spite of worthy accomplishments still produces often questionable results and at an ever diminishing return on resources invested in it. It is no wonder that our failures haunt us. But why should we continue to make our disease worse by constantly returning to the same quacks who helped get us into trouble in the first place and letting them continue to mislead us and tyrannize our future?

What are the alternatives to these modern self-defeating habits of life? How can we avoid being terrorized by the past and tyrannized by the future? Eliade's study contains the beginning of an answer. It does not begin with the terror of history, but ends there. It begins with an appreciation of the pre-Socratic and non-western cultures which, he observes, sought consolation for the existential fear that springs from the remembrance of history and a dread of the future. The members of these societies coped effectively, not by trying to rationalize the future and control it, as we do, but by relating all events to religious and mystical archetypes and the cyclical view of time that they represent. In this world view, if a misfortune befell a person he would console himself by thinking that this was a repetition of the divine drama, that the same thing happened to a god at the beginning of time and was all part of a great drama that would lead, ultimately, to the making and salvation of the world.† Of course we cannot, and should not, try to reconstruct the world view and ethos of the so-called archaic societies, but it would be foolish not to recognize the fact that there is more scope for cycles and repetition in modern life, and more virtue in this than our modern prophets would allow.

The cyclical view of time is basically feminine, whereas the linear view, which appeals to virtually all of our prophets, is masculine. The cyclical view therefore sheds a very different light on human development than that which comes from our prophets. Nothing illustrates this better than Aesop's fable about the ant and the grasshopper. Though he lived in the sixth century B.C., morally Aesop had a great deal in common with our modern day futurologists—the

---

† Eliade has observed that there are signs that the cyclical view of time is gaining some currency in the modern world, and he cites as evidence of this the writing of the historians Toynbee and Spengler, as well as the literature of T.S. Eliot and James Joyce. More recently, Milan Kundera in his remarkable best-selling novel, *The Unbearable Lightness of Being*, has made a sustained allegorical argument for the goodness of repetition in life.

seeds of their thinking have always been with us. This fable is very short so here is the whole thing:

> One fine day in winter some Ants were busy drying their store of corn, which had got rather damp during a spell of rain. Presently up came a Grasshopper and begged them to spare her a few grains, "For," she said, "I'm simply starving." The Ants stopped work for a moment, though this was against their principles. "May we ask," said they, "what you were doing with yourself all last summer? Why didn't you collect a store of food for the winter?" "The fact is," replied the Grasshopper, "I was so busy singing that I hadn't the time." "If you spent the summer singing," replied the Ants, "you can't do better than spend the winter dancing." And they chuckled and went on with their work.[7]

Aesop's fable, which is told in the familiar retrospective mode of the forecaster writing the history of future time, speaks volumes about the world view of the typical futurologist. The ants, to be sure, had a prophetic vision: they foresaw a grim and cruel future in the coming of winter and, in anticipation, planned for it by stocking provisions. The grasshopper, however, who lived only in the present, failed to see this vision, failed to take the necessary adaptive measures and therefore, from the ants' perspective, was destined to "deservedly" perish. But when you think of it, these ants were not really that insightful; they were, after all, preparing not for an unprecedented future catastrophe, but for the change of the seasons, for the winter which they had seen before and were to see time and again as it was to recur during their lifetimes. They were only your typical extrapolating futurologists, feeling clever about pointing to the obvious. That is the key: they were motivated not so much by insight as by anxiety, and even when they had a full storehouse that only needed ordinary maintenance based on received wisdom about preventing spoilage, their fear and grim vision drove them on to create a very narrow little world, to cultivate a narrow little niche and live a spiritually impoverished life-style.

This is the most charitable interpretation that one can give to Aesop's fable, but by neglecting other issues it gives him, as a moralist, far more credit than he deserves. Bear in mind how nasty these clever little ant-prophets were when confronted by someone whose world view was different from their own. They were reluctant to stop work even to consider her plight. They did not merely tell the grasshopper to go her own way, they mocked her about her life-style and on account of her profession. They were the prophetic ones; they had vision; they knew the world of the future would be cruel to such as she; they had anticipated it, had made their plans and preparations, and were ready for it. But when you consider the matter more closely, were they not purposive and logical to an extreme? They consulted their heads in all things, including the plight of a fellow creature, but not their hearts. Finally, they denigrated her work, her profession, which was singing; there was no room for it in their world, not in the present and certainly not in the future, where it is represented as being no more than mere folly.†

To see how typical they are of modern prophets one has only to recall Feigenbaum's similar tirade, which I quoted earlier: "These intellectuals who persist in their indifference, not to say snobbery, will find themselves stranded in a quaint museum of the intellect, forced to live petulantly, and rather irrelevantly, on the charity of those who understand the real dimensions of the revolution and can deal with the new world it will bring about." By now this vision should also sound familiar from other prophetic sources. The reader will recall that Plato, who was one of Aesop's spiritual heirs, took a similar view. In the *Republic* we also have an idealization of narrowly purposive behavior, but there, instead of tilling the soil, an activity which is denigrated, we have the single-minded pursuit of philosophy and athletics relating to military skills. Plato also, as the reader will recall, had no room in his vision for the arts, especially the so-called imitative ones. Similarly Richardson, in his City of Health, where the single purpose was to gear all life to the promotion and

---

† Incidentally, Aesop really had it in for grasshoppers. In another fable called *The Grasshopper and the Owl* he describes another scene in which the head, Logos, represented by the Owl, literally devours the soul, represented by another grasshopper who knows no better than to sing in this owl's presence.

sustenance of health, also had no room in his vision for the aesthetic side of life and so he promptly banished all decorations from its households.

There is something very troubling about these visions and the plans and schemes they legitimate and promote— aside from their prissy and uncharitable views, and aside also from the fact that they leave no room for aesthetics. It is not just that they are purposive and spell out future goals, but that their purposes are so very narrow, and their goals are to the exclusion of so many worthwhile other ones. Aesop, falsely but characteristically, makes this single-minded purposiveness a matter of life-and-death necessity; this kind of falseness, at bottom, is what the tyranny of prophecy is all about. More than this, these visions that claim to be very wise seem very foolish when one considers how the world really does develop. The arts, for example, are not a matter of mere luxury, but of necessity, and by saying this I mean more than that music and poetry and fine arts and theatre are good for you—even the meanest agricultural laborer knows the value of a barn dance. Not all of the drive for development comes from science. From the arts come also the creative forces in life, some of which have had profound practical impacts on even our technological and economic development.

Cyril Stanley Smith, the distinguished metallurgist, has documented a great deal of the history of how art has aided in the development of industry. He notes, for example: "Metallurgy began with the making of necklace beads and ornaments in hammered, naturally occurring copper long before 'useful' knives and weapons were made. The improvement of metals by alloying and heat treatment as well as most methods of shaping them started in jewellery and sculpture. Casting in complicated moulds began in the manufacture of statuettes. Welding was first used to join parts of bronze sculpture together—none but the smallest bronze statues of Greece or ceremonial vessels of Shang China could have been fabricated without the technique."[8] I noted above that the precursor for the modern digital computer was the Jacquard loom, and in this vein Smith also notes that most minerals and many organic and inorganic compounds were discovered for uses as pigments; wheels first appeared on toys; lathes were used for making snuff boxes before they were used for heavy industry; rockets for fun came before rockets for military use; the chemical industry grew from the need for dyes and mordants used in fine textiles; and electric generation was developed in response to the need for electricity for electroplating silverplate tableware.

The above examples should illustrate that a great deal of innovation is not purposive but adaptive in nature: whereas for the economist innovation may be a wilful trick, for the artist and craftsman of the finest order it is a response to present need and a natural part of their creative intelligence. All of the above innovations and countless others came from play and from the cultivation of known techniques by those who were intimately familiar with them. They were not attempts to "invent the future," as Stewart Brand claims many scientists and technicians are trying to do at MIT, because these innovators had no fixed idea in their minds of what the future should be like; they were only trying to be masterful, or, what is much the same thing, to enhance their present abilities, but ultimately their innovations were all used in unintended and unexpected ways.

These are important distinctions. The research that is going on now at the Media Lab at MIT and in a similar vein in many of our research and development establishments all over the world is all based on a paradigm of planning that is itself largely based on the paradigm of war. These research endeavors are generally parts of grim campaigns to be the first to occupy a rather unimaginative and narrow future industrial-technological niche: the clever telephone, the artless but glitzy robot secretary, mechanized graphics, and so on. The alternative paradigm of development, which is based on the artist's methods of cultivation and of play do not, because they cannot, have a prophetic quality and therefore are treated with indifference.

War is a seductive paradigm because, in a sense, it is the ultimate act of subjugating substance to form. And it is surely the intellectual basis of a great deal of modern planning, especially the grandest and most ambitious schemes. It is therefore no mere coincidence that many futurologists of our time—perhaps Herman Kahn is most prominent among these—started their careers in military planning. Nor is it accidental that those "think tanks" that have specialized in military research, like the Rand Corporation and the Hudson Institute, have also been major centers for work in futurology. If there is a god of warfare, he undoubtedly serves double time as the god of modern prophecy. And, since influence works in both directions, a great deal of modern futurology is rife with the "campaign" mentality, and the paradigm of war has in turn even invaded the thinking of other areas of futurology, like economics and health.

Planning today is based all too often on the war paradigm. It depends on prior destruction, on the obliteration of a great deal, if not all, present context and detail in order to achieve its ends. Planning, which usually relies heavily on forecasting, has become something of a fetish in social and economic thinking since the end of World War II. In recent years it has been argued, particularly by economic theorists like Professor Lester Thurow of MIT, that the main advantage that Japan and Germany have over the United States is that the former countries have national industrial plans whereas the American economy is developed on an ad hoc basis.[9] But there is no magic in planning. Whatever merit there may be in planning per se, its meaning and effectiveness will vary greatly from time to time and from place to place. More than goals, materials or objectives, and far more than any elaborate or simple concepts, planning, to be effective, requires *context*.

This fact is well illustrated by an examination of the outcome of the Marshall Plan and its descendents, some of the grandest economic plans of this or any century. Although the Marshall Plan was devised by the United States to assist all of the nations of Europe that had been devastated by World War II in their effort to build themselves economically, it is well known that it was not equally effective everywhere it was applied. Jane Jacobs, an economist who has a rare understanding of both the uses and the limits of planning, has summarized the different effects of the Marshall Plan in Europe in this way:

Some of the aided economies, such as those of the Netherlands, West Germany, parts of France and parts of Italy, did proceed to expand and develop

—as San Francisco did after its [1906 earthquake] disaster. But others did nothing of the kind. Britain received Marshall Plan equipment, as West Germany did, but this bounty did not make Britain's economy behave like West Germany's. Southern Italy received Marshall Plan aid, just as northern Italy did, but the sequels were strikingly different. Northern Italy, already the most prosperous and economically creative part of the country, proceeded to prosper, develop and expand further. Southern Italy, which had previously been persistently backward, poor and economically passive, stayed so. Insofar as Marshall Plan aid (or the much larger aid given later from the north of Italy) changed southern Italy, the changes did not transcend the gifts themselves, for southern Italy's economy did not take to expanding and developing on its own account or under its own steam . . .[10]

The gist of Jacobs's argument is that, in the different countries that were targeted by the Marshall Plan and by the subsequent Marshall-type plans that were aimed at Third World countries, these plans, in the form of economic and material aid, took hold only where there was context, where there were already enough people who had the necessary types of knowledge and skills to implement them, and in the context of networks and interactive systems in which this infusion of economic and material aid could take hold. In other places, like southern Italy, the Marshall Plan worked as effectively as sprinkling seed on rock or barren ground— in spite of the predictions.

My argument, of course, is not against planning per se any more than it is, in the final analysis, against being mindful of the future. Our experience with the Marshall Plan and similar enterprises has long demonstrated that, in spite of our fetishistic attachment to it, planning in and of itself is inherently neither good nor bad. Like regulation (a related process), planning can be either good or bad. The question is not whether or not one is to make plans. The question is, on what shall these plans be based? If plans are to be based on mere predictions then one must always ask: On what are these predictions really based? And whose interests will their fulfilment or self-fulfilment serve? But we should not delude ourselves into thinking that planning, per se, is always a good, always a virtuous thing to do. On the contrary, a significant part of planning is not only sterile, as was Marshall Plan aid to southern Italy, but often also debilitating, and even destructive.

Good planning should never unnecessarily limit choices; it should expand them. Ideally, good planning will not consist of that which is borrowed, but that which is bred. It will be a natural, concomitant activity, a by-product, if you will, of living as well as possible *in the present*; it will never be a substitute for it, which is often precisely what bad planning is about.

It is worth bearing in mind that the most effective method of combating the spread of AIDS has not been based on the war paradigm, so dear to the futurist. Even five years ago, the war paradigm dominated our thinking on how to deal with this challenge. Great cures were predicted. The disease would be knocked out by a heroic international research effort. But these predictions have so far come to naught. Meanwhile, the most effective means for coping with this disease have come from cultivation, which has led to changes in day-to-day habits of relationship. It is unfortunate that it has taken desperation for us to change in the present instead of continuing to wait for some future miracle to save us, but at least our experience with AIDS is teaching us that we can work effectively with present means, and that the present is the appropriate time in which to combat this or any future catastrophe. Unfortunately, in most other seemingly less desperate situations, we continue to wait for future miracles because we are told by our prophets that they will come.

The paradigm of war, which so many modern prophets invite us to worship, is also the ultimate depersonalizer of life, and therefore cares very little about relationships. It depersonalizes and trivializes all human relationships, all acts of nurturance and love that precede it and many that follow. That is why it is the ideal metaphor for our modern prophets—it fits perfectly into their psychology.

It is impossible to imagine a worse paradigm for thinking of the future, for growth and development, than the paradigm of war. One can say much against it, but basically it entails two main problems. The lesser of these is that it encourages us to put vast amounts of energy not only into preparation, but into overpreparation, to the point where our resources for other endeavors are sapped and we are never at ease to enjoy the fruits of our labor and the repose which should be the gift of everyday life. Those of us who think this is virtuous will stagger through life constantly pressed under the weight of their weapons; those who do not will simply retreat from life and try not to get trampled. No one has described this condition better than E.M. Forster in his novel *Howard's End*, where he writes: "Actual life is full of false clues and sign-posts that lead nowhere. With infinite effort we nerve ourselves for a crisis that never comes. The most successful career must show a waste of strength that might have removed mountains, and the most unsuccessful is not that of the man who is taken unprepared, but of him who has prepared and is never taken. On a tragedy of that kind our national morality is duly silent. It assumes that preparation against danger is in itself good, and that men, like nations, are the better for staggering through life fully armed."[11] Too many of us have completely forgotten the virtues of traveling light through life, relying on our character and inner resources rather than on externalities, on weapons.

The second problem with this mentality is, of course, that in any war there will be winners and there will be losers. In this context I have already mentioned the deadly dullness and homogeneity that results when all nations pursue the same goals; the world as a whole becomes the loser. The war paradigm, which has been a favorite among false prophets from Aesop on down, is not sometimes, but always, a recipe for disaster, if not your own than that of someone else.

The god of war has many attributes that have much to do with how we are today encouraged to regard the future. The god of war, the god of kill, is also the god of overkill, not only because fear of reprisal is a great motivator, but because relentless, blind pursuit is his nature. Even when the battle is going the wrong way, when the plan and the premises on which the plan were based are proving themselves to be useless, or worse than useless, the pursuit is relentless. Soldiers are told to ignore feedback that might distract them from their relentless course, and also to ignore details and context. Very rapidly, and increasingly, everyone becomes the enemy.

The alternative to the paradigm of war which has come to play such a great part in our contemplation of the future is Eros, who is commonly regarded as the god of love, but in this context can more generally be thought of as the god of connectedness. I will describe some of his attributes because they also belong to the alternative paradigm for thinking of the future. I have already mentioned two: repetition and the cyclical mode of living.

The uses of repetition are many in a world which strives for connectedness rather than merely for extension. It is used for gaining mastery and creating meaning, and repeated cycles serve the invaluable purpose of grounding life in the familiar rather than leaving it constantly subjected to the inherent strangeness of the novel. Open-endedness is another of this god's main attributes. Openness means that one never plans on arriving at a future encounter with the false prophet's ready-made answer, but alternatively on discovering the answer in the richness of exploring the new experience. But perhaps the most important attribute of this god which we must understand if we are to change our warlike mentality with regard to the future is cultivation.

Cultivation as an alternative paradigm to war for facing the future is different not only because it is ever constructive, but also because it is constructive by means of being respectful of context and paying close attention to detail. It is not like a moonshot, which is essentially an exercise in decontextualization through the creation of a self-contained environment. Few things in life are like moonshots. Most things are not like that, cannot be made like that because they are too complex, too dependent for their success on paying attention to and interacting with context, to the external environment—including the needs of other people—rather than subduing it by blasting through it. Because it examines context, cultivation requires attention to detail and interaction with that which is being cultivated, be it a school, a child, a tree, a car, a factory.

There is much talk today of competitiveness, of excellence, and much of this talk is patently war talk. It is talk about grimly purposive actions, about heroic acts of will geared towards the achievement of some future goal. But most goals are not achieved by single acts of will, even heroic ones. They are achieved by *sustained acts of will*, that is, by a change of habit, of custom and of culture. That is why all failures in achieving goals, that is, in mastery, be they in our ability to build cars or to make love, are based on failures in cultivation, in nurturance.

Cultivation takes time. Its effect or its failure are cumulative, even though sometimes expressions of the success that comes from it may be dramatic, as when you make a breakthrough in your piano-playing technique, or a tree that has for years been carefully pruned one year bursts forth in blossom and fruit. Sustained acts are necessary because nature is generally forgiving in the short run but not in the long. An occasional inappropriate response to the needs of a child will not permanently damage him or her, but persistent abuse or neglect will. The failures of nurturance, of cultivation, are persistent failures; they are failures which result from persistent neglect of the present.

Neglect and abandonment of the present are symptoms and necessary results of our obsession with the future, and with the relentless pursuit of narrow goals that we think will make the future for us. The heart of all prediction is a correlation of means and ends, but one of the pathologies of modern futurology is to think that means *are* ends. That is why every little innovation—which is usually no more than a disembodied means—gets extrapolated and lionized by our prophets. The tendency to think this way is deadly because it entails the subjugation of ends to means, of questions to answers. The search for applications for the latest innovation becomes not an associative but an exploitative search. Means masquerading as goals, means looking for ends, answers looking for questions, are all agents of exploitation. On the contrary, between ends and means should be continual dialogue. A good answer always changes the question which elicited it, and the changed question requires then a different good answer, until answer and question, means and ends, are entirely different from what they started as.

Tadao Umesao, a Japanese cultural anthropologist, considers narrow goal orientation to be the deadliest form of cultural habit we can develop. He writes: "To say that a goal is clear is to say that it is functional. To say that it is functional is to say that it is 'unifunctional.' What I believe is that at some point our world became filled exclusively with such unifunctional things, and it is this that has led to our present state of confusion." He then goes on to ask: "Is it really so absurd to envisage a plan which does not take a single goal as its final end, a plan in which each successive goal emerges and grows from the process of planning itself—i.e., a process which is rather like a succession of makeshift expedients?"[12] Those who understand Japanese culture on the basis only of the caricature that is presented to the West may find Umesao's contention puzzling, because Japan is usually portrayed in the West as being single-minded. This is true to a point, but it is only a recent development born of the desperation that arose in the aftermath of World War II. Japan has been successful in part because of its single-minded goal orientation, but in larger part because of its ability, like Sweden, to act concertedly as a nation. Umesao argues, however, that in the process of overplanning, Japan has worked itself into a very narrow niche, and he thinks that this will be deadly in the long run.

Context is the enemy of our prophets who like to oversimplify and trivialize everything. The rich, sticky and stubborn nature of reality is their bane. That is why so many of them are so enamored with systems and mechanical precision—yet one must never underestimate how close the precise can be to the petty. So in thinking about future atomic wars Nitze worried not only about controlling the situation with precise language, but also about how atom bombs could be dropped precisely enough to avoid civilian casualties. It is certainly a high-minded goal if you accept the premise of such a war itself and allow for the vanity in such thinking. Similarly Papert wants to decontextualize the future. Not only does he want to introduce his LOGO system into the schools, but he has predicted the abolition of the school system itself—and even our system of knowledge which took thousands of years to cultivate—in the process. That would certainly be a great exercise in decontextualization.

If we continue to follow the lead of prophets who trivialize and depersonalize future life in order to make it manageable, imaginable, then our goals will become simpleminded and we will continue to abandon the richness and complexity that works, albeit with difficulties, for a narrow future at best and an impoverished fantasy at worst. We will be sacrificing reality to fantasy. Present reality must be sacrificed, will be sacrificed sooner or later, but then this should be to a new reality, equally rich or richer—not to the impoverished visions of our prophets. There is room for any amount of innovation in this world, but in introducing it we should where possible follow the lead of our most sophisticated cultivators who are now practicing the art and science of intersowing. We should make our gardens richer and more diverse rather than always wanting to start with scorched earth and the new unknown crop.

When those who have power avoid responsibility for making the present work, those who are helpless suffer. The best years of the lives of a large part of the population are frittered away waiting for that miraculous time in the ever receding future when the economy will be ready to let them be a part of it; when society will be less alienating; the world will be safe; the education system will work; a cure will be discovered for the latest disease. There is an enormous amount that can be done with present knowledge, techniques and technology to significantly alleviate these types of problems *now*. Not to act now as best we can to deal with present problems is simply irresponsible. We do not know, cannot know, what will work to solve our problems in the future, but we can find out what will solve them in the present by working to solve them now, with proven means that are already at hand.

By being so enthralled by the future we have made a perversion out of what, when tempered with prudence, can be a virtue, that is, the postponement of gratification. Even on the level of the individual, decisions in which the importance of timing is fairly self-evident are very often indefinitely deferred for the sake of waiting for the "perfect moment," which is always at some time in the future. Countless numbers of people delay marriage and having children to the point where it becomes improbable, if not impossible, to make these decisions sanely and soberly—let alone on the basis of love. Greater numbers refuse to enjoy the daily gifts that life has to offer them for the sake of first completing the dieting or fitness regimen which they have persuaded themselves will make them more worthy people at some point in the future. This kind of thinking has become so prevalent in our society that for many it has become an almost lethal sort of second nature. By adopting this kind of thinking we deny not only our bodies, but our very souls; we postpone not only gratification, but the quest for meaning and fulfilment that should be part of our daily lives.

Furthermore, when it comes to thinking about the future—largely due to the way it is incessantly hyped by some of the most influential leaders in government, business and the media—we have become like impressionable children at a carnival, wildly dashing from one huckster to the next, never finishing a thing before dropping it and running off to grab at the next marvel or treat that is dangled before our eyes. With children, such mad dashing about usually leads to exhaustion and sore stomachs. Is this really the way we want to develop our lives and culture?

This last question is a paraphrase of Tolstoy, who asked not, What does the future hold in store for us? but, What shall we do and how shall we live? If the futurologists who tell us that the future has endless possibilities are really right, we need not wait to hear from them what the future ought to be like. This, as Tolstoy suggests, is a question we should pose to ourselves. Unless we do so, unless we exercise the real freedom we have *at present* to shape our destinies according to the way we want to live, rather than acting on the basis of our prophets' versions of the good and the "inevitable," the less freedom in the long run we will have to exercise. Talk of the inevitable is cheap, but it is also insidious. When we hear it we would do well to ask ourselves: What does the promoter of a particular inevitable scenario have at stake in having it realized? What do they have to gain? And, perhaps more important, because there is no such thing as a neutral future, what do other, undoubtedly more helpless members of our society, have to lose?

In the Jewish tradition, waiting for the Messiah, that is, for the salvation of the future, is now considered to be morally corrupt. One must make the most of the present, not only because it is the given, but in order even to be worthy of the Messiah's coming. There are also similar precepts in Christianity (even though that religion believes the Messiah has already come), and in the other major religions of the world. These religions consider true prophecy to be the highest calling because they recognize that all questions surrounding the uses of prophecy are ultimately moral questions, questions that are concerned with what we want to become. In this sense prophecy that is not grounded in morality is always false. Far from being foresightful, it is myopic and evasive to forget that most questions that can be posed about the future can more meaningfully and forcefully be posed about the present. It is only at our peril that we forget that if we used only the knowledge we now have, and used it only for the good, we could have heaven on earth, without one further innovation or discovery, and thereby create a better world than any of our false prophets are capable of envisioning. This may be a truism but cannot successfully be evaded. It is a matter not of ingenuity but of character, and it is the key to any and all possible good futures.

NOTES

1. Ivan Illich, *Limits to Medicine: Medical Nemesis: The Expropriation of Health* (Harmondsworth, England: Penguin Books, 1977).
2. Henry Kissinger, "American Strategic Doctrine and Diplomacy," in Michael Howard (ed.), *The Theory and Practice of War* (London: Cassell, 1965), p. 277.
3. Edmund Burke, cited by Karl Popper in *The Open Society and Its Enemies* (Princeton, N.J.: Princeton University Press, 1966).
4. See Michael Fullan, *The Meaning of Education Change* (Toronto: OISE Press, 1982), p. 4. Fullan estimates there are tens of thousands of members of what he calls the "innovation establishment" working in the United States in the field of education.
5. Mircea Eliade, *The Myth of the Eternal Return* (New York: Pantheon, 1954), pp. 147–148.
6. Eliade, p. 148.

7. *Aesop's Fables* (trans. V.S. Vernon-Jones) (London: Heinemann, 1912), p. 125.

8. Cyril Stanley Smith, "Aesthetic Curiosity—The Root of Invention," in *The New York Times* (August 24, 1975).

9. Lester Thurow, *Zero-sum Solution: The Route to Economic Growth* (Harmondsworth, England: Penguin, 1987). Actually America does have a national industrial plan—but it is embedded in its military planning. It may not be a *good* plan, but it is national in scope and intervenes heavily in the economy.

10. Jane Jacobs, *Cities and the Wealth of Nations* (London: Viking, 1985), p. 8.

11. E.M. Forster, *Howard's End* (New York: Bantam, 1985), p. 101.

12. Tadao Umesao, "Soul and Material Things," keynote address to meeting of International Council of Societies of Industrial Design, ICSID '73 (Kyoto: Congress Report Japan Organizing Committee for ICSID '73), pp. 17–18.

INDEX

Hugo, Victor, 119**n**
Huxley, Aldous, 119, 143, 206
Hygeia, 177
Hygeia (Richardson), 177–86,
    187, 192, 194, 199
Hypnopaedia, 143

IBM Corporation, 141–42, 145,
    164, 171, 172
Ideological prophecy, 27, 81–104
Illich, Ivan, 96, 248
Illiteracy, 222
Immortality, 71–72
Individualized learning with
    computer-aided instruction,
    152–62
  branching tutorials, 155–56
  courseware based on game
    theory, 156–57
  generative courseware, 156
  linear courseware, 154–55
  LOGO system, 157–62, 167,
    273
Industrial society, 220–22
Inevitability, 44
  of change, 20
  ethic of, 30
  rhetoric of, 30, 31, 37–38, 41–
    42, 275–76
Inflation, 36–37
Information society, myth of,
    222–23
Innovation, technical, *see*
    Science
*Inquiry into the Human Pros-
    pect, An* (Heilbroner), 216
Insight into human nature, 11
*Invasion of England: A Proph-
    ecy in Two Acts, The*, 129
Iphigenia, 109, 110, 138
Iphigenia in Tauris, 138
Iran, 24, 133**n**
Iraq, 133**n**
Isaiah, 10–11
Israel, 9, 11**n**, 112**n**, 133**n**
  kibbutz in, 149
Italy, 267–68, 269

Jacobs, Jane, 45, 267–68
Jacquard loom, 253
Japan, 3, 23, 38, 41, 119, 131,
    273
  economy of, 22, 33, 267
  mastery of received technol-
    ogy in, 256–57
  resource dependence of, 24
Japanese Fifth Generation proj-
    ect, 96
Jargon of futurology, 89–93, 137
Jephthah, 110**n**
Jevons, Stanley, 212, 216, 217**n**
Jews, 225–26, 276
  Hebrew prophets, 10–11
  see also Israel
Josephus, 226
Jouvenal, Bertrand de, 43
Joyce, James, 262**n**
Julius Caesar, 226

Kahn, Herman, 42, 92, 94–95,
    266
Katz, Michael, 171
Kennedy, John F., 116, 121,
    121**n**
Kibbutz, Israeli, 149
King, T.J., 236
Kingston *Gleaner*, 6–7
Kissinger, Henry, 14, 41, 128,
    134–35, 255–56
  limited nuclear war, doctrine
    of, 121–24, 125–27
  prophetic role assumed by,
    29–30, 31
Koch, Robert, 180, 181
Korean War, 131, 134
Kundera, Milan, 262**n**
Kushner, Kathy, 214–15
Kuttner, Robert, 38–39

Laffer curve, 34
Language
  jargon of futurology, 89–93,
    137
  learning of, 158
Laski, John, 166
Laszlo, Ervin, 43

Learning theory, 163
Lebanon, 112n, 133n
Lentulus, 88
Le Roy, Louis, 19n
Less developed nations, 218, 219
Lesse, Stanley, 31n, 200–2
Leviticus, Book of, 225, 226n
Lewis, C.S., 16
Limits of Growth (Club of
　Rome), 216–17
Limits of Medicine (Illich), 248
Linear projections, *see* Present
　trends, prophecies based on
Liotta, Domingo, 195
Living in the future, 259
LOGO system, 157–62, 167, 273
Luehrman, Arthur, 168
"Lying in Politics," 99–100

Machines, 151, 250, 252
　assimilation of, 163
McNamara, Robert, 14n, 116–17
Malthus, Thomas, 82–83, 216,
　217n
Managers, middle, 61–62
Manhattan Project, 235
Manifest destiny, 27–29
Marcuse, Herbert, 40
Marshall Plan, 267–69
Marx, Karl, 108, 153, 171, 212
Marxism, 84–87, 153
　environmental matters and,
　212
　theory of revolution, 85–86
Mason, Roy, 66–67
Masuda, Yoneji, 102–3
Mathematics, learning of, 158
Maxmen, Jerrold, 32, 194, 202–
　3, 255
M'Bow, Amadou-Mahtar, 43
*Media Lab: Inventing the Future
　at MIT, The* (Brand), 75–
　76, 77–78
Medical technology, 187, 188–
　91, 193, 194–99, 202
　artificial heart, 195–99
Medical terminology, 93

Medicine, *see* Health and
　medicine
Megatrends (Naisbitt), 188n
*Mémoire sur la fermentation ap-
　pellée lactique* (Pasteur),
　180–81
Mental illness, 183
Messiah, 108, 276
Metallurgy, 265
Mexico, 26–27, 32
Middle managers, 61–62
Military, futurology and the,
　107–39, 266–67, 273
　in ancient times, 108–10, 112
　arms race and, 116–19, 121–22
　end of war with advent of nu-
　clear weapons, 120
　"limited nuclear war," 119,
　120–29, 132, 273
　military intelligence, 116–17
　preparation and start of wars,
　107–10, 112
　technological innovation and,
　112–19, 122–23, 131, 134
Mindstorms, (Papert), 158
Minsky, Marvin, 70
"Missile gap," 116
MIT, 65, 71, 76, 150–51, 266,
　267
Mob psychology, 46
Moral argument in prophecy,
　10–11, 276
Moravec, Hans, 68–69, 70, 71
More, Sir Thomas, 178
Moses, 10
Moto-oka, Tohru, 96, 97
Moynihan, Daniel P., 136
Mumford, Lewis, 163
Mutual deterrence, 120, 128,
　130n
Mutually assured destruction,
　128, 130
Myth of the Eternal Return, The
　(Eliade), 260

Naisbitt, John, 2–3, 4–5, 8, 13,
　188n